ROY PEDERSEN was born in Ayrshir‹ where he graduated from the Unive in Geography and Economic History. where he created and published the fi ......g Gaelic map of Scotland, he has spent most of his working life based in Inverness. There he pursued a successful career in the economic, social and cultural development with the Highlands and Islands Development Board and its successor, Highlands and Islands Enterprise. In the course of this career, he was the original architect of the ferry charging system, Road Equivalent Tariff (RET). He was also intimately involved with the community co-operative scheme and revival of Gaelic including acting as Development Director of Comunn na Gàidhlig. More recently he has been proprietor of a consultancy business covering the diverse fields of transport and cultural development and has served as a Highland councillor. He writes, publishes, speaks and broadcasts on a variety of issues connected with world affairs and with the history, present and future development of the 'New Scotland' and its wider international setting.

He is Chair of Ainmean-Àite na h-Alba (Gaelic Place Names of Scotland) and he specialises, among other things, in maritime issues, serving on the Scottish Government's Ferry Industry Advisory Group.

JOHN ANGUS MACKAY was born in Shader, Barvas on the west side of the Isle of Lewis in 1948. He was educated 'painfully' at Airidhantuim Primary School and the Nicolson Institute in Stornoway. He graduated with an MA degree from Aberdeen University and then gained his teaching qualification at Jordanhill College of Education in Glasgow. He also subsequently gained a Masters in Media Management at Stirling University. His varied professional career evolved from Sales Rep for DC Thomson, secondary teacher in Glasgow where he rose to assistant principal teacher of English, after which he returned to his native Lewis as community co-operative field officer with the Highlands and Islands Development Board and subsequently Senior Administrative Offices responsible for that organisations Western Isles activities. He was then appointed founding CEO of Comunn na Gàidhlig, CEO of Gaelic Television Service, serving also as Chair of Acair Publishing, the Gaelic college Sabhal Mòr Ostaig, An Lanntair multi-media arts venue and Western Isles Heath Board. If that was not enough, he was until recently an active crofter and now spends part of each year in his beloved Italy.

Non-fiction

One Europe – a Hundred Nations (Channel View Books, 1992)

Loch Ness with Jacobite – A History of Cruising on Loch Ness (Jacobite, 2007)

Pentland Hero – The Saga of the Orkney Short Sea Crossing (Birlinn, 2010)

George Bellairs – The Littlejohn Casebook: The 1940s (self-published monograph, 2010)

Who Pays the Ferryman? – The Great Scottish Ferries Swindle (Birlinn, 2013)

Western Ferries – Taking on Giants (Birlinn, 2015)

The Pedersen Chronicles – A Family History of the Pedersens of Ardrossan (For the Right Reasons, 2018)

Fiction

Dalmannoch – The Affair of Brother Richard (For the Right Reasons, 2012)

Sweetheart Murder (For the Right Reasons, 2013)

The Odinist (For the Right Reasons, 2019)

Gaelic Guerrilla

John Angus Mackay, Gael Extraordinaire

ROY PEDERSEN

Luath Press Limited

EDINBURGH

www.luath.co.uk

First published 2019

ISBN: 978-1-913025-39-7

The paper used in this book is recyclable. It is made from low chlorine pulps produced in a low energy, low emission manner from renewable forests.

Printed and bound by Ashford Colour Press, Gosport

Typeset in 11 point Sabon by Lapiz

The author's right to be identified as author of this work under the Copyright, Designs and Patents Act 1988 has been asserted.

Contents

Acknowledgements

IT IS NORMAL for an author to thank numerous individuals who have helped in bringing their text into being. In this case the list is relatively short. The one individual above all who merits a very special thanks is John Angus Mackay himself. He was unstintingly generous with his time in relating evening after evening the amazing episodes of his life. On John's behalf, I must also thank Sarah and Donnie Macdonald and his uncle Norman Mackay for sharing their research into the history and torpedoing of the armed merchant cruiser F94 *Salopian* on which John's father served alongside Norman's father John.

Thanks are also due to John's son Derek for making available his History of Gaelic Radio Broadcasting by the BBC, to Leighton Andrews, now Professor of Practice in Public Service Leadership and Innovation at Cardiff Business School, for crucial detail on aspects of the lobbying challenges that John faced in securing funding for the Gaelic television service, as well as to John's wife Maria who sourced several photographs and illuminated a number of episodes that John had skirted over, particularly with regard to their mutual Italian experiences.

The photographic illustrations were culled from a number of sources, many from my own or John's collections, others are credited where the source is known.

I must of course record my grateful thanks to my publisher Gavin MacDougall of Luath Press and his staff for enabling the extraordinary achievements of John Angus Mackay to be recorded for posterity. As the book was the distillation of countless conversations between John Angus and myself, Gavin suggested that we exemplify a few of these conversations. While this involves some repetition, John and I have provided such examples in the form of five Cabadaich (Blethers) sprinkled throughout the text.

I also thank Marie Kilbride, who was an invaluable sounding-board as the text progressed and John Storey, son of our mentor, the late Bob Storey, who proofread the draft manuscript and uncovered and corrected many a factual, typographical and grammatical blunder. The responsibility for any remaining errors that may surface is mine alone for which I hope I will be forgiven.

Preface

IT IS MY privilege that John Angus Mackay has been a colleague and my very good friend for more than two score years. This is his story; that of the ultimate Gaelic guerrilla (OED definition: 'Guerrilla, noun, a member of a small independently acting group taking part in irregular fighting, especially against larger regular forces'). It was Gaelic writer and broadcaster, the late John Murray of Barvas, who first likened John Angus' regular forays from the Western Isles to Westminster as guerrilla tactics – rather like an old-fashioned *creach* or Highland raid.

That was John Angus' working life to a T. His fight to save our rich and venerable Gaelic tongue and its culture was not of the military kind, but instead utilised psychology, subterfuge, persuasion, passion, tenacity and, above all, courage in achieving its ends. In pursuing this struggle, John was not just one of the small and committed group that turned round the cause of Gaelic against almost impossible odds; he was *the* pivotal lead figure during the critical few decades in which a thousand-year history of persecution and decline, instigated by a hostile and powerful establishment, was halted and, if the momentum is maintained, it is hoped, reversed.

Before John's unique and vital role in this remarkable turnaround is forgotten, I just had to put it on the record. This book is the result. Whilst telling the story of one individual, there is no denying the fact that many individuals and organisations have made very significant contributions over the years to supporting the Gaelic language. This book seeks to illustrate the change in institutional attitudes towards, and support for, Gaelic which created the context in which John Angus Mackay's efforts, with the help of others, achieved what had previously seemed impossible. It's just a pity that we don't have more John Anguses.

Of course, as the saying goes, no man is an island and that is no less true of John Angus. His skill lay in drawing on the achievements and efforts of other individuals and organisations in creating an environment in which his own efforts could get results. Among the key institutions are An Comunn Gàidhealach who for decades kept the cause of Gaelic alive. Comhairle nan Sgoiltean Araich, CLI and the Gaelic college Sabhal Mòr Ostaig undertook pioneering work in pre-school and adult education while the Bilingual Education Project in the Western Isles paved the way for Gaelic medium education. The Gaelic Books Council helped to keep Gaelic writing and publishing alive, while the *fèis* movement co-ordinated by Fèisean nan Gàidheal and the initiatives of the National Gaelic Arts Project created a foundation for the development of the confident young talent that today act as such splendid international ambassadors for Gaelic.

Individuals who drove the cause forward are too numerous to mention and many kept a low profile, working effectively, but unsung, in the background. A few, however, stand out. Brian Wilson's advocacy for community co-ops on the Irish model was taken up by Ken Alexander, Chairman of the Highlands and Islands Development Board (HIDB). The model was skilfully adapted by the HIDB's Bob Storey, thereby creating the career opportunity which gave John invaluable experience in community work and dealing with institutions. This experience was to stand him in good stead in tackling the immense challenges of managing the co-op programme and HIDB's Stornoway office, Gaelic development through Comunn na Gàidhlig and the Gaelic Television Committee, rescuing the Western Isles Health Board and finally further advancing Gaelic as CEO of Bòrd na Gàidhlig. Of these individuals, a special personal debt of gratitude is due to the late Bob Storey, who not only mentored John and me, in the art – and it is an art – of community development, but set a standard of integrity and discipline that we have tried to emulate, not always successfully on my part.

In the national political arena, cross party-political support for Gaelic was, and still is, an important factor. Special credit must, however, be given to Malcolm Rifkind for assiduously pursuing the case within a sceptical Government, and in the face of Treasury opposition, for the creation of the Gaelic Television Fund. At the regional level, local authorities, came to play a vital role, most notably Highland Regional Council, Comhairle nan Eilean (Western Isles Council) and Strathclyde Regional Council, the latter being influenced by the Labour Party Gaelic Policy which had been drafted by Brian Wilson. And, after considerable persuasion, the broadcasters BBC, Grampian and Scottish Television also took up the Gaelic cause to incalculable positive effect.

Notwithstanding John's guerrilla capabilities, one secret of his success was his ability to work within the system, even when the system was ranged against him. When the system became too obdurate or political routes failed, however, alternative means were adopted. For example, the possibility of a hunger strike and the response to the minister who suggested that the Gaels lacked the fire of the Welsh – 'Are you inciting us to arson, Minister?' – opened closed minds. So the willingness to consider more extreme measures, implied or intended, demonstrated that the Gaels might not have been as quiescent as they were, had things not panned out as positively as they did.

Anyway, my job as scribe has been to put John's amazing story into written form. To save the blushes of some individuals, a number of the most hilarious, or alternatively most gut-wrenching episodes, could not be included, but those episodes aside, what has been recorded is a cornucopia of adventure that would fulfil the lifetimes of several lesser beings.

I hope you enjoy the saga of the Gaelic guerrilla.

Roy Pedersen
September 2019

List of Acronyms

BBC: British Broadcasting Corporation
BEA: British European Airways
BNG: Bòrd na Gàidhlig
BPS: bits per second
CBE: Commander of the British Empire
CEO: Chief executive officer
CLI: Comunn an Luchd Ionsachaidh (Gaelic adult learners organisation)
CNAG: Comunn na Gàidhlig
CNSA: Comhairle nan Sgoiltean Airich (Gaelic playgroups organisation)
COSLA: Convention of Scottish Local Authorities
CTG: Comataidh Telebhisean Gàidhlig (Gaelic Television Committee)
DCS: Distinguished Service Cross
DG: Director General
DSO: Distinguished Service Order
EIS: Educational Institute for Scotland
FOI: Freedom of information
GME: Gaelic medium education
GMS: Gaelic Media Service/Seirbheis nam Meadhanan Gàidhlig
HIDB: Highland and Islands Development Board
HIE: Highland and Islands Enterprise
HMI: Her Majesty's Inspector (of Schools)
HMS: His Majesty's Ship
IBA: Independent Broadcasting Authority

IDP: (European) Integrated Development Programme
ITC: Independent Television Commission
ITV: Independent Television
MP: Member of Parliament
MSP: Member of the Scottish Parliament
NHS: National Health Service
NTL: National Transcommunications Limited
OBE: Order of the British Empire
PA: Personal assistant
RN: Royal Navy
RNR: Royal Naval Reserve
RTD: Retired
S4C: Sianel Pedwar Cymru, meaning 'Channel 4 Wales'
SCU: Scottish Crofters Union
SDN: S4C Digital Networks
SMO: Sabhal Mòr Ostaig (Gaelic college)
SMT: Senior Management Team
SNP: Scottish National Party
STV: Scottish Television
TG4:   Irish Gaelic television channel
UHI: University of the Highlands and Islands
VAT: Value Added Tax
VHF: Very high frequency

A Modern Miracle

OF THE MULTITUDE of television channels now available to us, one of the most fascinating is BBC Alba. This channel, which was launched in 2008, is watched regularly by over half a million viewers, yet, astonishingly, it is provided for Scotland's small and dispersed community of just under 60,000 Gaelic speakers.

It seems that it is BBC Alba's quirkiness that has attracted this unusually large and diverse viewership. Of course, as might be expected, a channel aimed at this small linguistic minority covers a mix of Gaelic music, news, current affairs, entertainment, education, religion, children's programming, sport, drama and documentaries. The channel is normally broadcast between 5.00pm and midnight. But BBC Alba is far from inward looking. It regularly covers major sporting events, including top level Scottish professional football and other major sporting events. It features regular and highly popular Country and Western fare and the unique *Eòrpa* Gaelic current affairs programme, which uncovers otherwise unreported political, social and cultural issues across Europe – a format not found on any other channel.

The station is also unique in that it is the first channel to be delivered under a BBC licence by a partnership and is also the first multi-genre channel to come entirely from Scotland and with almost all of its programmes made in Scotland. As a means of broadening its reach, most programming features on-screen English subtitles although, for reasons of language development, children's programmes are not subtitled.

What is so remarkable about all this is that until recent years, it was commonly thought that the Scottish Gaelic language was in such steep decline that it would be extinct within a couple of generations. And it is true that, while in the 12th century Gaelic was the language of almost all of Scotland and the tongue of kings, court and scholarship, it, and the rich culture it carried, had subsequently been the focus of relentless official policies aimed at its extermination. Such was the success of this sustained 'ethnic cleansing' that, towards the end of the 20th century, the transmission of the language to the next generation was approaching the point of no return. The ancient language, it seemed, was doomed.

Then something amazing happened – a miracle one might say. Through the actions of a small group of individuals, acting in concert, the process of linguistic destruction was challenged. New means were created to rebuild that which the powers-that-be had sought so long and so hard to destroy. By the first decade of the 21st century, the Scottish Gaelic language and culture was turning the corner. The number of young Gaelic speakers was on the increase.

How this was achieved will be described in the pages of this book but, in a nutshell, it involved achieving community, institutional and cross-party-political support for new policies and organisational structures, to aid the development of Gaelic medium education, promotion of Gaelic arts and culture and, to support all this, the creation of a Gaelic television service. The unexpected success of these efforts has silenced many detractors.

Many individuals have contributed to this linguistic and cultural renaissance. One man, however, stands out. Without his heroic efforts, a whole range of key Gaelic development initiatives could never have achieved the success they have. The most audacious of these initiatives, and against huge odds, was the campaign for a Gaelic television service, summarised by Brian Wilson in the West Highland Free Press as a '...textbook lobbying exercise'. The man in question has an unlikely pedigree. He comes from a humble rural Hebridean background, from childhood short-sighted, hard of hearing and often lacking in self-confidence; yet his courage, intelligence, humanity, political nous, people skills, wit and steely resolve were such that, what lesser beings regarded as impossible, he made possible. That man is John Angus Mackay.

Community Roots

LOWER SHADER IS a crofting township on the west side of the Outer
Hebridean island of Lewis and it was there in the early years of the
20th century, at Newpark, Lower Shader, that the Mackay household dwelt. The address was later known as number 43. The head of
the household was Roderick 'Rodaidh' Mackay. In the late 1890s,
he had enclosed the land at Newpark and renovated the old school
building there to create a family home. His wife Annie bore him
six children. Two girls Annie and Catherine followed the seasonal
herring fishery from Shetland to Yarmouth; another, Peggy, was a
nurse. Of the boys, John died as a result of an accident at a relatively young age, while Donald emigrated to America. Then there
was Alexander Mackay, more commonly known as Ailig Rodaidh,
or to give him his Gaelic *sloinneadh*: *Alasdair Ruairidh Bhig 'An
Bhàin*. Like many another young Lewisman in the 1920s, Alexander Mackay followed his brother and went to the United States in
1929 to seek a better life.

At first, he found work as a sailor on the Great Lakes, but before
long he got a job in Detroit with the Ford Motor Company. Even after
the Great Depression struck, he was fortunate enough to keep his job,
latterly as an engine polisher. That was Alexander's job – a dream job
in many ways – but for all that, with the gang-warfare that was rife at
the time and then the Great Depression, America was not the land of
milk and honey that it had promised to be a decade earlier.

In 1934, Alexander Mackay decided to come back home to Lewis.
He had probably been carrying on a correspondence for some time
with Mary Macdonald who was then working in Glasgow as cook
to the family of a professor in medicine at that city's University. In
the last year of primary school, Mary had gained a bursary to go to
school in Stornoway. When she came home all excited and told her
mother, the response was: 'But who will help look after the cattle?'

And that was the end of that. Years later, John was to have a similar experience with *his* mother causing him to sidetrack his ambition in similar circumstances.

Alexander and Mary married in 1935. Initially on return home, Alexander bought a loom and, whilst working the land, he weaved Harris Tweed, at times cycling to Stornoway for 16 miles to pick up the wool and cycling back to Shader. As was commonplace among the men of Lewis' west side, Alexander enrolled with the Royal Naval Reserve (RNR) which entailed the pleasant and valuable diversion of periodic paid training sessions at Chatham in Kent. As events will reveal, the training and discipline gained was to prove invaluable.

The couple's first son, Angus, was born in 1937; the second, Roddy, in 1939. Alexander also created a family home by building on to the side of his own father's house, a task that was interrupted by the outbreak of the Second World War.

War inevitably meant call-up to serve King and country and although it seems almost unbelievable to us today, the 1939 to 1945 War Roll of Honour Ness to Bernera records that no less than 50 men and one woman from 27 homes in the village of Lower Shader served – including two homes which each gave four men, and six which each gave three men. Three gave their lives, including one of the five who were Prisoners of War. In the wider community of Lower Shader, Upper Shader and Ballantrushal respectively, three men were especially recognised for acts of bravery, Alan Morrison DSM, Alexander Macdonald DSM and Angus Macleay the George Medal. Of the Lower Shader total of servicemen, 38 men served in the RNR. One of those was Alexander Mackay who was assigned to the armed merchant cruiser F94 *Salopian*.

HMS *Salopian*, formerly the 10,000-ton Bibby Line passenger motor ship *Shropshire*, had been hastily requisitioned and renamed by the Admiralty at the outbreak of hostilities and, like over 50 other similar vessels, converted to serve as a ship of war. A major function of such vessels was to act as escorts to protect convoys. What was remarkable about *Salopian* after conversion at Birkenhead was that, of her 200 plus complement, 41 were from the Isle of Lewis.

In October 1939, *Salopian* sailed north on her first deployment. As she passed through the Minch, Alexander and his Lewis shipmates could witness the tantalising sight of Loch's villagers busy with the harvest. But there was no stopping and soon they joined the great Home Fleet at Scapa Flow. They had not been long there when the German U-boat, U-47, under the command of Korvettenkapitän Günther Prien managed to penetrate the 'impregnable' defences and put four torpedoes into the battleship *Royal Oak*, sinking her with the loss of 850 lives – an ominous indicator of the perils that lay ahead for *Salopian* and her men. The fleet was immediately ordered to sea and *Salopian* took up patrol duties in the Denmark Strait.

By all accounts, notwithstanding the dangers and the harsh weather conditions, *Salopian* was a happy ship. With several bards on board, the rich banter and hilarity can be imagined, as described in the song 'Oran a' Chrùsair', composed by Alexander's shipmates John Mackay and Calum Maclennan. By virtue of *Salopian* being a former passenger liner, conditions on board were well above the norm for a warship. No hammocks here, but two berth cabins for the men and single first-class staterooms for the officers.

After her initial winter duties in Arctic waters, *Salopian* went south to West Africa and then Bermuda where thick ganseys and duffle coats were exchanged for tropical whites. It was not long, however, before she was transferred back in northern waters to join the Halifax Escort Force to support the transatlantic convoys. These duties involved escorting each convoy from Canada to the western edge of the U-boat danger zone where it would be handed over to a British destroyer escort. On 12 May 1941, after such a handover of convoy SC30, *Salopian*, under the command of Captain Sir John Meynell Alleyne, DSO, DSC, RN, turned at 3.30am to head back to Halifax.

Twelve days earlier, on 1 May, unknown to *Salopian*'s happy crew, the German submarine U-98 sailed from Saint-Nazaire for operations in the North Atlantic under the command of Kapitänleutnant Robert Karl Friedrich Gysae.

Gysae's log describes how at 4.00am on 13 May, a shadow was identified at 30° on his port bow. The shadow became larger, taking the form of a large passenger liner with no running lights steaming fast and making strong zigzags. It took until 5.30am to get into a position to fire a double salvo of torpedoes which missed because the enemy changed course at 90°. The U-boat had to move fast on the surface to get another opportunity to fire which she did at 6.22am. These two torpedoes also missed their target which steamed away in the dawning light, undamaged as a mist descended. Gysae kept to his course, reloading the tubes as he proceeded, and suddenly at 7.20am the lookout spotted the steamer through the mist on the port bow. Five minutes later, two torpedoes were fired in succession and this time they found their target. The first hit amidships and the second detonated under the bows. The ship stopped, listing slightly to starboard, but showed no sign of sinking. Gysaes noted men scurrying on deck, boats being readied and guns manned. Just as the hatch was sealed for diving, two impacts from the ship's shellfire were felt with splinters clattering against the hull. U-98 dived to safety.

On board *Salopian*, Gysae's first four torpedoes had been unnoticed and it was only during the third attack that a suspicious object was sighted on the starboard beam. Action Stations were sounded and the helm put hard aport, but too late. Both torpedoes struck, the first bringing down the wireless aerials and putting the engines out of action. Allayne ordered all his men into lifeboats except key officers, damage control parties and gun crews. While a large war ensign was raised defiantly on the foremast, all hands worked with quiet efficiency and the advance party got their boats away in good order.

The U-boat surfaced and *Salopian's* six-inch guns opened fire, causing the German to submerge. It was only a matter of time before he would strike again. The order was given for final abandonment. The next torpedo hit the ship aft which caused the ship to heel slightly making the lowering of the last two boats easier. During the whole abandonment process, several men were able to get to their quarters to retrieve personal items. Time was also taken to load petrol for the motor boat. Once all the boats were away, another torpedo struck, but still she floated. And then the *coup de grâce* broke her back. Both halves stood on end and disappeared in less than a minute.

To the credit of the U-boat's commander, he left the occupants of the boats unmolested. Robert Gysae in command of U-98 sank ten Allied merchantmen between October 1940 and February 1942 when he handed over command to Oberleutnant ZS Kurt Eichmann under whose first deployment U-98 was lost with all hands. Gysae survived the war serving in the post-war Bundesmarine in which he reached the rank of Flottillenadmiral. He died in 1989.

On the motor boat's emergency wireless a signal was transmitted 'AMC torpedoed 56°43N 38°57W'. For the rest of that day they waited. When the boats clustered for the night, a roll was called and it was discovered that they had lost three men – engineer, fireman and bosun's mate. The following day, 14 May, the boats stretched out on a north south line to make it easier for searchers to find them. The men were rationed to half a biscuit, an inch cube of corned beef and two half-measures of the water dipper per day. The ship's doctor checked the condition of the survivors and on examining Alexander, he declared that if the privations continued, he (Alexander) would be the last man alive on account of his strong and heavy build. These comments were not wholly welcome, for the looks and hostile comments of the other men displayed little empathy with the doctor's prognosis.

Next morning, the motor boat was dispatched to steer south as far as fuel would permit, in the hope of intercepting a convoy that they knew was on its way. Thankfully they made contact with a destroyer, HMS *Impulsive*, which picked them up and then rescued the others. *Impulsive*, running low on fuel, headed for the nearest landfall at Reykjavík in Iceland where *Salopian's* commander and 277 officers and ratings were disembarked.

Alexander Mackay and his shipmates, including another 40 Lewismen, were taken to an army camp at Hafnarfjörður some seven miles from Reykjavík, where they were clothed, fed and found welcome sleep. On 26 May, the *Salopian* survivors boarded the *Royal Ulsterman*, departing early the next morning for Gourock. In peace time, the *Royal Ulsterman* and her consort, *Royal Scotsman*, were the nightly mail ships on the Glasgow-Belfast run. It is an interesting coincidence that the *Royal Ulsterman* was the first ship on which I sailed as a toddler to visit relations in Northern Ireland.

Alexander Mackay was fortunate to have survived the U-boat menace and there was joy in that a further son Kenny was born in 1942. The family was not, however, without its share of personal grief. John's mother Mary had suffered the death of two brothers, who were lost aged 21 and 29 years in the space of five weeks between October and November 1944. Both served in the RNR. As we shall see, this was the beginning of a series of heartbreaks due to loss of young lives which were to plague the family in years to come, and which could not but have had emotional consequences for family members.

On the cessation of hostilities, Alexander Mackay returned home to Mary and his young family to resume weaving. They were blessed with a fourth son, Donald John, in 1946 and, on 24 June 1948, their fifth son John Angus, the leading character in our story, was born. In 1953, the last of the Mackay siblings was born, Annie Henrietta or Annette, the only girl in the family.

The Young John Angus

IN HIS EARLY years, John Angus Mackay was unlucky with his health, and seemed also to have a propensity to land himself in the wrong place at the wrong time – a marked contrast to the serendipity he demonstrated in his later professional life, learning from his own, and others' experience. From birth, John Angus was very short-sighted. Later his mother told him that she had suspected from early on that her fifth son could not see very well. She would wave a teddy or some toy above his head and his eyes never moved, whereas if she did something with a toy that made a sound he could hear and follow it. To add to this sensory impairment, in the course of an epidemic, John contracted measles and mumps around the age of two. This caused a burst eardrum so that his hearing was henceforth seriously impaired.

Worse was to come. As was usual at that time, the house had an open fire on which his mother cooked. He was about three when his brother found a pipe, which was an occasion for excitement among the bigger boys. Angus sat on the chair by the fire pretending to smoke the pipe, which of course led to much hilarity. As John jumped up to try to grab the pipe, Angus pushed him off such that he fell right back into the fire and overturned a boiling kettle This scalded him very badly on and under the shoulder, to the extent that he nearly lost his arm. That was bad enough and extremely painful but the wound started to go septic with proud flesh exposed. The treatment at that time was harsh. The nurse came every day with a pumice stone to scrape proud flesh off the raw wound.

On the nurse's arrival, John would try to hide in terror in the barn behind the Jersey cow, covering himself in straw. His brother always found him and pulled him out as he screamed 'a' chlach ghorm! a' chlach ghorm! (the blue stone, the blue stone!)'

Poor eyesight and hearing, plus this accident and later experiences left him sub-consciously wary and frightful of close relationships, even although needy of them, in case he was hurt or caused hurt. Recognising this later in life was a cathartic experience, albeit tinged with regrets.

In some ways, the young John was relatively unaware of his handicaps. His earliest indoor memory was the still incomplete house in which he slept in a box bed under the stair and from which he could hear the Gaelic conversations of the adults – a haven of physical and emotional safety. Of course, at that time, Shader was a wholly Gaelic-speaking community.

Outside the house, the memory of horses and carts passing to collect peats was to be a lasting one. What to him were gigantic animals pulling carts with very big strong men on the carts made a powerful visual impression on one whose sight was poor.

In 1955, the family was plunged into grief when the nine-year-old Donald John died under anaesthetic in Woodend hospital in Aberdeen. His mother never fully recovered from this, coming after the loss of two of her brothers in the Second World War some eleven years previously, and consequently this affected her youngest son deeply. Island communities at this time were struggling to build lives after the ravages of two wars in which heavy losses had been inflicted with hardly a family untouched. Family deaths were the subject of outpourings of grief which were terrifying to young children.

The next accident occurred when John was about nine. The milk lorry came to the school every day to deliver the milk and, on the way back, stopped to collect the empties. Somebody thought of the bright idea of hanging on to the back of the lorry and then to let go. All the boys got engaged with this until one day John's cousin suggested that there should be a competition to see who could stay on longest. John was determined to make his mark so he grabbed the back of the lorry. The others dropped of one by one, but John still hung on. The lorry started to pick up speed, however, and he realised that after a while he had to pass the post office where there were always people standing outside yacking. He then had the picture in his mind's eye of people standing there. They would all wave at the driver and then say, 'Goodness gracious' (or Gaelic expletives to that effect), 'there's someone hanging on to the back of the lorry.' What consternation that would create! To avoid the impending embarrassment, John let go and hit the road hard, probably bouncing in the process. Head and knees were hurt, but no lasting damage except for a life-long scar on his forehead. It is with some irony that John Angus states that there are not many people who can claim that they fell off the back of a lorry. This incident showed he had a propensity to hang on in there when others let go – even to the detriment of his health. He was to demonstrate this same characteristic in adult life.

In later years, John Angus recalled that the happiest times in his childhood were usually in the company of adults and animals. Among his own age group there was quite a lot of rough and tumble. The older boys stirred things up and encouraged fighting each other or lining up in teams to emulate Rangers and Celtic. When not doing that, fights took place with the boys from the neighbouring village of Borve, which involved chasing each other with clods and stones until the Shader gang escaped over their home boundary.

From an early age, John had the benefit of the experience of growing up and participating in a working crofting community where the pattern of the year was dictated by the seasons. In the spring, manuring the fields, ploughing and planting, lambing and calving; followed by the peat-cutting and gathering and sheep gathering and shearing in the summer; hay and oats scything and stacking, potato digging and storing in the autumn; and in the early winter, sheep going to the tup and subsequent daily feeding of sheep and cattle.

Most of this work was done by hand with tools which are common to rural communities throughout Europe. Initially ploughing was by horse, though by his mid-teens John's father had purchased a Massey Ferguson tractor and implements which made life easier. For years, his brothers being at sea, John had to draw household drinking water from a well about quarter of a mile from his home and, until the advent of electricity in the '50s, lighting was by Tilley lamp or lantern. From resenting the drudgery of having to do what was demanded, John grew to love crofting life and gradually took on responsibilities on his own initiative.

As for school, John hated it. This is understandable when, like the other crofter's children, he went in to Airidhantuim Primary School not speaking any English, other than his mother's coaching on how to ask to go to the toilet. From the day of entry into that system of cultural annihilation, English was all these five-year-old Gaelic-speaking pupils heard until they returned to their families in the evening. With hindsight, it seems astonishing that this deliberate official policy of undermining Gaelic, and the rich culture it carried, was accepted with little demur from those on which it was inflicted.

One small but important official crumb that was on offer to the Gaelic community was the radio. John remembers people being practically glued to the receiver to listen to what little Gaelic was then broadcast on it.

At school, due to a lack of confidence due to poor eyesight and hearing, John instinctively sat unobtrusively at the back of the class until it was discovered that he was struggling with the work. He was thereafter moved to the front and was prescribed glasses. From that time, John has had the strong belief that, when a person has weaknesses or deficiencies, they either go down or fight against them. What seems to have grabbed John was a survival instinct that urged: 'Don't let this get you down'. Out of that instinct, a spirit of rebellion seemed to have emerged rather than a desire to achieve or to be something. Now that he had glasses, John could read; and he read books avidly – books, it has to be said, that were well above his level. This strength became an antidote to the bullying, which took advantage of his weaknesses.

Although the communities of rural Lewis were immersed in a rich corpus of Gaelic song, verse and lore, this was ignored almost totally by the Anglo-centric school curriculum. As an example, even the music lesson, provided by a peripatetic music teacher, could hardly at times have been more alien and inappropriate to young children who were supposed to be learning English.

De Camptown ladies sing dis song
Doo-da, Doo-da
De Camptown racetrack's five miles long
Oh, de doo-da day.

Gwine to run all night
Gwine to run all day
I bet my money on de bob-tailed nag
Somebody bet on de bay.

Thus they were exposed to verse that was not only incomprehensible and lacking in relevance but exhibiting a similar type of racist ridicule to which the Gaelic community itself was being subjected.

One song that John recalls that did have a Scottish connection was 'Will ye no come back again?' But again, although of some cultural relevance, there was little explanation as to who 'Bonny Cherlie' was, or why he had gone away in the first place. And why *that* song, when there are a hundred well-known Gaelic songs about the campaign of 1745–6 and its aftermath? In fact, throughout the primary school experience, there was next to no Gaelic until Primary 6 or 7 when the headmaster would read some Gaelic from a book and then ask each pupil to read a section.

For all these deficiencies in the primary education system and for all his own handicaps, the eleven-year-old John Angus Mackay survived scrapes and scraps, while his own reading, coupled with his growing experience of agriculture and community life, had given him a breadth of learning that was unusual.

In those days at the end of the primary stage of education, all Scottish children sat an exam which would determine whether their secondary education would be in an academic or non-academic institution. This exam was known as the Eleven Plus. When John sat the Eleven Plus, he got exceptionally high marks; on the strength of which he was bound for the Nicolson Institute in the island capital of Stornoway. His brother Angus had also attended the Nicolson, but due to chronic asthma, had missed many of his classes and left at the age of 15 to become a sailor. Ultimately, when John was in his mid-teens, Angus emigrated to New Zealand, where the climate suited his health better.

Cabadaich 1: Nuair a Bha Mi Òg

Blethers 1: When I was Young

ROY: Rural Lewis in your youth was very different from today. Remind me of some or the characters.

JOHN: I lived in the village of Shader where work revolved around the land, animals – cattle, sheep, horses – and the seasons dictated how people lived. When I was very young, we had no mains water or electricity – the *tobar* (well) and the Tilley lamp were the order of the day. When I looked out from our house, I could see people working on their crofts. I could see peat smoke rising from the chimneys. From this you could tell that people were alright. Life revolved around the land and the simple equipment that we used. Most crofters were also weavers of Harris Tweed. And, of course, Gaelic was the language of the community.

One of my earliest memories is watching a competition between my aunties – my father's sisters – and my father. It was just on the cusp of when we were changing from sickle to the scythe. My father, however, used the scythe. The aunts who used the traditional sickle said, in Gaelic of course, 'This will never work. It'll make a mess of the corn.' So there was a competition. The two aunties were bent double cutting away with the sickles, while my father walked swinging the scythe – swish, swish. My father won! That was my first experience of tradition versus modernity. Then my father used the horse for ploughing until within ten years the tractor arrived. Of course, people were saying the same thing: 'The tractor will ruin the land.' The tractor then was the small Ferguson.

ROY: You don't see many horses about crofts today. How prevalent were they in your young day?

JOHN: When I was very young, there were a lot of horses used for cultivation. In the winter, they wandered freely around the village. I well remember a white mare, I used to be lifted on to its back. It was quite docile and it belonged to a guy called Dolly Tee. Now Dolly Tee was famous in the village because, during the First Word War, he saved the life of his brother by attacking sailors with a marlin spike who were about to throw his wounded brother overboard.

Then there was my grandfather's cousin Alexander Mathieson. He was known as Suft. He was the spitting image of my grandfather. Both of them had huge moustaches and they smoked pipes. His wife had died in childbirth and he had to bring up the twin children on his own. In these circumstances, Suft had to rely on his animals and he developed an amazing relationship with his dog and with his horse, because the three of them understood each other. He trained his dog to go out on its own to the moor for miles to find and round up the cattle, because he couldn't leave the house on account of the children. I used to spend a lot of time with this old man. I asked Suft how he trained the animals and he told me, 'You talk to the animals as if they were friends and eventually you get on the same wavelength.' All he had to do then was to say to the dog, 'Go and get the cattle.' And the dog went out for miles and brought the cattle home. Later, I got a dog from Skye. Now in our village there were about 40 Ayrshire cattle that all looked alike. Anyway, the dog learnt when I said 'bò (cow)' it would go and pick out the right animal and bring it home. My father was amazed.

Another time I was sitting with Suft in his old house eating potatoes when there was a knock at the door. Suft said 'Oh that's the horse.' When he opened the door sure enough, the horse stuck its head through the opening. Then Suft said 'Thig dhan dorus eile' (Away to the other door). Suft said, 'Faic seo' (See this). We went down through the house to the barn where he opened the back door and there was the horse waiting for him.

ROY: You speak a lot about the land, but I know your brothers were sailors.

JOHN: Yes, when I was very young, my brothers went to sea, so the sea also played a big part in our lives. Living on an island, the sea was all around us. Most families in the village had sailors serving with cargo or passenger lines like the New Zealand Shipping Company, P&O and so on. Most houses had a picture of Sydney Harbour Bridge or some other memento from foreign parts.

One of the most notable guys in the village was known as Aonghas Deed. He was big in every way – tall, strong, broad. He had been a boxer in the navy and seemingly won boxing competitions. People were wary of him, but they also liked him. The story goes that Aonghas Deed and his pal Aonghas Dhaidh, another huge man, when they fetched up in Liverpool after a voyage, they used to take on the Liverpudlians in the pubs for a fight. Aonghas Deed had a problem, in that when he drank too much, he lost the power of his legs. So he sat on a table at the back of the pub with his back to the wall. Aonghas Dhaidh would pick up one of the Liverpudlians and throw him to Aonghas Deed who would then punch the unfortunate local man. Anxious to keep the fight going, Aonghas Deed would shout to Aonghas Dhaidh, 'An Diabhal, Aonghais; sad fear eile thugam! (The Devil, Aonghas, throw another one to me!)' Then there was a riot and more and more Liverpudlians piled in to take on these Lewismen, so they eventually escaped using dustbin lids as shields, to fend off the stones and bottle that were being hurled at them.

ROY: Some character. Not a man you would mess with.

JOHN: Indeed not. In fact, the same could be said of many another sailor as well. When they were home, they entertained us landlubbers, gathered outside the Post Office, with colourful yarns of distant lands and foreign ports. This stimulated yearning within youngsters to follow in their footsteps. Prince among the story tellers in our village was Tarmod Stufain (Norman Macleod) who entertains people with his tales, poems and wit to this very day.

ROY: What other forms of entertainment did you have?

JOHN: For young people, *danns' an rathaid* (dancing on the road to melodeon music), more generally Calum Kennedy concerts and the radio. On the other hand, the Church played a large part in dictating the rhythms of community life: mid-week prayer meeting, two services on Sunday, monthly and quarterly meetings, and twice-yearly communions. These sessions gave people a societally legitimate excuse to dress up and go out as well as allowing open expression of their religion. The communions especially gave the womenfolk an opportunity to compete by showing off their latest hats. Who needed Ascot, canapes and champagne when you had Communions, crowdie and cream!

ROY: Who indeed?

Stornoway

STORNOWAY AND THE educational experience it was to provide exposed John Angus to a wholly new environment. For one thing, the town of Stornoway was very different from the rural community that had been his life up until that point. There was much Gaelic to be heard in the town of course but, at its core, the ruling ascendancy was largely non-Gaelic-speaking. Indeed, there was among many of the townspeople a snobbish disparagement of the Gaelic-speaking country 'Maws'.

John's father took him to Stornoway for enrolment in the Nicolson Institute – to him a massive school with hundreds of children milling around. John had never seen anything like it before. The closest experience hitherto would have been the fank (sheep pen) into which hundreds of wayward sheep were corralled. Of course, by this stage, his English was pretty good on account of the large number of books he had read – books that his brothers had brought home, or books borrowed from the mobile library.

At the enrolment session, the Rector advised that John study Latin as he already spoke Gaelic, to which his father concurred. And so John was put into the Latin class, thereby taking him completely out of his familiar milieu; linguistically, culturally, emotionally and sitting with the largely non-Gaelic-speaking children of professional people – doctors, lawyers, headmasters and such like. As will be recorded, compared with the small village primary school, the Nicolson Institute, with its significant record of educational achievement presented a new range of challenges to the young John Angus, as it did to many others before and since. So once again, having been a misfit in primary school, he found himself out of place in this new environment, a circumstance which had its own negatives and positives.

Of course, hearing problems and poor eyesight continued. With the exception of a few teachers, there was little allowance made or support given in ameliorating these handicaps. Although given an NHS analogue hearing aid, this did little to help as it magnified every noise and did not have the capacity to isolate speech.

At first, John struggled in the Latin class and he was terrified by the teacher, Mrs Urquhart, such that he frequently got nose-bleeds. In time, however, as he came to grips with Latin, he grew to like it. By the fourth year stage, John got tonsillitis and had to go to hospital in Inverness for treatment, such that he was two weeks late in returning to the new term. Because of this late start that term, and the rigidity of the system, John became a nuisance to the teacher, Bill Macleod (known as Bill Soft, as he spoke with a soft voice), who took a strong dislike to John.

John was placed on a seat beside the brightest pupil, but as the teacher was not able to control the class, his pupils played games and indulged in pranks, making concentration difficult, and lessening John's motivation. Because of this, John was demoted to a lower class where he was given more support and gained better marks. At one point, John overheard a furious argument between the two Latin teachers, one saying that he was the worst in his class and the other saying that he had been the best in hers.

When it came to the O levels, John did not distinguish himself, but discovered that others who had played around in class had been studying at home and had done relatively well in their exams. From then on, John decided to turn his back on the teachers and his classmates to undertake self-study in the library. He started to dodge classes and to study past papers. This strategy yielded success in Highers in the fifth and sixth years. This experience of self-learning, whilst borne more of pressure of circumstance than personal choice, was to stand him in good stead in future years as both student and teacher.

With regard to Latin, Bill Soft had lost no opportunity to inform John that he had no chance of passing his Higher in the subject. John was determined to prove him wrong and he worked really hard to learn all the relevant Latin texts by heart. After the exam was over, John was quietly confident that he had at least passed the 50 per cent mark. On the day the results were to be announced, Bill Soft, John's nemesis, climbed the stairs to the Latin classroom. As he reached the top of the stairs, he collapsed with a heart attack and died, clutching the briefcase which contained the exam results. When they were finally revealed, John had scored highly but he was denied by fate the satisfaction of acknowledgement from Bill Macleod.

One of the features of attendance at the Nicolson by pupils from the country areas was the requirement that pupils board throughout the week in the school hostel. Children from the parishes most distant from Stornoway, like Uig and South Lochs, stayed the whole term. Few found this a happy experience, though it may have been character building. The contrast between the harsh discipline of this environment, dormitory life and regimented study contrasted greatly with the family life most rural children had experienced up to this point. Some pulled out, and some persevered. In some ways, John lived a Jekyll and Hyde existence.

In school and in the hostel, he reverted to being a rumbustious teenager. In fact, John hated the whole set-up, often rebelled and came close to expulsion after he and another boy were held up to be ring-leaders in causing trouble for the young teachers assigned to live in and manage the pupils. The intervention of a Dingwall-based Deputy Director of Education from Ross and Cromarty brought a cessation of hostilities. John was able to demonstrate that the charges brought against him – smoking, shouting in the corridors and dumb insolence – could equally be levelled, perhaps with the exception of the latter, at the teacher leading the inquisition. On a promise of future good behaviour, the miscreants were pardoned. Perhaps the boys had begun to appreciate advice given to them previously by one of the hostel wardens, a bluff Yorkshireman who demonstrated the only practical use of Latin that had been encountered so far when he, on listening to complaints, said, 'Always remember boys – *Illegitimi non carborundum*: don't let the bastards grind you down.'

At home, at weekends and during holidays, he worked with older people on the croft: in the spring spreading manure, planting potatoes, sowing corn and cutting peats; in the summer gathering the peats, gathering and shearing sheep; in the autumn scything the corn and the hay, and lifting the potatoes.

An aspect of the school curriculum that had a deep, almost uncanny influence on John was one of the set books for the Higher English course. That was Lewis Grassic Gibbon's *Sunset Song*. As he studied this book, he realised that it was the first of the *Scots Quair* trilogy, set in the east of Scotland. It may have been the fact that he read this trilogy whilst sitting with his back to the biggest stone of the ancient stone circle of Steinacleit, which was located just behind his parent's house at Shader, that he felt a great connection to the novel's main character. He read about the life of the heroine Chris Guthrie, a woman from the north-east of Scotland during the early 20th century, in which standing stones featured as her haven from the vicissitudes of life. Her husband had returned from the Great War a changed and damaged man, and to re-orientate herself, she used to go to a stone circle, so linking into her heritage and culture. As he read on, the hair stood up on the back of John's neck, as he shared this experience, albeit in the Western Isles. When John touched the stone, he felt what seemed like an electric current running through him that appeared to link him and Chris Guthrie.

In these final two years in the Nicolson Institute, John had gradually taken more control of his own life: for some time, he had been smoking on and off – more on than off – but made the decision to give it up, in which course, although temporarily excruciating, he succeeded. He took up running and other physical exercise and, as we have seen, took responsibility for his own learning. This laid the foundation for developing physical and mental stamina, which was to stand him in good stead in later years.

Alma Mater

AFTER SUMMER WORK on the land at Shader, John Angus, in the company of a group of school leavers, like countless young Lewismen before them, ventured forth from Stornoway just before midnight on David MacBrayne's Royal Mail ship *Loch Seaforth*. A number of the group disembarked at Kyle of Lochalsh at the ungodly hour of 4.00am, the steamer thereafter continuing her scheduled passage to Mallaig, whence others of the group were bound for onward connection to Glasgow. The Kyle group had to hang around shivering on the pier until boarding the 6.20am slow train to Inverness, where, following another two-hour wait, they caught the Aberdeen train to arrive in the Granite City later that afternoon.

In the ensuing days, John commenced his studies for an Arts Degree at the University of Aberdeen. He stayed with his old school mate Peter Smith, also from Shader, in cold, inhospitable digs in Springbank Terrace. In his first academic year he studied English, Psychology, Logic and French. John studied hard. He had a fear of failing and letting his family down, more than a desire to succeed for his own sake. The Rector of the Nicolson Institute had warned the departing scholars, that gaining a University degree, and particularly at Honours level, was very difficult. He had also given some sage advice about being gentlemanly when seeing a young lady home, but certainly never to accept at the door the offer of a 'fatal' cup of coffee. John has little recollection of drinking much coffee under such circumstances, nor it being offered either. As with many another Aberdeen undergraduate before and since, his social life centred mainly around the Marischal Bar in the Kirkgate, the Blue Lamp Bar in the Gallowgate and playing snooker in the Students' Union.

After completing his first year, John naturally returned home to Lewis for the summer break and, to fund his future studies, he sought work for that three-month period. He called at a number of building sites and in due course got a labouring position with Stornoway Builders who were building Stornoway Primary School. His first assignment was to work with an older man from Shader, Ailig 'an Chaluim, to rake the stones off what was to become the school playground. Fortunately, John was familiar with raking stones as he had raked stones raised up after ploughing on his father's land and he set to it with gusto. Ailig 'an Chaluim, who had worked on several of the hydro schemes and other big civil engineering projects throughout the Highlands, took John aside with:

'Air do shocair, a bhalaich, na marbh thu fhèin – no mise! (Take your time, boy, don't kill yourself – or me!)'

Thereafter they both proceeded at a steady pace, which gave breathing space for the older man to pass on tips from his wealth of experience, including how to stand up for himself – a lesson which stood John in good stead in later years. Later, on another building site, John saw Ailig putting his own advice into practice, squaring up to a gaffer who demanded his shovel as it was obviously well sharpened. Ailig's response was that he could have it – if he was prepared to take it on the top of his skull! That was the end of that episode.

When they stopped for lunch, the foreman took John aside and said, 'I been watching your work and you've passed the test. You're a good grafter.'

John's next task was the rather dangerous business of treating building blocks with acid and then washing the acid off with water to bring out the texture of the stone.

On subsequent summer breaks, John again worked with Stornoway builders and in the process learnt the skills of working with concrete, driving dumper trucks, diggers and other tricks of the building trade.

By the start of his second year at university, John Angus was 19 and, having had enough of digs, he moved into a flat with another Lewisman, Dusty MacLeod. Dusty was into boxing in a big way and John became his out-of-the-ring sparring partner for which purpose John toughened up his stomach muscles so that he could receive Dusty's punches. John also took on the role of Dusty's cook. Dusty particularly liked mashed potatoes at 11.00pm to sustain him into the following day, such that John regularly served him a substantial portion of his favourite dish at that hour. These administrations must have been helpful, for Dusty became the University's middleweight champion.

In his second year, too, John felt his bad eyesight to be a continuing handicap. Perhaps the city would have better facilities for addressing such problems than were to be found in Lewis at that time. After an unhelpful encounter with one optician, who laughed and said he had never seen such poor eyesight, John was fortunate to find another who was more sympathetic, knowledgeable and accommodating. This man said, 'Look, I have a practice in Gibraltar. Is there, by any chance, a history of cross-fertilisation in your family where people have been too closely related?'

John answered in the affirmative in that his father and mother were second cousins.

'Ah, I suspected that,' acknowledged the optician. 'We have been doing a research project in Gibraltar about such consanguinity and we have found that it can cause eyesight difficulties of the kind you are experiencing. There is, however, a positive side to this. Think of it. In any film you have seen featuring professors – often absent-minded professors – they all wear glasses. So people like you who are seriously short-sighted, and if they have brains at all, compensate by focusing on problems and try to understand them in a different way from perfectly sighted people. That leads to intellectual development. So don't despair. Take it as something positive.'

From then onwards, John did.

He graduated in 1969 from the University of Aberdeen with an MA Degree in English Literature and Psychology.

He had initially intended to study French to Honours level, but that was set aside after he had announced to his mother that he was to spend three summer months in France. His mother was alarmed, pointing out that his grandfather had spent more than four years in France as a prisoner of the 1914–8 war, and that it was a very different place culturally as well as linguistically. The final straw was that his father was unwell with an ulcer and he needed help with the summer croft work. John gave up French and fledgling aspirations to do Honours. This was a significant decision – family loyalty before career. This was to place him in the position of taking a number of career risks, which ultimately bore fruit, as this tale will reveal.

A steady job as a French teacher was not to be. In later life, however, as will be revealed, his discovery of the allure of Italy and its language and culture was to offer ample compensation.

The School of Hard Knocks

A PROFESSIONAL CAREER path was not immediately in view, so John Angus went round various factories and building sites in Aberdeen to look for a job. When he arrived at the gate of one building site in the Torry area of the city, he encountered one man who was apparently departing from the site and another shouting after him, 'Fuck off and don't come back.'

The shouter turned out to be the site manager. John addressed him by saying, 'It looks as if you have a job vacancy for a labourer here.'

The site manager agreed that this was so and asked, 'Are you a labourer?' to which John replied that he had worked with Stornoway builders. He was hired and delegated to the concrete squad. The gaffer of the squad, a big well-built man of six foot two seemed to take an instant dislike to John, although John could not understand why.

He was given a series of difficult jobs, but each time was able to cope and exceed expectations. It was extremely hard work, 12 hours a day, seven days a week, six of which were on concrete and, on the seventh, ten hours on shuttering. On one occasion, John was told that a lorry load of cement bags had arrived and that he and another older man who was the gaffer's pal were delegated to unload the hundred-weight bags. Unloading commenced and the older man had a bag placed on his shoulder and then ran with the bag to deposit it where required. John picked up his first bag and walked to deposit it, in response to which his 'mate' exclaimed, 'Hurry up, we haven't got all day.' To demonstrate the supposed urgency the other man ran to deposit a second bag.

John, who was extremely fit and used to lifting heavy loads as a result of croft work, his sessions with Dusty and with weightlifting and running, said to the lorry driver, 'Give me two bags.'

'Are you sure?' said the driver.

'Yes, give me one under each arm.'

And so commenced a pattern of John delivering two bags for each one of the other fellow, so trumping the gaffer's friend's efforts. When John pointed this out, his opponent walked away.

After one more delivery, the gaffer appeared and called John off the unloading job. A point had been proven.

That was by no means the end of hostilities, however. John graduated to driving a dumper truck, which is quite tricky as it had rear wheel steering. One day, John parked the dumper truck as usual to take his lunch break. On return from lunch, the dumper, with the load of sand that was in it had been tipped into a large and deep hole. The gaffer come over and accused John letting the machine fall into the pit, when clearly someone else had deposited the dumper there out of malice.

The dumper was duly pulled out of the pit but the gaffer said, 'Teuchter, you go down there and shovel out the sand.'

John climbed down into the pit and started shovelling the sand, but such was the steepness of the sides that the sand hit the sides and fell back in again, which enraged the gaffer.

'Come on, do it properly.'

'I'm doing my best,' said John, 'but I don't know how to do it.'

'I'll show you,' said the gaffer, as he climbed down the ladder and John climbed out.

The gaffer duly shovelled the sand out of the hole, observed by John standing on the edge of the pit with the quip, 'Who's the fool now?'

Matters came to a head one day in the site hut over lunch. John was in the habit of eating corned beef and used a sharp knife to open the tin. This was in line with advice John's father had given him: always to carry a sharp knife, a piece of string and a box of matches. Each day one particular workmate sat beside John and ridiculed what he was eating. John knew that this was the man who had tipped the dumper into the pit. On the day in question, the comments recommenced:

'Oh aye, fits Teuchter eating the day, oh aye corned beef. You're nae ees here...'

Meanwhile the atmosphere in the hut grew tense. A silence reigned.

John, who had ignored these provocative comments hitherto, turned to him and said, 'You know, day after day, you have sat beside me and criticised my food and now I'm getting angry. And when I get angry, I'm not responsible for my actions. I have a very sharp knife here, which I sharpen every night. If you carry on with what you're saying, this knife might just slip and stab your side.'

With that, John made a thrust with the knife onto his persecutor's side, but John had deftly turned the hilt foremost, not the blade. The bully went white and walked away shaken.

Immediately after this event, two of his workmates took him aside and said, 'Let's go for a pint after work'. One of the two, Norman Law, was a cousin of the famous footballer Denis Law.

That night at the pub, the pints were lined up and Norman said, 'Well you really disappointed us today.'

'What do you mean?' said John.

'Well,' explained Norman, 'this was the big day. We had worked out how many of these guys we could knock out before they could take us and you went and defused the situation. You should have hit that guy. What did you do?'

John explained that he had turned his knife hilt first.

Norman then said, 'Look, do you understand what's been going on here?'

'No.'

'Well there's 73 men on this site and we three are the only ones who are not masons.'

It is a testimony to John's determination that he had stuck the poisonous situation so long, but after 12 weeks on the site, having made quite good money, he quit.

John then went on the dole while he applied for jobs. In fact, he applied for 42 jobs with 41 rejections; on the grounds that he was overqualified for some of the posts he had applied for and too inexperienced for others. Eventually he got a job as a circulation representative with DC Thomson, the publishers of *The Sunday Post* and other well-known journals and comics. In his application for the job, he had said that although he had a degree, he downplayed its value. The recipient of the letter, his future boss, apparently liked this because he did not have a degree and felt that those who had were over-rated.

As circulation representative with DC Thomson, John remained based in Aberdeen covering both the city and the rural hinterland of north-east Scotland. In this new role, his exposure to Doric (the very distinctive Scots dialect of Scotland's north-east) confronted him with a new reality and problem of communication in situations where the language of two people in dialogue were incompatible with full comprehension. Negotiations required patience and compromise on both sides but instilled in John an abiding respect for the Doric tongue and its down-to-earth speakers. Much of the job entailed going round the paper shops promoting the company's products and ensuring that they were displayed prominently. One of the aspects of DC Thomson's methods that John did not like was that there was no sale-or-return policy, such that if retailers were left with unsold stock, the profit on sales made could be wiped out. This practice seemed particularly unfair, as other suppliers did not pursue it.

It was while travelling round rural Aberdeenshire, among the Doric speaking country folk, that John remembered Lewis Grassic Gibbon's *A Scots Quair* that he had read in his schooldays. He realised that although he spoke Gaelic, he and his people had shared links going back thousands of years, with the people of the Doric-speaking north-east of Scotland as embodied by the standing stones that abounded throughout rural Scotland.

The period with DC Thomson was undoubtedly a learning experience in terms of sales skills, business and the quirks of human nature. With the security of a salaried position, John got engaged to Joan Martin. She was from Kilmuir in the north of Skye and they had met at university. The young couple were married in Skye in 1971.

John worked for DC Thomson for two and a half years in all, until his brother Roddy was lost at sea on 5 May 1971 at the age of 32. This was another tragic blow to the family, John especially, as he and Roddy had become close in his teenage years on Roddy's home trips between spells at sea. At that point, notwithstanding a career path with good prospects, John became very unsettled, felt he had had enough of Aberdeen and decided to go to Glasgow, where his brother Kenny lived. In that city, he would take up teacher training at Jordanhill College.

Glasgow

IN THE SUMMER of 1973, John Angus and Joan set up home in in a room and kitchen, which he bought for £750 on a £75 deposit. The flat was in Blantyre Street just beside Glasgow's Kelvin Hall. The mortgage was paid to the former owner who called for his money weekly accompanied by a large and fierce-looking Alsatian dog. John described him (the man, not the dog) as smooth talking and handsome, but with a distinctly menacing demeanour beneath the veneer.

John's year at Jordanhill Teacher Training College was funded by a Government grant. On completion of the course, he commenced a teaching job in North Kelvinside School on Oban Drive. He and Joan then bought a larger flat in Fergus Drive conveniently located across the road from the school. This was to be the Mackay family home for the next five years, initially with wife Joan and latterly with the addition of their baby son Derek. John had already experienced this school when on student placement. As it happened, his commencement at the school coincided with its conversion to comprehensive education. Over that summer, the builders had been busy on a large new extension and in converting the existing and fairly elite grammar school building to cope with an influx from four former tougher and more working-class junior secondary schools. As a consequence of this amalgamation, the school role had risen to 2,200 pupils.

At the start of term, conditions were challenging. Builders were still at work; paint pots were everywhere and discipline was difficult to maintain. The change in status to comprehensive was particularly difficult for the teachers who had formerly taught in the original and relatively genteel senior secondary (grammar) building.

Of the 14 teachers in the English Department, John and the head of department were initially the only two men. The stress of the new regime was such that teachers were going off sick. Classes had to be doubled up and sometimes John had to supervise three classes simultaneously by sitting up on the windowsill of his own class to supervise the other classes through a glass partition.

There was one class in that first year of comprehensive education, that John was given, that presented a particular challenge. This was a group of 13 sixth year boys and girls who had scraped through their O Grade English, but who were regarded as having little if any hope of passing their Higher Grade. The challenge was exacerbated by the fact that at Jordanhill, John's course had covered only first and second year secondary teaching. John started by doing poetry with them by reading Matthew Arnold's 'Dover Beach'. By the time he had reached the fourth line, the reading was interrupted by a large boy sitting at the back of the class, who exclaimed:

'That's a load of crap, Sir.'

John asked the boy to repeat what he had said, which he did. John closed the book and said, 'Why do you say that?'

'Well I don't understand it.'

Responding that there must be a lot of crap in the world in that case, John then had a discussion with the class along the lines of did they want to sit Higher English or were they there just because they had to be there? There was a consensus in the class that they were all 'no hopers' and had no chance of passing their Highers.

'Who told you that?' enquired John.

'Oh, we've been told that since we started secondary school, Sir.'

John then asked, 'Well if you thought you had a chance of passing your Higher, would you have a go?'

A number did want to have a go and John said, 'Well I'll be happy to work with those who want to make the effort. If the rest aren't interested, then it's no skin off my nose. I don't care if you turn up or not.' Three opted out, but with the group who agreed to stick with it, John struck a bargain to do his best to encourage them to develop the skills to make a go of their Higher English.

Mulling this episode over, John realised that the teenagers he was working with saw no more relevance on first reading in Mathew Arnold's 19th century poem than he had found as a child in 'Camptown Races'. His training in Jordanhill College had been geared towards project work, though in the context of early secondary years. This technique he adapted to targeting Higher passes for his students. John analysed past Highers papers and tested them a bit to see what their strengths and weaknesses were. Some were quite good at interpretation and some did not have a clue. Armed with this information, John split the group into small groups and got those who were reasonably good to help, in their own words, those who were struggling. John then went round the groups checking and helping where required.

When it came to the prelims, nine of the class got passes. A few days later, one of the other teachers with whom John had a good working relationship called into his classroom to tell him that there was speculation within the department that the papers had been leaked to his class. She personally did not believe this theory but wondered if the success rate was more something to do with John's teaching methods.

John retorted, 'Well *I'm* not teaching them. They're teaching themselves. That's after all what education should be about.'

'How are you doing that?'

'Well, I've got them working in groups, helping each other and working to their strengths. If they have an issue or a problem, I'll answer their questions and discuss it with them.'

Around this time, the three who had opted out of the class, opted back in and when it came to the Higher English exam, nine out of the 13 passed and a tenth passed on appeal. Motivated self-learning had worked for most of this class as it had earlier for their teacher.

During that first year at North Kelvinside School, the teachers went on phased unofficial strike, because the pay was so low and the EIS (the teachers' union, the Educational Institute of Scotland) was doing nothing about it. A group of teachers, including John, went to London to demonstrate.

The chant was 'What do we want – fifteen pounds – When do we want it – Now!' Ever the Gael, John and some others called out: 'Dè tha sinn ag iaraidh – coig nota deug – cuin a tha sin na iarraidh – an dràsda!'

The outcome of the teachers' strike which started off as unofficial without union backing, but was skilfully led by Keir Bloomer, was the Houghton Commission's recommendations on improved pay and conditions for teachers. The example of Keir Bloomer's skill in leadership and negotiation was in due course to inspire John as to how to go about political lobbying and to achieve positive results. When the dust settled, and John had secured his full teaching qualification, he secured a post as Assistant Principal Teacher of English in Colston Secondary in Springburn.

In the meantime, however, John's brother Kenny, a latent epileptic, had collapsed and died at the age of 31 on 10 May 1973, climbing stairs to his fourth-floor tenement flat on his way to lunch. They had been close since John's move to Glasgow, and John had noticed from time to time that Kenny seemed to be far away for fleeting moments. Each time when asked, his response was 'I'll be alright.'

On arriving home from school on that beautiful summer's day, John was met at the door of his flat by two policemen, who said they were there about his brother who had had a fall.

John said, 'But he'll be alright.'

The policemen took their hats off and gave him the news of his brother's death.

The shock of this third family tragedy had a major impact on the whole family, and left John feeling as if fate was stalking them all. One outcome of this, he subsequently recognised, was that he was dogged by fears of not being able to meet family commitments, with consequent feelings of insecurity which had a detrimental effect on his closest relationships, particularly his own marriage.

In retrospect, this led to his trying to put the most into – and get the most out of – life while he still had it, a motivation that was to shape his behaviour and outlook for years to come. Consequently, he was riven by fears bordering on depression, while driven by determination to contribute while he had the opportunity.

John's tales of his five teaching years in Glasgow are legendary and would merit a book of their own – a cross, one might imagine, between *Blackboard Jungle* and *The Tales of Para Handy*. Townhead and Albert Secondaries in which he did student placements were tough environments; North Kelvinside and Colston where he taught English were no less so. On one occasion, for example, he carried out what he considered to be a 'citizen's arrest' taking a rowdy boy back to school in his car to remonstrate with him. The boy's poor mother appeared at the school in her dressing gown and slippers half an hour afterwards and both boy and teacher were interrogated in her presence by the headmaster.

When the mother heard what her son had done and the insults he had thrown at the teacher, she brought the session to an abrupt end, ordering the boy out: 'Jist you wait till your faither hears whit you sayd tae yer teacher.'

With reputation at stake in the classroom jungle, and the risk of losing classroom discipline with tough teenagers, the young teacher had felt he had no option but to confront the boy. In modern times, this may well have led to more serious consequences for the teacher than a stern word of advice from the Headteacher.

In that time, his weekday evenings were split between teaching in night school, beginner's Gaelic and Higher English and work with the BBC as a radio requests programme presenter and actor in the first Gaelic radio drama series. The latter was to be a harbinger of greater things to come in the field of Gaelic broadcasting.

Weekends were given to sport – skiing in winter, running and football in the summer – and the lively social scene pursued by teachers and other professionals in the West End of Glasgow.

In many ways, life in Glasgow had been rewarding, but John had a hankering to get back to Lewis and to bring up his family in a proper Gaelic environment. He also felt an obligation to support his ageing parents while he could and to try to recover emotionally from the grief he felt at the loss of siblings. He had applied for teaching jobs in Lewis as they arose but had been unsuccessful. Then newly promoted, he applied for promoted posts, but it seems was regarded as too inexperienced.

In frustration John contacted Norma, his old headmaster's daughter, now married to Dr Finlay Macleod, himself an inspiring and innovative teacher. Norma was by this time Deputy Head of Social Work in the recently created Comhairle nan Eilean (Western Isles Council) and she suggested that John sign up to Counterdrift. What was Counterdrift? It was a scheme, of which John had been hitherto unaware, devised by the recently created Highlands and Islands Development Board (HIDB) to attract skilled workers back to the Highlands and Islands. Acting on Norma's advice, early in 1977, John filled out the form and dispatched it to the HIDB office in Inverness.

The outcome of this application was that Bob Storey, a senior officer from HIDB, called at John's flat in Glasgow. In the course of the ensuing informal interview, Bob described a new and experimental scheme that his Board was about to embark upon – namely, to encourage the creation of community-based co-operatives in the Western

Isles. John indicated an interest in becoming involved in such a venture, in response to which Bob assured him that a formal interview would take place some months hence.

Bob Storey was as good as his word. As will be described shortly, a formal interview did eventually take place and the HIDB offered John the post of Community Co-operative Field Officer for Lewis and Harris, initially on a two-year contract.

Meanwhile, over the previous several months, John's involvement with the BBC and with broadcasting flowered to the extent that he was given a bit part in a Gaelic radio soap drama called *Na Moireasdanaich* – a kind of Gaelic *Archers*. The programme was scripted by Dolina MacLennan and was the first ever Gaelic drama series, as distinct from one-off plays. Dolina had persuaded Fred MacAulay, the Head of Gaelic in the BBC to run with it.

John's part was that of an off-shore oil worker, such that in the early episodes he appeared intermittently. As the series developed and John's role increased, Dolina approached him to say that she was intending to split *Na Moiresadanaich*. Half of the action would take place in the Western Isles, instead of Glasgow as hitherto. She explained that she had been reading about the HIDB's proposed community co-op project in the West Highland Free Press and was going to have John's character going off to the Western Isles to become a community co-operative field worker.

She was astounded when John told her, 'Well actually. I am going back to the Western Isles to work as a community co-operative field worker. I've been offered a job by the HIDB. You must be psychic.' Dolina has since confessed that when John told her of this uncanny co-incidence, a shiver went up her spine. A shiver went up John's spine too.

HIDB

THE HIGHLANDS AND Islands Development Board (HIDB) was to have a major influence upon John and he in turn was to have no little influence in shaping various aspects of the Board's mission.

The Board had been created in 1965 by Harold Wilson's Labour Government under the Highlands and Islands Development (Scotland) Act 1965 in an attempt to address long-standing problems and decline experienced by this large indented and mountainous area on the very edge of Europe. In landmass, the Highlands and Islands cover about one sixth of the United Kingdom and about half of Scotland, featuring lochs, glens and about a hundred inhabited islands. Over the previous century, for all the area's natural beauty, it had suffered from under-investment and consequent chronic population decline, through out-migration, from 423,880 in 1857 to under 300,000 in 1966.

These circumstances had been recognised in a series of measures and legislation dating back into the 19th century. Of such measures, the HIDB was to have by far the most dramatic effect in turning round this decline and engendering a process of development that was to transform the Highlands and Islands into one of Scotland's most dynamic regions.

The principal objects of the HIDB were defined as: firstly, to assist the people of the Highlands and Islands to improve their economic and social conditions; and secondly, to enable the Highlands and Islands to play a more effective part in the economic and social development of the nation.

The Board had wide-ranging powers. These were principally: the provision of financial assistance in the form of grants, loans and/or equity to businesses expanding or setting up in the area; undertaking development projects carried out at its own hand; advisory functions, social planning, research and long-term economic promotion.

What was unusual, if not unique, about the Board, was that it was designed to be people-orientated and had a social as well as an economic remit. In its early days, however, the social remit was not pursued very actively as indicated by the fact that only two thirds of a page of its first annual report was devoted to 'Social Aspects'. This made reference only to medical services, education and youth activities. It seems to have been assumed that social development would somehow follow if the area's economic conditions were improved.

Undoubtedly, injection by the Board of capital into businesses, or creating facilities (such as factory units), saw an almost immediate leap in economic activity over a wide spread of industries such as manufacturing, agriculture, fisheries, tourism and community amenities. The discovery of North Sea oil and the establishment of oil terminals and production platform construction yards further accelerated the rate of economic activity, as a consequence of which, by the 1970s, the area's population was growing rapidly, largely as a result of inward migration to man the new and growing industries.

This advance, which had been particularly strong in Inverness, Easter Ross, Shetland and certain other so called 'growth poles', hid a continuing decline in a number of the more peripheral or deeply rural parts of the area. The Western Isles, with its largely Gaelic-speaking crofting/fishing community was one part of the Board's domain that was not benefiting from the upsurge in economic activity experienced elsewhere. It seemed that with the strong egalitarian tradition prevalent in the Western Isles, individual entrepreneurship was relatively undeveloped and even regarded with some suspicion. In that circumstance, despite the availability of maximum levels of grant and loan, applicants were not coming forward at the rate experienced elsewhere. Furthermore, a number of incoming small businesses failed due, in part at least, to the difficulty of controlling a distant operation from a head office in the Home Counties or English Midlands.

This presented the HIDB with a dilemma. Since the normal methods at its disposal did not seem to be having the required effect in the Western Isles, was there some different approach that could be followed?

It has been noted that, at the outset, the Board's social development role had been somewhat side-lined, a circumstance that was uncovered in 1967 when Jo Grimond MP, then leader of the Liberal

Party and member for Orkney and Shetland, asked in the House of Commons how many of the Board's staff were employed to address the Board's social role.

In answer, it was confessed that none were so employed. To rectify this omission, the Board took on, as Social Development Consultant, Robert (Bob) Storey. Bob, who was a social anthropologist by training, had been Development Officer with the then Zetland (Shetland) County Council. It is of interest that, while in Shetland, Bob wrote a report on the economic and political possibilities for Shetland based on a study visit he had made to the Faroe Islands in 1964. The Faroes model was subsequently and successfully used by Shetland to promote ideas for small businesses and ventures.

Once ensconced within the HIDB structure, Bob undertook research into the social conditions of some of the Highlands and Islands' more fragile communities, hence the highlighting of the circumstances whereby the Western Isles were not benefiting from the Board's programme of incentives as then made available.

A possible new approach came to light around 1975 when Brian Wilson, founding editor of the then recently launched radical West Highland Free Press, visited the Irish Gaeltacht (Irish-speaking) communities in the west of Ireland where community-owned multi-functional co-operatives had apparently turned round the fortunes of remote and formerly depressed districts. On his return to Scotland, Wilson met with Professor Kenneth (Ken) Alexander, the then Chairman of HIDB, and suggested that a similar co-operative approach might be worth trying in the more peripheral and Gaelic-speaking parts of the Highlands and Islands.

There ensued a series of fact-finding visits to Ireland by Board Chairman, Professor Ken Alexander, Iain MacAskill, the Board's Gaelic-speaking Secretary and by Bob Storey, who by this point had been made a permanent member of the Board's staff and provided with an assistant in the form of Alasdair Munro. The visitors were impressed by what they learnt.

These Gaeltacht communities had lacked basic services such as electricity and piped water and, with few employment opportunities, had, like many rural Highland and Island communities, suffered chronic out-migration. As there was at that time little prospect that the Irish Government would provide such services within a foreseeable timeframe, a number of these Gaeltacht communities took the initiative to provide such amenities for themselves. Energetic parish priests had generally provided leadership and, by adopting a democratic one-person-one-vote co-operative structure, shares were issued on a subscription basis to raise the funds necessary firstly to install the desired service infrastructure and then to develop employment generating enterprises. Activities varied from co-op to co-op, but included knit-wear production, fish farming, agricultural equipment hire and provision of summer schools for learners of Gaeilge (the Irish language).

The impact of the multi-functional community co-operative, or Comharchumann, model was impressive. The HIDB visitors learnt that emigration had been reduced. For the first time in a generation, young couples were staying, marrying and having children and in a number of cases emigrants returned from America or England to take up employment in these new enterprises. If community co-operatives could have such a beneficial social and economic effect in the Irish Gaeltacht, why not in, say, the Western Isles?

Thus inspired, Bob Storey and Alasdair Munro, with the backing of the Board's Chairman and Secretary, conceived a scheme to foster the creation and development of community co-operatives in the Western Isles. The concept was that of community self-help but backed by a package of advice and generous financial assistance.

Bob Storey was given the responsibility for managing the scheme and this he did with great thoroughness and insight into the art, and it is an art, of community development. A loose-leaf handbook or manual was written by Gaelic-speaking journalist and broadcaster, Martin Macdonald, on the steps that needed to be taken by community groups interested in establishing a community co-operative. This handbook was published in both English and Gaelic, a radical step at that time, and the word 'Co-Chomunn' was adopted as the generic Gaelic term for a community co-operative.

It was around this time that I myself was drawn into the project, firstly to draw illustrations for, and otherwise contribute to, the handbook and then, with legal advice, to create special model rules under the Industrial and Provident Societies Acts and to get these rules approved by the registrar. One difficulty was that the civil servant in the Scottish Office who had been asked to secure the registrar's approval of the rules had failed to persuade that official that the rules

came within the scope of the Act. It fell to me to go to London to negotiate with the registrar. Perhaps he was impressed that someone had
come all the way from the Highlands to see him, but after explaining
the purpose of the proposed co-ops and the remote rural environment in which they were to operate, the registrar agreed to sign off
the model rules as acceptable under the Act. I felt very pleased with
myself, until boarding the BEA Inverness-bound Trident at Heathrow,
the steward whispered, 'Sir, your fly is undone.' I looked down and it
was. The zip had burst. *Sic transit gloria.*

Under the rules, membership was open to all adult residents and
former residents of the community served. It was expected that a
substantial proportion of households would subscribe shares in the
enterprise. Shareholders would then be entitled to elect a management
committee to agree the policy and general development of the business. The management committee would then appoint a paid professional manager who would in turn engage such employees as might be
required to enable the co-operative to grow and carry out its business.
Unlike a conventional company where shareholder voting is normally
in proportion to shares held, member voting in a co-op is strictly on
the basis of one-person-one-vote. In this way, local democratic control
takes precedence over powerful financial interests.

Strange as it may seem today, the HIDB at that time was a highly
centralised concern operating almost exclusively from its Inverness
headquarters, although an area office had been opened in Stornoway. Thus if a fisherman from, say, Uist sought financial assistance,
he would have to make the long journey by steamer and bus or train
to Inverness to be cross-examined as to his credentials and the anticipated viability of his business proposals by an official of quite different cultural background – a highly intimidating process. By the same
token, it was equally difficult for Inverness-based officials to identify
and communicate with potential clients in the peripheral areas.

To overcome this inherent difficulty, on Bob Storey's advice,
the Board decided to take the radical step of appointing two young
Gaelic-speaking graduates as field officers who would be based in the
Western Isles. Their job would be to act as, in effect, double agents by
identifying and working with local groups who might be interested
in setting up community co-operatives and at the same time liaise
with officials in the HIDB's headquarters in Inverness to unlock the

package of financial and other assistance required to capitalise and support the co-op.

While this preparatory work was underway, the concept of community co-operatives had been publicised in the West Highland Free Press as a possible answer to some of the problems faced by crofting communities. This undoubtedly helped in opening minds to this novel socio-economic model. Before the scheme was operational a further mind-opening exercise commenced in the form of a chartered Aer Arann Islander aircraft with six Irish co-op activists on board. The flight was routed from Galway to Glasgow to clear customs and to pick up Bob Storey, and then onwards to Barra. The famous landing strip on Barra is An Traigh Mhòr, an extensive beach and, not having been to Barra before, the pilot on making his approach, suddenly pulled back on the joystick with a 'B'Jaysuss that was the wrong beach.'

Safely landed on the correct beach, the Irish party met local people in Barra, discovered a culture and language very similar to their own and a warm-hearted welcoming people who were fascinated to hear about the Irish experience with community co-ops. The partying went on well into the night. The next day, the Irish contingent set off northwards, up the Long Island (Outer Hebrides) to find a similar response in other communities. By the end of the week, they had reached Ness at the northern tip of Lewis and left an impression of a way of doing things that enough local residents thought might just work in some of the communities of the Western Isles.

Recruitment of field officers commenced in the late spring of 1977 and in due course they were appointed. Coinneach Maclean was first to arrive in Inverness for familiarisation of the work of the HIDB. Uist and Barra was to be his patch. Meanwhile, Bob Storey had identified a man who he anticipated would work in Lewis and Harris. His name, of course, was John Angus Mackay.

Back To Lewis

AS ALREADY MENTIONED, John Angus had been keen to get back to Lewis, partly so that he could bring up his family in a truly Gaelic environment; partly to get his life back on track after the painful period following the deaths of his brothers. His parents, too, were getting older and he wanted to be closer to them.

The prospect of an interview with the HIDB in Inverness for the post of Lewis-based community co-operative field officer was a very attractive one. Meantime, however, John had also applied to the Highland Regional Council for a job based at Ullapool teaching French. As it happened, both interviews were scheduled for the same June day in 1977.

Over the summer holidays, John had been in Lewis and, while shearing sheep, had hurt his back. So on the day of the interviews, it was with a bad back that he crossed by ferry, which by this time was routed to Ullapool, rather than to Kyle and Mallaig as formerly. He drove to Dingwall for the first interview – that for the teaching post.

When he arrived at Dingwall, just before the interview, he confessed to the Director of education that he had applied for two jobs and that the interviews were on the same day and that his preference was for the HIDB job, because that would take him back to Lewis. The deputy Director thanked John for his honesty and they proceeded to the interview, where this circumstance was announced at the start of proceedings. By the end of the interview, John was offered the job. He explained that he would need to see how he got on with the second interview but agreed to let them know whether or not he would accept the job by 5.30pm the same day.

By now tired and sore of back after the morning's early start, travel and first interview, off went John to Inverness, where he was met by Bob Storey and escorted to an interview room. There he was introduced to the Secretary of the Board, Iain MacAskill and to Tudor

John, the Head of Personnel. The interview commenced and with the back pain and his impaired hearing, exacerbated by traffic noise coming through the open window, John found it difficult to understand Iain MacAskill who spoke with a low voice. He persevered and came to a point at which Iain MacAskill asked, 'If you had the job and were sent out to a community that you didn't know, say, an island like Berneray, what would you do? Who would you meet?'

John answered, 'Well that depends on the weather.'

With a scowl it was clear that MacAskill thought John was being flippant and Bob Storey intervened: 'Could you explain?'

John elucidated, 'Well if it was a nice day, for example, and there's a fank (sheep penning) on, or fishermen were working at the harbour, I'd stand around, observe and work out who the leader was. Because there's always a leader in these circumstances and these are the guys who make things happen in crofting and fishing communities. What I would not do is go immediately to the manse or schoolhouse, because the people in these places think that they are the leaders, but really they are not. They might be titular leaders, but the real leadership is usually elsewhere.'

The interview continued and then came to a conclusion. Bob Story escorted John out of the room and told him that it would be a few days, perhaps weeks before he would get a response. John explained that he needed a response by 5.30pm. Bob asked why and John explained that he had been offered another job and the Education people in Dingwall were waiting to hear whether he was going to take it or not.

Bob made it clear that the Board did not offer people jobs on the day of interview, to which John said that he was the preferred candidate for the Ullapool job and would have to accept that if the Board could not let him know immediately.

'I'll see what I can do,' said Bob. 'Wait here.'

And by 5.30pm, Bob had managed to persuade the others that John was worth taking a chance on.

Not long afterwards, John came to Inverness for a week's initiation into the mysterious ways of the HIDB. Bob Storey took him round the building to be introduced to a myriad of strange faces, including my own. John was then given the handbook and told that this was the co-op 'Bible' which set out the steps by which a community co-operative could be set up. It was stressed that co-ops had to be multi-functional or they could not survive.

Thus equipped, John was sent back to Lewis to work out of the office which had recently been opened by the HIDB on South Beach Street in Stornoway.

John was of course joined by his wife Joan and his little son Derek and, after initially renting in Barvas, he wasted no time in building a new house in his home community of Shader.

Sometime after he had been in post, John asked Bob Storey, why he had been appointed.

To this, Bob replied, 'I detected in you a touch of madness' – presumably seen by Bob as a useful attribute.

Bob had a point though. To give up the prospect of a secure pensioned job for an insecure two-year contract on a highly speculative enterprise was, if not madness, certainly a gamble. Bearing in mind that the community co-op scheme was regarded by the Board very much as an experiment and that the appointment of the field officers was for two years only in the first instance, John's decision to accept the HIDB job rather the permanent post in Ullapool was a considerable risk for a young professional who had become an Assistant Principal teacher of English within three years of commencing teaching, and demonstrated considerable courage on his part and faith in the potential of the project. It was also indicative of the strength of John's feeling about going back home. Again, family loyalty and the desire to do something for Gaelic-speaking communities had underpinned his decision to take this big personal and professional risk into the unknown rather than take the safe path – a trait that was to develop as a defining characteristic as subsequent events unfolded.

The Co-Chomuinn

ONCE THE PROCESS of familiarisation with HIDB procedures and co-op principles had been absorbed, one of John Angus' first tasks in his new role was to attend a meeting in Ness, at the northern extremity of Lewis. Ness is a large crofting community where there had been an immediate interest in the HIDB scheme. John was accompanied by Bob Storey and it was the first time John had been at the official side of a table in Lewis, facing a group of crofters.

Bob started telling the story of the co-ops in Ireland and the similarities between Ireland and the Highlands and Islands and the economic problems that they shared. John noticed that there was one man in particular, an active crofter, grazing clerk and ex sailor who was nodding and listening to Bob with rapt interest. At one point, Bob used the term 'out-migration'. John then saw this man's eyes blinking and a cloud coming over him as he tried to figure out what this term meant, which took a couple of minutes, by which time he had missed the thread of what had been said.

On noting this, John thought to himself that he would need to speak to these people in their own language and not in terms of out-migration and other jargon words used by economists and sociologists. From that point, he decided that he would use Gaelic at such meetings and would have to turn the official pitch into simple language so that he could translate it into intelligible parlance.

By adopting this Gaelic policy, John found that the meetings could get to the point more quickly and more effectively. Where meetings were held in English, the more articulate monoglot incomers invariably hogged things. Holding meetings in Gaelic, on the other hand, changed the atmosphere and validated people's own experience. Thus, John came to realise that language and culture were essential parts of the development effort.

After the Ness meeting, John went round the various communities in Lewis and Harris, mainly alone, to ascertain what interest there might be in community co-operatives. In Uig, there was no interest. In South Lochs, there *was* interest, as there was in Harris. In other communities such as Point, interest was lukewarm. As a result of this initial foray, three communities in John's patch – Ness, South Lochs and Harris – emerged as promising in exploring the co-op idea further.

This was in any case as much as could be coped with at one time. John met with individuals, such as grazing clerks, in the first instance and councils of social service to get a handle on community dynamics. Out of these conversations and by drawing on existing local committees, like community associations, public meetings were held to judge the potential level of community support. In these cases where support was indicated, steering committees were appointed to research what potential there might be in establishing this new model of community-owned enterprise.

Under the terms of the HIDB scheme, there were a number of steps that communities had to go through if the Board was to be persuaded to fund a community co-op and to support its creation and development. Once a steering committee had been formed, it would explore what trading activities might be carried out profitably. If a credible portfolio of trading projects could be assembled, a business plan would be prepared, with the help of the field officer and specialist board staff. This would be submitted to the community for consent to proceed with an application to the HIDB board for its consideration. The field officer and an HIDB Board member would then attend the community meeting to judge the level of community support, including pledges to purchase shares, and would then report back to the board in Inverness when it considered the application.

Under the laid down procedures, if the application was approved, the steering committee would stand down and a community meeting would agree to the registration of the co-op and the election of the management committee, whose job was to set policies, targets and budgets and look after the development of the business. It was, thereafter, the responsibility of the management committee to appoint a paid manager to set the business up and handle its day-to-day management.

This was what happened in all three cases. I was a demanding process for all concerned. Besides the advice that field officers and other

HIDB staff could offer, there was a generous package of financial and other assistance available, namely:

- Establishment Grant, matching pound for pound shares raised by the community
- Management Grant to meet the cost of employing a manager
- Project finance for the approved projects undertaken by the co-op
- Training Assistance for managers, employees and committee members

In the light of John's early and close working relationship with Ness, this was the first community to present an application to the Board in April 1978. The proposed projects were a garage, a workshop making woollen items, a mobile snack bar, a horticultural nursery, agricultural machinery hire and supply of agricultural requisites. An establishment grant of £15,000 and a management grant of £7,500 were approved the following month, with provision for further management grants on a reducing scale for up to five years. The co-op was registered as Co-Chomunn Nis in June amid press euphoria and trading started in December 1978 when the first manager James MacLeod, a local man, took up his duties.

Such rapid progress confounded the scheme's many nay-sayers and was undoubtedly a feather in John Angus' cap. The Co-Chomunn's share subscription target of £15,000 was exceeded and the apparent success of the co-op inspired other communities to proceed with their own applications.

The next co-op to be approved was in Coinneach MacLean's area, namely Co-Chomunn Bhatarsaidh (Vatersay Co-op) serving the most southerly inhabited island of the Outer Hebrides. As it happened, Vatersay was the home community of Bob Storey's wife Lisa, a noted Gaelic activist and scholar who was subsequently to pioneer Gaelic medium education.

Vatersay was closely followed by Co-Chomunn na Pairc (Park or South Lochs, Lewis), the second in John's area. This community of about 500 inhabitants had identified several potential projects, including agricultural machinery hire, hand and machine knitting, sheepskin curing, mechanical peat cutting and possibly salmon farming. Five disused school buildings were available potentially as bases for these activities.

John Angus was also working closely with steering committees in Harris and Scalpay. As volunteers, steering committees invariably met in the evenings, often Fridays in Harris and South Lochs, and at times going on until late, which meant a long drive to reach home in the small hours of the morning. The work with the Harris committee was protracted and not without its difficulties. This was complicated by the fact that when meetings were held in English they tended to be dominated by the more articulate incomers or local professionals.

To test the strength of wider community feeling, John advertised a meeting in Leverburgh as a Gaelic event. It started badly. A local teacher spoke first and advised that a Gaelic-only meeting was a mistake as it meant a number of important people could not participate. Nevertheless, John and the meeting Chair, Donald Maclennan, persevered.

Then a voice came from the back of the room: 'Excuse me, could you speak in English so I can understand you?'

This caused a hubbub. It was explained that another meeting would be held in two weeks' time through the medium of English, but this was billed as a Gaelic meeting and so it would continue, with John adding that if it was to be otherwise, he for one was going home. The issue was put to the vote and the overwhelming majority voted in favour of continuing in Gaelic. A very positive meeting ensued.

Subsequently, a well-attended public meeting was held in Tarbert in November 1978. Also present was HIDB Chairman, Sir Kenneth (Ken) Alexander (who was highly supportive of the whole idea of community co-ops), myself and of course John Angus. Many questions were asked, quite a few of the more vociferous and self-important were hostile, suggesting that the co-op concept was bordering on communism. In the end, however, the silent majority prevailed, with an overwhelming vote in favour of issuing promissory notes for £25 shares, with a target of £10,000.

After the meeting, we retired to the Macleod Motel in Tarbert where we were staying. With a sense of relief that the evening's business had concluded successfully, it has to be admitted that we rather let our hair down amid much hilarity as drink was consumed and songs were sung. The situation was rescued in the wee small hours by our landlord, John Macleod, bringing a tray of sizzling succulent deer livers to absorb the worst of the toxins. His wife, Catriona, who had in her early years been John's family's next-door neighbour in Lower Shader said, 'Mo chreach! Bha mi an duil an fheoil sin a' chleach-dadh airson an dinear a maireach. (Good grief, I intended this to be tomorrow's dinner.)'

At 9.00am the following morning, John was roused by our Chairman Ken Alexander (who had of course retired at a civilised hour) to attend a meeting of the Co-Chomunn steering committee. That John was able to rise to the occasion says much for his stamina. I lay abed until the late morning.

Co-Chomunn na Hearadh was registered shortly thereafter. Proposed projects were a bakery, bait production, horticulture and a tea-room/craft complex possibly utilising the Board's new Craft Centre at Leverburgh.

Diverse Dealings

IN THE AUTUMN of 1978, John Angus had the good fortune to be invited to attend an international conference in Prince Edward Island, Canada. The main theme of the event was examination of the impact of the growing global influence of multinationals on governments and economies at national and even local level. It was attended by delegates from some 30 countries. This was a hugely enlightening experience both from the lessons learnt from shared experience and also the friendships forged.

With so many nationalities represented, there were inevitable linguistic difficulties, and not all languages could be served with simultaneous translation. John found himself translating from English to French for a small group of people whose grasp of English was very limited. One of those was Dr Adriano Gallevi, a field worker on a programme in Southern Italy where co-operatives were being created in isolated rural areas. Adriano had studied French in school, but had very little English; John, as we know, had studied French to University level and had no Italian. So, they communicated in French, forming a lifelong friendship which continues in get-togethers most years in Italy, fresh buffalo mozzarella and organic wine helping to cement the relationship!

One particular lesson which stuck with John from the conference in Prince Edward Island was that, while the overwhelming evidence was that multinationals exerted overbearing control wherever they could gain it, there were some examples given of 'friendly' multinationals which worked with local communities. That there may be some potential for co-operation between local communities and multinational companies was an eye-opener which stayed with John and was to be explored a few years later in the context of the community co-operatives.

Meanwhile, in South Lochs, where the population was much smaller than was regarded by the HIDB as viable in terms of establishing a Co-Chomunn, John worked with a determined, dedicated and forward-looking committee. This was the first community group in the Western Isles to pioneer fish farming, initially one trout cage. The Co-Chomunn's other projects entailed plant hire and sale of locally produced knitwear. On the day when the Co-Chomunn was to be established John was surprised to hear his Vice-Chair, David Dunbar Naismith and Bob Storey voicing private concerns about the viability of the project. John argued vehemently that the quality of the people involved far outweighed the community size and demographic, and this argument won the day, despise continuing misgivings.

As the Co-Chomunn progressed, the development of salmon farming in the Western Isles had taken off in leaps and bounds with generous grant aid under the European funded Integrated Development Programme (IDP). At one stage, the Co-Chomunn was advised by a colleague of John's that they could not compete in the environment when small producers were up against multinationals. The committee was advised that their hatchery, trout cages and sea sites that they had taken out leases on were worth no more than £10,000. The Co-Chomunn Chair approached John and asked for his advice as he felt that they would be selling themselves short. John, who chaired the inter-agency fish farming development group for the IDP, concurred. He took a list of the community-owned assets to a local Accountant, Jackie Mackay and asked him to assess the potential of the holdings and draw up a business plan.

This plan was taken to Dr David Horrobin of Scotia Pharmaceuticals which had taken on the lease of the HIDB-owned factory at Callanish, where a research facility based on the evening primrose plant was established. Dr Horrobin agreed to invest in the business plan to develop a salmon farming enterprise in partnership with the Co-Chomunn. A friendly multinational was thus enlisted to meet the threat of the predators. In the event the Co-Chomunn's assets were converted into £100,000 of share capital in the new company.

Ultimately, the venture was sold out to a major fish farming multinational, as competition in the marketplace militated against all but the very large, multi-site producers.

John's faith in the community and his support for it was borne out, despite the early misgivings of Inverness-based HIDB staff. Above all, it is a tribute to the tenacity of the people of South Lochs that Co-Chomunn na Pairc continues in operation to this day, serving the community from the shop established in the old school at Ravenspoint, Kershader.

All in all, of those communities in Lewis, Harris and the Southern Isles who had shown an interest in the scheme, the response had been impressive, but there is no doubt that their ultimate success could not have been achieved without the intense input by both field officers.

Thus far, each of the co-ops had been pursuing its respective path in isolation. In an attempt to ameliorate this isolation and to provide a forum for exchange of experiences, an assembly of representatives from each co-op or steering committee was held in Stornoway in February 1979. It was a revelation to the participants that many of the problems and issues that they each saw as solely their own were in fact shared with others. The co-ops now began to sense that they were part of an important movement that was to grow over the ensuing years.

John's participation in the assembly was curtailed by the birth of his second son, Peter.

The review of progress scripted by Bob Storey and presented to the Board on 27 February 1979 stated that:

> The field officers, who had proved of high calibre, have worked long hours, often including weekends, on a task that requires much sensitivity and understanding of local conditions. Both have come fairly close to exhaustion.

It had indeed been a hard slog for the field officers, but the review continued:

> Fortunately recent progress of the scheme has been such as to raise the field officers' morale.

That review of progress, also noted that:

> One of the field officers, Mr John A Mackay, based in Stornoway, has recently been appointed to Finance Division [of the HIDB] as an investigating officer on the understanding that for some time to come he will continue to work on co-operatives.

John Angus became more involved with the wider aspects of development in the Western Isles. A young graduate Agnes Gillies was taken on as community co-op field officer for Lewis and Harris. Agnes hailed from Galson on the west side of Lewis, not far from John's Shader and was of course a Gaelic speaker from a crofting background. John and Agnes worked well together and in due course Agnes was to become a leading figure in promoting the social and cultural development of her native island. Around this time, too, interest emerged in developing community co-ops in other parts of the Highlands and Islands. At first, it fell to me to deal with such initiatives as part of my other duties but, in due course, an additional full-time field officer was taken on. His name was Chas Ball.

With his transfer to the Finance Division, the main thrust of John's work was dealing with applicants, from the length and breadth of the Western Isles, for financial assistance towards the development of new or expanded businesses. This involved investigating the feasibility of the projects proposed and, if proceeded with, writing a GPL (grant and loan paper) with a recommendation to the Board in Inverness for approval or rejection.

John still, however, kept an eye on the Co-Chomunn and one in particular was giving cause for concern. Co-Chomunn Nis, the first to have been created and the one given most publicity, was in difficulty in terms of finance, management, trading and personnel. It fell to John to wrestle with this difficult issue, often late into the night after his more routine work had been dealt with.

At this time, the Board, which had previously offered a flexible working hours policy, changed to a policy of regular 9.00am to 5.30pm hours. The Stornoway office manager, who had been drafted in from Inverness for a period and who was not renowned for proficiency, was determined to apply this new policy to the letter.

One morning, when John turned up at the office at 10.00am, he was taken to task by the said office manager.

'But I was working until two o'clock this morning' was John's response.

This was immaterial. All staff were to be in the office at 9.00am.

As may be imagined, an uncompromising argument ensued and to resolve the matter, Bob Storey arranged for Tudor John, who had oversight of HIDB's personnel, to come to Lewis to shadow John while undertaking his duties. Bob subsequently reported that such were John's long and intense hours of work that Tudor had to take two days off to recover. Needless to say, John was then given special dispensation to work flexible hours.

Promotion

IN 1982, JOHN took over as manager of the HIDB's Stornoway office. The experience gained while working at this level was to prove invaluable, not just in carrying out the extremely varied aspects of the Board's work, but in preparing John for the various roles he was to fulfil in future years. On the one hand, he had to learn how to deal with senior members of his own organisation, including the Chairman and Board members, but also local authority members and officials, community representatives and the business community. On the other hand, he was introduced to business tools such as accounting, business plans, profit and loss accounts and balance sheets and, as interim manager of Co-Chomunn Nis, day-to-day management skills, from human resources issues to computing payslips and putting cash in wages envelopes at the end of each week.

From time to time, John had to act as guide to visiting Board members and senior staff from Inverness. On one such occasion, he had to escort the Deputy Chairman Rear Admiral David Dunbar Naismith and Iain MacAskill on a tour of developments in Lewis and Harris. Both were big men and as John's car was a small one, he hired a large and comfortable car from Mitchell's, the local bus operator and car hire firm. The car in question was in fact Mitchell's personal car. The visit went well and the VIPs returned to Inverness well satisfied. Some days later, there was a phone call from Mary Geddes, who handled the HIDB's expenses claims. Such was Mary's hawk-eyed vigilance that no irregularity escaped her notice.

She asked John, 'How many people were in your group?'

'Just three of us – and there was another chap for part of the journey.'

'Why did you hire a bus?'

'I didn't. It was just a big car.'

'Well the voucher says "hire of one bus".'

'Ah, yes 1 BUS. That is the 'cherished' registration number of the car – Mr Mitchell's own car.'

Deputy Chairman Rear Admiral Dunbar Naismith was a striking figure. He always wore a kilt and exuded an air of enthusiasm. During another visit by the rear admiral, accompanied this time by David Pirnie of Highland Craftpoint, he had asked various contacts in Harris for their ideas for development, agreeing that he would look into them. Not long into the return leg of the trip, the rear admiral asked John to stop the car, whereupon the former sailor strode up a nearby hillock. There the kilted figure stood for some time taking in the view.

John grew anxious about flight connections and shouted to the rear admiral, 'Well David and I are off. When you come up with a good idea, we'll come back and pick you up.'

David Pirnie, sinking down into his seat with acute embarrassment, muttered, 'You can't speak to the Deputy Chairman like that.'

But the rear admiral laughed, taking it in good part, conceded it was a fair point to put to a man in his position and he returned to the car.

As will be noted, John was never one to let seniority divert him from the proper course of action. Rear Admiral Dunbar Naismith's well-meant promises to 'look into' any development ideas brought forward during or after the public meeting in Harris were yet to be fulfilled. On his next visit to Inverness, John sought him out and, as it happened, he was about to rush off to the railway station to catch a train to Edinburgh, explaining that he did not have time to talk. He told John to take the issues presented to him by people in Harris to various Board departments. Undeterred, John accompanied him along the street, pointing out that the rear admiral had said that he himself would look into such matters, that the promises made to follow up development ideas needed to be kept or the Board's credibility would be lost, and there would be no point in his continuing to try to do his job in Harris. The deputy Chairman was somewhat irritated at John's persistence, but finally commented that he admired his officer's determination and commitment to the community he sought to serve. On his return from Edinburgh, the deputy Chairman duly arranged for the various proposals to be considered and the originators responded to.

There was more to the role of manager of the Stornoway office than dealing with applications for grants and loans and escorting senior members of the Board. In the course of his travels, and sometimes travails, throughout the Western Isles as Senior Administrative Officer for the HIDB, John met many interesting characters. One of them was especially unusual.

When in Barra, John usually stayed at the Clachan Beag Hotel in Castlebay. There, he enjoyed the tales of seafaring and deep diving with which the proprietor Donald MacNeil regaled him. One evening, as they sat over a meal the telephone rang. Donald excused himself to answer it and when he came back, he looked perplexed. He explained that the call had been from George MacLeod, owner of the Isle of Barra Hotel. George was in a quandary and sought advice. He had a guest staying in the hotel who had drunk six bottles of wine and wanted another one to accompany his meal. What should he do? They had discussed the man's mobility, speech and general behaviour and decided that, as his faculties did not seem to be seriously impaired, he could have another bottle. Donald, who in his time had been able to sink a few, though now abstemious, was of the opinion that the man was probably accustomed to heavy drinking. As it transpired, he was right!

The next day John was flying back to Stornoway via Benbecula. The only empty seat on the plane was the one beside him. After a few minutes the pilot apologised for a slight delay as an additional passenger had checked in somewhat late. Minutes later this passenger boarded, red-faced and harassed-looking and sat down beside John. In those days the pilot flew solo and also carried out the safety announcement which in other circumstances would be done by cabin crew.

When he turned to do so, he excused himself and, addressing John's companion, said, 'Excuse me for asking, sir, but are you Langan of Langan's Brasserie in London by any chance?'

The response was 'Yes, I am.'

'Well congratulations!' said the pilot. 'I have eaten there and I am saving up to go back again.'

It turned out this was, indeed, Peter Langan, the famous rumbustious hard-drinking Irishman whose partner in business was actor Michael Caine, and whose restaurant had become London's most fashionable haunt for stars such as Elizabeth Taylor, Marlon Brando, Mick Jagger, Muhammad Ali, Jack Nicholson, David Hockney and many others – quite a contrast with landing on Barra's beautiful but elemental expanse of Traigh Mhòr.[1]

Langan was well known for eccentric behaviour. On one occasion, he ordered everybody out and guarded the front door to keep them out. Unknown to him, Michael Caine let the guests back in through the back door, and when Langan finally decided to re-enter the place was full of quietly spoken diners. It seems he enjoyed the joke as much as everyone else!

During the flight, John and Langan, two larger-than-life Gaels, chatted and got on well. When asked why he was in Barra, Langan said he had got fed up and taken the first flight out of Heathrow to get away from the 'bastards'. The first flight was to Glasgow. Sure they would follow him, he took the next flight out of Glasgow, which happened to be the Barra flight and, to confuse them even more, he was on his way to Benbecula, before returning to Glasgow. John persuaded him that he might as well carry on confusing and accompany him to Stornoway, to which Langan readily agreed. They had lunch in the Royal Hotel, Langan with wine and John, who was working, with water. When John mentioned the previous evening and asked Langan if he had by any chance stayed in the Isle of Barra Hotel and drunk at least seven bottles of wine, Langan responded that indeed he had and that that was not unusual – in fact, he usually had six bottles of white wine before lunch!

After lunch, John excused himself to check in at his office, but promised to return as Langan had been interested in John's account of the fresh fish of various kinds being landed in Stornoway, and in the hand knitting projects throughout the islands. When John returned, there was no sign of Langan but the barman handed John a small jotter bought by Langan in Woolworth's, in which he had written a 'Dear John' letter explaining that he had phoned his restaurant and needed to go back urgently. He gave John his telephone number and said he would be very welcome to visit him if he ever came to London. At the time, John's work did not entail visits to London.

---

1 Traigh Mhòr – the great strand that serves as the runway for Barra's airport and on which flights are timed to land and take off only at low tide.

Years later, when he was visiting Westminster on a regular basis, Langan had, regretfully, succumbed to depression and had died. Langan's Brasserie was never the same again, and whilst cherishing to this day the time spent in the company of this complex and entertaining companion, John did not have the heart to go there.

Other Developments

FROM CHILDHOOD, JOHN had been all too aware of the importance of broadcasting to the Gaelic community and when the first television programmes were broadcast in Gaelic, this had been of huge interest in Gaeldom. The fact that five young singers from his own village – the Macdonald Sisters – appeared on television programmes, created a marked impression. John thought back, especially to the time when these girls appeared on television on the back of a tractor, driving through his own village singing Gaelic songs.

There was, however, a growing awareness, that with the rapid spread of universal English language television, children were being drawn away from the Gaelic environment and into a box that spoke English. The seriously erosive power of this new medium of television became very apparent to those who were trying to bring their children up with Gaelic.

In 1979, John was invited to serve on the BBC's Gaelic Advisory Committee under the Chairmanship of Dr Finlay Macleod. At this time, the committee had changed from simply advising on existing programming to identifying gaps. This new approach was led by Dr Finlay Macleod with strong support from John Murray, Ina MacIver and Colin Spencer, and with input at various times by Father John Archie Macmillan, Gordon Donald from Tiree and others. What the committee drove toward was the expansion of Gaelic programming on both radio and television. By the early 1980s, in order to free up Finlay to take a more active role in debate, John was invited to become the committee's Chair and, to be frank, a more neutral one. Backed up by sound advice from successive committee secretaries John Adams and John McCormick, this position gave John insights as to what it was like to deal with the mysterious inner workings of the BBC. John McCormick was later to become BBC Scotland Controller, a position in which he was supportive to Gaelic broadcasting.

In this way, the early groundwork was laid for John's later engagement with the broadcasting industry, giving him an understanding of how it operated. Dr Finlay Macleod, himself politically astute, advised repeatedly that the only way to change institutions effectively was from the inside, no matter how much noise was made outside – although external noise was important also. As will become evident, both were needed to effect significant change in the direction of broadcasting policy and practice.

In 1984, when John was grazing clerk in his own village, there was a meeting of the Crofters Union in Lewis held at the Retirement Centre in Stornoway. It was chaired by Angus MacLeod. The meeting turned out to be something of a disaster, demonstrating that the Union was in considerable disarray.

Afterwards, Angus, who had been one of the committee members of Co-chomunn na Pairc, came to John's office and said that he felt the Lewis Crofters Union needed to be sorted out and that it would need HIDB help. John advised that Angus should go to Inverness to speak with the HIDB secretary, Iain MacAskill, because such a radical and politically charged initiative was beyond the remit of the Stornoway office.

John phoned Iain MacAskill and told him that Angus MacLeod was coming over to Inverness to see him. Iain's antennae were so tuned that he already knew. John explained that Angus would ask for support for the Crofters Union, but his (John's) advice was not to give them support directly, but rather offer assistance to do an investigation as to how to reinvigorate the union. This line was duly pitched to Angus Macleod when he met with Iain, to which Angus responded that that was exactly what he wanted because he felt that there was no point in continuing with what existed.

On the spot, Iain and Angus agreed to set up a small working group to look at what might be done. The group was made up of Hugh Maclean, a thoughtful Gaelic-speaking Tiree man who was Head of Land Use at HIDB, Angus MacLeod and John Angus. As the group deliberated, it was agreed that someone would need to be appointed to go round the crofting areas to talk to people and look at re-inventing the Crofters Union idea. The first name that came up on the list was Dr Finlay MacLeod but, on being approached, Finlay did not feel able to commit to such a task. Then Angus Macleod to his credit suggested Dr Jim Hunter author of the seminal work *The Making of the Crofting Community*.

All agreed that this was a good idea. John was asked to contact Jim Hunter, who was at that time a journalist with *The Press and Journal*. John made contact and spoke to Jim about the proposition. He was quite surprised and pleased to be approached and decided to take on the job. Once in post, Jim visited the various crofting communities, ascertained their situation and their views. His recommendation was that a new member-led organisation be established dedicated to promoting crofting, a proposal that was unanimously accepted. When the new Scottish Crofters Union (SCU) was formed in 1985, Angus MacLeod became its first president with Jim Hunter as first Director.

* * *

Whilst proving successful in career terms, John's work ethic remained strong, but the move back to Lewis had not succeeded in healing the emotional scars left by previous experiences, and John found his marriage increasingly untenable.

With the break-up of his marriage in the early '80s, the house that he had had built was given to Joan and John moved out. He remained on Lewis to maintain contact with his young sons, Derek and Peter, with his parents and to continue his career with HIDB. He stayed initially in a caravan, after which he got the temporary tenancy of a holiday chalet until he eventually won the tenancy of a new council house in Arnol on the west side of Lewis.

Here he was joined on a permanent basis by Maria, an Italian/English interpreter, whom he had met on an exchange visit between Scotland and Italy, the circumstances of which are described in the next chapter. Maria subsequently qualified as a Social Worker at the University of Aberdeen, and the couple married in 1986. Their first son Ciaran was born in 1987 and their second, Michael, in 1990. By then, John and Maria had built a new house in Arnol, where they were able to bring the children up bilingually. Contact was also maintained between John and his two older sons on a regular basis, such that there was a close and lasting bond between father and all four sons.

Italian Interludes

IN THE TIME when John Angus was community co-op field officer for Lewis and Harris, the Land Use Division of the HIDB had arranged a visit for people from Italy, active in rural development, to come to Lewis to learn about the HIDB's involvement with co-operatives.

The key figure behind this exchange was John Bryden, an economist by training, who was a senior official with the HIDB, interested in land reform and active in developing links with the European Commission. John Bryden had links with an organisation called the Arkleton Trust which organised international seminars for senior civil servants and others on rural issues. At one of these seminars, John Bryden had met Guiliano Cesarini, head of the Cassa per il Mezzogiorno – an organisation established to fund rural development projects in the impoverished south of Italy.

And so it was in spring 1981 that an Italian delegation arrived in Lewis on a wet and windy day. John Angus accompanied the party as they visited the co-ops in Lewis and Harris and then onwards to Uist, where they were handed over to Coinneach Maclean.

To enable the formal information exchanges to function, translation was provided by Maria Ferguson who also accompanied the group. She knew little about agriculture having been brought up in Lenzie in the central belt of Scotland. As it happened, however, Maria had been in Rome to teach as part of her Italian degree course and had lodged with the Cesarinis.

The following year, at the suggestion of Giuliano Cesarini, a return visit was made by a group of individuals from the Western Isles and the College of Agriculture. The group was made up of active crofters and others involved with co-ops and agriculture, with John Angus and Agnes Rennie (formerly Gillies) representing the HIDB and the community co-operative scheme. Again, Maria accompanied the group. The representatives who came over from the college of agriculture kept using technical terms such as the number of lactations a cow would have in a day. Maria and John hit it off because he was able to translate the technical terms into everyday English thereby allowing Maria to translate into Italian. The bond thus established between John and Maria was in due course to blossom to the extent that Maria would become John's second wife.

The Scottish group was taken to Naples and then further south to the mountains of Campania. They spent the best part of a week there, meeting many of the same people who had visited the Western Isles on the previous year. Visits were made to co-ops, mainly agricultural co-ops, but including one which made jam from fruit.

John found that he got on well with the co-op development workers and in particular with Adriano Gallevi, whom he had met previously at a conference in Prince Edward Island in 1979. As Adriano spoke no English and at that time John spoke no Italian, they communicated through French when formal translation was not available and by this means they were able to translate exchange of information for the benefit of others.

John also established a rapport with another development worker, Teodoro Vadala, who was based in Naples and had established links with the communities destroyed by earthquake not long before, in 1980. Some of the group were taken to the devastated area where they experienced heartbreaking scenes in which many houses and in some cases whole villages had collapsed, leaving behind heaps of rubble. In some areas dazed people were observed, picking about in the rubble looking for mementos of their past lives. This development officer asked John to go back to accompany him on visits which John duly did to show solidarity.

Many had been killed, but the earthquake also changed the lives of those who survived, because a huge international relief effort initiated a massive rebuilding programme. A lot of money had been collected worldwide. Many relief workers came to help with the relief and rebuilding effort. Many of the relief workers were young people who brought with them values and modes of dress that had previously been unknown in that deeply rural and conservative area. In particular, young American and British women who behaved as equal to men were a revelation to the Italian peasant women. When some of these local women started to assert themselves, this naturally caused ripples in families.

Other more general forces were at work that would change the traditional way of life of southern Italy. The building by the Government of a north-south Autostrada del Sole (motorway of the south), which connected with local authority-built side roads, revolutionised the access of hitherto rather isolated villages.

As one villager put it to John and Maria on a later visit, 'Before the road came, I would spend half a day going down by donkey to the nearest town with my milk, cheese or other produce. After a few hours selling these, it would take several more hours to get back to the village. Now with the road and co-op in place, a milk tanker comes to my door to pick up my milk.'

The group was fascinated, however, that such traditional equipment as scythes and shears, as were still in use, or were in museums, were exactly the same as the traditional implements that had been used in the Western Isles. Such was the universality of rural tradition that went back centuries, if not millennia.

Two years later, Guiliano Cesarini asked John and Maria to return to Campania to look afresh at the co-ops and on their return, supported by the Arkleton Trust, Maria again took on the role of interpreter. Their key informant was again Adriano Gallevi – a dotore (PhD). He was very clever, intense and seemed to know everything about agriculture. Working under the auspices of Guiliano Cesarini of the Cassa per il Mezzogiorno, Adriano had become the kingpin of the Cassa supported co-op movement in the south of Italy. He worked out of Eboli on the coast south of Salerno. He enthusiastically explained how he had facilitated the creation of four tiers of co-op activity – first the primary production, then processing, and then marketing and finally an administration co-op – the co-op of co-ops – of which he was the president, with his office in Eboli.

As he described all this, as translated by Maria, John asked her to ask him, 'Does it work?' to which the answer was 'No.'

John sought an explanation as to why it didn't work, to which the answer was 'Too many tiers!' or, more accurately, that there was not enough critical mass at each level for it to be viable.

One problem faced was that when they sought answers to specific questions such as number of hectares under different crops, yields and such like, to define the scope and scale of activity, it was difficult to get accurate information.

Over the ensuing years John and Maria returned to Italy on a number of occasions. They visited several of the agricultural co-ops that had been assisted by the Cassa and also one involving textile production. This women's co-op made clothes and accessories for the Milan fashion market. When visited, however, no work was being done because they had no orders at that time. The women preferred to stay at the factory because it had given them a degree of independence and they did not want to go back to being controlled by the men.

It became clear that while the co-ops that Giuliano had started were agricultural co-ops, in which land had been made available to create larger and more efficient units, run on traditional lines, this ran counter to the women's wish to get away from traditional mores and to gain some independence. In the aftermath of the earthquake, the external influences referred to earlier, coupled with new economic opportunities, had created a different social, cultural and economic environment to that which pertained when the agricultural co-op model was originally designed.

There was another dimension, as voiced by at least one individual. When enquiring about this, John and Maria were directed to the office of a publisher, Lorenzo Barbera. When they arrived at his office and asked the secretary if they could speak with the person they had been directed to, she looked frightened and evasive and said that he was at a meeting and did not know when he would return. Explaining that they were from Scotland, John and Maria said they would wait.

After some time, they returned to the office, and the secretary was more forthcoming. It transpired that Barbera was at a meeting of what appeared to be the Italian version of the European Integrated Development Programme, which was at the time in progress in particular areas of Scotland and France. She explained that he was involved to try to keep the Mafia out. After some time, John asked how much longer he might be, at which point the secretary burst into tears and said that he might never be back as he might be shot. Eventually, however, as evening approached, the man arrived and in the ensuing conversation he confirmed that he had been publishing anti-Mafia material in Sicily and had to go on the run, hence ending up in Campania, where he continued publishing anti-Mafia literature.

It was clear from the information provided by Adriano that the co-ops had to increase output and needed more Government money to be able to do so. Things took a turn for the worse, however, when the Government in Rome that had been providing the funds through the Cassa per il Mezzogiorno stopped the funding, insisting that local authorities should provide the support to the co-ops instead. In the end, John and Maria decided that the research project had deviated so far from the original brief of how the co-ops were faring, to issues of women's liberation and the Mafia, there was no way in which they could write it up without considerably more research which they did not have the time and resources to conduct.

A few years later, however, John and Maria went back to Italy and contacted Adriano. He was delighted that contact had been re-established as he had arranged for a gathering of co-op people from various parts of the country to celebrate his birthday. Guests brought wine, cheese, ham and other products. John brought malt whisky. On that balmy night under the trees, Adriano's beautiful daughter, Maria Sole, who subsequently became an accomplished opera singer in Brazil, sang, captivating the assembled group.

Such was the allure of this and previous experiences that Italy was to exert a lasting pull on John and Maria.

Cabadaich 2: *Bella Italia*

Blethers 2: Italy

ROY: For a boy born and raised in the furthest Hebrides, Italy has become a big part of your life. What attracted you to the place?

JOHN: This all started with the HIDB and John Bryden of the Arkleton Trust. He set up a chain of events that over the years set me on a path to buying an apartment in Italy which has given huge pleasure to Maria and me.

It all started when John Bryden asked me if I would go to a conference in Prince Edward Island. The conference was about the influence of multi-nationals on rural communities. At the conference I met an Italian, Adriano Gallevi. We conversed in schoolboy French. He didn't speak English and at that time, I didn't speak Italian. We got on famously to the extent that I ended up translating for him or explaining to him some of the English contributions to the conference.

At a subsequent conference Ken Alexander, then Chair of HIDB, met Giuliano Cesarini who was the equivalent of John Bryden at the Casa per il Messogiorno. The two of them agreed that there should be an exchange visit between the community co-ops in the Western Isles and co-ops in the south of Italy. So that's how I went over to Italy for the first time.

One of the people I met up with again was Adriano Gallevi who was involved in setting up co-ops and eventually became the president of the federation of co-ops in the south of Italy. So a friendship developed between us that continues to this day.

When we were in Italy, what we saw was that there were similar traditions to our own in the rural communities. People were working with much the same kind of implements as we had at home. I mentioned to you before sickles and scythes and they had those and hoes that very much resembled the *cromans* that we used to dig the

mance where people took the
animals up into the mountains in summer the same way as our people
took the cattle out onto the moor in the summer too. So I felt that
we had an empathy with the people and them with us. So in a way,
although I was in a foreign land, we felt at home.

ROY: And I believe there was a certain young lady who came into
the picture.

JOHN: Well yes. Maria had been the translator for the Italians when
they came to Scotland and for us when we went to Italy. That's how
we met up. The whole thing was much easier for me because of course
Maria was fluent in Italian, and we relied on each other in these circumstances. Anyway, as you well know, Maria and I married and our
mutual interest in Italy led us to find a place there. This we did in the
beautiful little hillside town of Pacentro in the province of Abruzzo. It
is reckoned to be amongst the ten most beautiful little *borghi* (towns)
in Italy.

Then of course one big attraction of Italy for someone from the
Western Isles was the sunshine, the food and the wine.

ROY: Well that's three attractions, but having stayed at your lovely
apartment in Pacentro with its views over the valley and mountains
beyond, it's idyllic and I know you and Maria have become part of the
community there with new friendships. So people and place must be
part of the draw. Anyway, I can only say your Italian bolthole is well
deserved after all your hard work over the years.

Cor na Gàidhlig

FROM THE HIGH point in the 11th century when Gaelic was spoken by the king, court and the great majority of the Scottish people, an inexorable decline followed partly as a result of official policies to 'extirpate' the language. The 1981 Census confirmed this downward trend and occasioned serious concern about the future survivability of the language. Whereas the 1891 Census enumerated 254,415 Gaelic speakers in Scotland, the number had reduced to 79,307 by 1981. Such was the rate of decline.

Efforts to support Gaelic had existed for some time. An Comunn Gàidhealach, had been founded in 1891 to help preserve and develop the Gaelic language. Its highest profile activity was the National Mòd, the annual Gaelic competitive festival that provided a platform for Gaelic singing and other arts. It was becoming clear, however, that new approaches were needed.

During the 1950s, '60s and '70s, a number of individuals and groups had begun to consider what fresh actions might be taken to address Gaelic's chronic decline. Among these initiatives, Professor Derick Thomson founded the Gaelic Books Council and edited the Gaelic quarterly magazine *Gairm* as a vehicle for Gaelic writing and dissemination of ideas. Among students and Gaelic learners, the radical approach by language activists in Wales prompted thoughts about trying to emulate such an approach in Scotland, albeit in a more muted form. Agitation began for Gaelic road and other signage, which resulted in some direct action. A Gaelic book club, Club Leabhar, and a Gaelic newspaper, *Sruth*, both relatively short-lived initiatives of An Comunn, attempted, and to an extent succeeded, in encouraging Gaelic authors and increasing the range of reading material available. One group coalesced around the venerable Gaelic Society of London and the Gaelic classes of the City Literary Institute. Among its members were Professor Ken Mackinnon who was later to undertake much useful Gaelic socio-linguistic research and, for a short period, myself who created and published the first Gaelic map of Scotland, which was to sell some 30,000 copies.

These efforts were insufficient to stem the attrition, but they did raise Gaelic's profile and sowed seeds of hope that were later to germinate. It was to be a series of bold initiatives by the HIDB in partnership with others, however, that first put in place the means by which Gaelic's decline might be halted and reversed.

As has been noted, in the first few years after the creation of the HIDB, the main thrust of the Board's effort was focused on physical regional planning concepts. There was little or no thought as to the significance or value of Gaelic.

In 1968, the Board, under its scheme of grants for non-economic and social projects, assisted the costs of Mòds when held in the Highlands and Islands. In 1969, the Board mounted a major exhibition aboard the MacBrayne car ferry *Clansman* moored at Tower Pier, London. One unintended outcome of this event was that it provided a forum for those Gaelic activists, then resident in London, to meet with Board personnel initiating a two-way awareness raising process. At that time, too, an HIDB booklet describing the new area tourist organisations listed the name of each area in Gaelic. These initiatives were essentially accidental, as there was not then, or for some time to come, any conscious intent to develop a Gaelic policy.

Within local government, matters regarding support for Gaelic had been no better. The rural county councils were dominated by aristocrats and landed gentry, for whom, in general, Gaelic was an alien concept with which they had no sympathy. Furthermore, the Outer Hebrides (Western Isles) were split between Inverness-shire and Ross and Cromarty, whose headquarters were located in distant mainland Inverness and Dingwall respectively.

Then, in 1975, the old regime was swept away with a radical reorganisation of local government. This saw the creation of a new all-purpose local authority for the Western Isles, which was given the Gaelic name Comhairle nan Eilean. New top tier regional authorities were also created Scotland-wide, of which Highland Regional Council and Strathclyde Regional Council, the latter of which also covered Argyll, were to have a much more supportive attitude to Gaelic.

With the appointment of Professor Kenneth Alexander as Chairman of the HIDB, the social emphasis of that organisation was refocused. This featured firstly, at Bob Storey's behest, the renaming of the Board's 'non-economic grants' as 'social grants' and more ambitiously the launching in 1977 of the high-profile community co-op scheme, which, as has been described, is how John Angus' appointment as field officer was to influence how the Board approached other aspects of development at community level.

Gaelic policy and development effort within the HIDB was to evolve through the vision and pioneering efforts of a small number of individuals within the staff compliment. Sometimes these efforts faced a climate of indifference or even hostility; at other times, they echoed a consensus of support. In the course of this process, the HIDB and its successor HIE became recognised internationally for their innovatory approaches as the prime movers in the re-generation of Gaelic. How this came about is described later.

The publication of a wholly Gaelic version of the community co-operative guide and the naming of most co-ops as *Co-chomunn...* using the Gaelic term, together with the inclusion of Gaelic articles in the Board's magazine *North 7*, was the first time that any Board programmes had an explicit Gaelic dimension. Other Gaelic projects were helped on an ad hoc basis, such as Gaelic publishing, drama and *Fèis Bharraigh* (an instructional Gaelic arts festival in Barra inspired by Father Colin MacInnes). Most notably, however, landowner Iain Noble was creating a number of other Gaelic initiatives, including the genesis, from a derelict barn in Skye, of what was to become the Gaelic college Sabhal Mòr Ostaig (SMO). A key concern, however, was the ineffectiveness at the time of An Comunn Gàidhealach in promoting the development of the language, as confirmed by the markedly reduced number of Gaelic speakers in the 1981 Census.

In the light of this and following discussion with several prominent Gaels, Iain MacAskill, the pro-Gaelic HIDB Secretary and Bob Storey, supported by the Board Chairman Sir Kenneth Alexander, resolved to seek advice on how the Gaelic community could be supported to develop through the medium of its own language. And so, in June 1981, the Board commissioned a group to advise on the need and scope for more effective help for developments in the Gaelic community linked with the Gaelic language.

The members of the group were appointed on a personal basis. They were: Donald John Mackay (Chairman); The Rev John MM MacArthur (Highland Regional Councillor); Fred MacAulay (Manager, BBC Radio Highland and Head of Gaelic at BBC Scotland); Catriona MacDonald (Gaelic teacher); Dr Finlay MacLeod (Deputy Director of Education at Comhairle nan Eilean); Duncan MacQuarrie (Head of Gaelic and Guidance at Inverness Royal Academy); and Cailean Spencer (Education Director at An Comunn Gaidhealach). Journalist and broadcaster Martin Macdonald was appointed reporter/secretary to the group and Iain MacAskill and Bob Storey acted as assessors.

This impressive muster of talent set to their task with great diligence and, by November 1982, produced a report that was to have a major and positive impact on the future development of the Gaelic language, culture and community. The report was entitled 'Còr na Gàidhlig' (The Condition of Gaelic) and was the result of a wide programme of research and consultation with organisations and individuals actively involved with the Gaelic community and knowledgeable about various aspects of the linguistic situation.

The report considered the cumulative effect of erosive factors behind the decline in Gaelic in recent generations. These included negative official attitudes, the refusal, under the 1872 Education Act to allow Gaelic in schools, depopulation, inward-migration by non-Gaels, a predominantly English mass media and a fatalistic attitude by Gaels themselves.

On the other hand, more recent supportive factors were also identified, such as increased Gaelic broadcasting: the success of the Gaelic rock group, RunRig; the impact of the drama company, Fir Chlis; and the creation of the Celtic Film Festival in Benbecula in 1979. In the educational field, Sabhal Mòr Ostaig at the further education level and the emergence of pre-school playgroups, promoted by a redoubtable Gaelic activist Finlay MacLeod, were pioneering instruction of young people through the medium of Gaelic.

One important, and as it would turn out, pivotal finding of the research data showed a desire among a significant group of parents for Gaelic instruction of their children at statutory (school) level. This desire was accompanied by growth in assertive action in favour of the language by community groups, student organisations, language promotional bodies, pressure groups and individuals. The report noted that, in response to these actions, official attitudes to Gaelic were softening and political support seemed to be growing.

The 'Còr na Gàidhlig' report led to the formation of a number of Gaelic policy initiatives within HIDB. A series of Gaelic officers were appointed and, with ministerial backing, the decision was taken to create a new Gaelic development organisation to be called Comunn na Gàidhlig (CNAG) tasked with a new proactive and professional approach to Gaelic development based on a partnership of HIDB, three local authorities, An Comunn Gàidhealach and the Scottish Office.

The first of the Board's Gaelic officers was Allan Campbell, engaged on a short-term contract primarily to bridge the diplomatic gulf between the promoters of CNAG and An Comunn Gàidhealach, who saw CNAG as a threat to their supposed authority and status. The next was Aideen Ò Malley, again on a short contract, to aid the drafting of HIDB Gaelic policy, deal with applications for assistance from Gaelic projects and to help the process of creating CNAG. These and subsequent Gaelic officers were located within the Board's Social Development Branch led by Bob Storey and assisted by me.

After the creation of CNAG, which is described in the next chapter, a full-time Gaelic officer post was created in HIDB to deal with applications for a variety of Gaelic projects then being created by activists. These included CLI, a new Gaelic learners initiative; the introduction by Comhairle nan Sgoiltean Àraich (CNSA) under the radical Finlay MacLeod of the first of a network of Gaelic medium playgroups; *fèisean* which grew from the pioneering tuitional festival, Fèis Bharraigh, to a evolve into a nationwide network of (to date) some 40 *fèisean* Scotland-wide. The *fèisean* in turn led to an upsurge in performance of traditional music and other Gaelic-related arts. The first full-time Gaelic officer was Myles Campbell followed by Margaret MacIver and John Shaw.

Besides handling applications of these kinds, the Gaelic officers undertook translation work, policy drafting and animation at community level. The Head of Social Development (by that time myself, following Bob Storey's retirement) steered the direction of development and initiated new projects such as the staged development of courses and infrastructure at Sabhal Mòr Ostaig, which was beginning to foster the development of a new generation of young professionals confident to use Gaelic in their workaday lives.

Comunn na Gàidhlig (CNAG)

COMUNN NA GÀIDHLIG was created as a not-for-profit company limited by Guarantee in 1984. It was structured as a partnership of HIDB, Highland Regional Council, Comhairle nan Eilean (Western Isles Council), Strathclyde Regional Council and An Comunn Gàidhealach. From the start the company used the acronym CNAG (pronounced 'krack'), which in Gaelic conveys the sense of the heart or nub of the matter as in the phrase 'cnag na cùise'. CNAG's first Chairman was Donald John Mackay, with Duncan MacQuarrie as secretary. One of the first actions of the company's board was to advertise the post of Director.

The chance to head up a new organisation aimed at riding the growing wave of interest in Gaelic was too tempting for John to turn down. Interviews were held and John Angus Mackay, HIDB's now Senior Administrative Officer and Area Officer for the Western Isles, was the winning applicant. There is no doubt that John's own seniority and profile within the HIDB machine added to the development clout of the post.

After working out his notice with HIDB, John started in the post of Director of CNAG in January 1985, based initially in the office of CNAG's Chairman, located in Academy Street, Inverness. Donald John, as housing association Chairman amongst his many commitments, secured for John one of the association's houses in Invergordon.

In many ways, this job was another brave departure for John. His educational and community development credentials were well proven. The irony was that, as a fluent speaker of Gaelic from his mother's knee, he had never received any formal education in Gaelic. His ability to read and write his native tongue was, therefore, very limited. Painstakingly, John taught himself to read and write his own language. He took time each evening to read a chapter of the Bible. As for the more challenging task of beefing up his skill in writing Gaelic, he sought advice in correcting the various letters, reports and other documents he created. It goes without saying that he quickly reached a professional standard in written Gaelic.

Both Donald John Mackay and Duncan MacQuarrie were a considerable help to John in explaining the purpose and ambitions of CNAG and making a number of key contacts. Early in this process, Donald John accompanied John Angus down to London where they met Russell Johnston, Liberal MP for the Inverness area, and also other MPs to open up cross-party links. This was to become very fruitful in the ensuing years. Another useful contact made in London at that time was Finlay Maclennan, Head of Security in the House of Commons. He took them out to lunch on that first visit.

Highland Regional Council's representative on CNAG was Councillor Reverend Jack MacArthur. He was the council's Gaelic-speaking Chairman of Education and a Church of Scotland minister. Jack had many influential contacts and was very supportive of John, particularly during CNAG's early period.

Srathclyde Regional Council appointed Councillor Bernie Scott as that organisation's representative on the CNAG board. Donald Mackay, Chair of Education at Comhairle nan Eilean, was the Western Isles representative and Neil MacKechnie represented An Comunn Gàidhealach. Each of these brought experience in Gaelic, education and public service as well as a range of contacts which collectively opened many doors. In those first early months, John learnt a great deal very quickly from this impressive array of expertise.

CNAG focused on three key strands of development. These were Gaelic medium education, the Gaelic arts and Gaelic broadcasting. CNAG appointed staff who knew about education and who were helpful in developing that strand, including youth work. In some ways, it was quite difficult to find a locus in education because that was a local authority responsibility. The key to progress was growing parental demand, in part fostered by CNAG. To facilitate progress CNAG set up Comunn nam Parant as a Gaelic medium education promotional and support organisation, and set up home visiting schemes so that knowledgeable and committed people, mostly mothers, visited parents in their homes to demonstrate the growing availability of Gaelic children's books and to discuss the benefits of Gaelic/English bilingualism. For the children, CNAG set up after school clubs, Sradagan

(Sparks) youth organisations and summer camps, where the language of activities was Gaelic.

One early initiative in that first year was a conference that came on the back of an invitation by Iain Noble to Secretary of State for Scotland, George Younger, to visit Skye. Iain Noble was a merchant banker and owner of a considerable estate in Skye. Unusually for an aristocratic landowner, Iain had learnt Gaelic to a high degree of fluency, was an influential advocate for the language and had inspired the idea of the Gaelic college, which was duly created in one of his properties – the now famous derelict barn called Sabhal Mòr Ostaig. By the time CNAG had been created, the college was already functioning as a small-scale further education establishment providing courses through the medium of Gaelic, and John Angus had become part of the advisory group working on the development of the college.

In the early 1980s, George Younger had attended the Oban Mòd. He had listened to some of the competitions and the singing and was taken by the emotion of the occasion. He realised that there was something in Gaelic that struck a chord with him.

A merchant banker himself, George Younger knew Iain Noble through the close-knit world of Scottish financiers. Thus, when Iain Noble asked him to come to Skye to be seen, not just among his own circle, but on a public platform, a conference was organised by John and his board at CNAG at the Sabhal Mòr with George Younger as keynote speaker. George Younger willingly agreed and was receptive to CNAG's ideas on Gaelic medium Education, promoting Gaelic arts and looking at the case for a Gaelic television service. It was noted, however, that his civil servants were anything but receptive to these ideas.

At the conference dinner, after general discussion about the Gaelic situation, George Younger asked, 'What do you want?'

Rev Jack MacArthur responded with the approach previously agreed with other CNAG Board members. 'We want you to come off the fence. Benevolent neglect is choking us. We want you to support us actively.'

George Younger replied, 'If you continue to do what you are doing just now, I'll ask my civil servants to support you. If you ask, we will try to give you what you want, but don't go for a Gaelic language Act because, if you do, a lot of energy will be diverted towards that. You might even win it but, in the meantime, nothing will have happened in education, the arts or broadcasting. So, I would advise you to work hard in developing these fields and eventually the Act will follow.'

This was to prove prophetic, although it was to be another 20 years before the whole process came to fruition.

George Younger explained that it was important that so long as the Gaelic-speaking community pushed forward and demonstrated a demand for Gaelic services, then the Government would do its best to respond. He explained that it was not the Government's job to lead Gaelic development, but to respond to a demonstrable need.

After internal debate within CNAG, this was seen as sound advice, which John and his advisers took on board.

Gaelic Education and Arts

THAT YEAR OF 1985 was also the year in which Highland Regional Council and Strathclyde Regional Council agreed separately to support Gaelic medium education by setting up Gaelic primary school units in the Central School in Inverness and John Maxwell's school in the Southside of Glasgow, with less than 20 children between them. The situation in Glasgow demonstrated that the recommendation to set up CNAG as a quasi-public body with Strathclyde Region as a member was an inspired one. The composition of the Board with high-level representation from its membership gave John as CEO unprecedented access to political leaders, such as CNAG member Councillor Bernie Scott, Social Work Chair, James Jennings (Convener) and Charles Gray, Leader of Strathclyde Regional Council and Chair of COSLA (the Convention of Scottish Local Authorities). Thus, John, whilst also attending evening meetings with parents in Glasgow, was able to meet other key personnel in the Council.

The parent group advocating creation of Gaelic medium education in Glasgow met with Charles Gray and his officials to hear the outcome of a report prepared by Frank Pignatelli, Director of Education, and his Deputy Keir Bloomer. John had fortuitously asked for an interview with Charles Gray beforehand and after some chat, Charles Gray told John that, regretfully, the report did not recommend establishing Gaelic medium education (GME) that year due to space and financial constraints but recommended applying for European funding. Realising how devastating this would be for Glasgow parents, and potentially demoralising for Inverness parents, John argued that Strathclyde – to whom the rest of Scotland looked for leadership and innovation – should lead the way politically and practically. Charles Gray indicated he was personally sympathetic but could not promise anything at that stage.

The meeting became very fractious when parents, supported by Brian Wilson, heard the outcome of the report. After listening to the heated exchange, Charles Gray stated that his officials had done a lot of good work for this report and had shown why it might not be possible to start Gaelic medium education that year. Nevertheless, a political decision had been taken that day, and officials would now be tasked to work with parents, if they were willing to pull their weight, to work out what could be done. A crucial intervention by renowned Gaelic singer and activist, Anne Lorne Gillies, who had identified empty classroom space in Sir John Maxwell School, meant the meeting closed on a positive note to underpin the political decision.

It is no exaggeration to state that the commitment by George Younger at Sabhal Mòr Ostaig to support Gaelic actively and the establishment of the first Gaelic medium primary school classes marked 1985 as a turning point in the changing fortunes of Gaelic. Out of that came a drive to persuade other local authorities to support Gaelic medium education with the establishment of Gaelic medium education units in primary schools spreading across Scotland.

Around this time John Angus moved out of Donald John's office to the offices of An Comunn Gàidhealach where he was given some administrative back-up and then more permanent support, in the form of Jessie Morrison to be joined shortly afterwards by Ceiteag MacGregor. Outgrowing the space available in the small An Comunn office, John and his small team moved to a room in Cauldeen School. After a while the CNAG team moved back to the Inverness town centre, firstly to rooms in Academy Street and then to one of the National Trust for Scotland's Little Houses in Church Street.

With this succession of moves, the staff grew. A strong, though small, development team was created, such that John was able to delegate responsibilities. In 1987, CNAG, jointly with An Comunn Gàidhealach, set up Pròiseact nan Ealan (Gaelic Arts Project) with Malcolm (Malkie) Maclean, an accomplished artist and former art teacher, as its Director. Within a year, the Gaelic Arts Project came wholly under the wing of CNAG. The Gaelic Arts Project liaised with the Gaelic arts community, identified aspirations and barriers to their realisation and sought to meet the needs identified. In particular, it set out to support Gaelic singers and musicians, develop Gaelic drama and set up relevant training courses. Thus, the project helped young artists to develop professional skills and equipped them with the ability to work and make a living in the arts marketplace. The drama summer schools, run at Linaclete School in Benbecula by the Gaelic Arts Project, engaged professional Directors, actors, and experienced writers as tutors. This was to bear fruit in a flowering of stage and screen talent which ultimately provided the backbone of the first Gaelic serial television drama, *Machair*. This series was pitched initially at the same time as *Eastenders* on the BBC and secured higher viewing figures than that programme in Scotland.

Support was also given by way of school drama and a children's magazine to the growing Gaelic medium education sector. Talent development was central to the success of these ventures, and the project also encouraged the spread of *Fèisean*, the music tuition festivals. This culminated in the establishment of a stand-alone support structure for the individual *Fèisean* – Fèisean nan Gaidheal – which has grown from strength to strength and now provides tuition for thousands of youngsters, as well as running a major annual event *Blas*, with dozens of performances throughout the Highland area.

CNAG also established a publishing programme partnership with the Stornoway-based publisher Acair. In this period too, John was the Secretary to the UK committee of the European Bureau for Lesser Used Languages, during Rev Jack MacArthur's tenure as the President of the Bureau. Following a successful international conference on minority language children's publishing held in Stornoway, Acair and CNAG jointly funded, on a shared profit basis, commissioning and publication of a new strand of books. This led to regular mutually supportive communication and action between the two organisations, culminating in John's joining the Board of Acair and acting as Chair between August 1990 and September 1991.

With the requirement to travel to carry out his duties, John was an early adopter of the now ubiquitous mobile phone. The mobile then was not the handy pocket device of today, but a formidable object the size of a brick, featuring a long retractable aerial and held in a body holster when not in use. John used to hire one at Glasgow Airport. Cumbersome it may have been, but it proved its usefulness on the occasion of a meeting of the main committee of the European Bureau for Lesser Used Languages in Glasgow.

On the occasion in question, this international group of linguists was walking west down Argyle Street towards the Hielanman's Umbrella.[2] One of the group was a tall, blond member from the Netherlands Friesian minority who spoke in English with what, to the untrained ear, sounded like a fairly posh English accent. This seemed to enrage a gang of young toughs, whose ears, it seems, were of the untrained variety. The gang started following the group, hurling insults. This was a somewhat alarming turn of events as the group was mostly composed of academic rather than athletic/Rambo types. As a countermeasure, John pulled out the phone which with its aerial had the appearance of a police radio. He pretended to call up reinforcements.

This did the trick. One of the more aware of the hobbledehoys shouted, 'Hey boys, he's polis!' and they ran off before the imagined reinforcements materialised. Necessity, then, as in so many other instances, was the mother of invention.

All the while John Angus worked closely with HIDB and, in particular, with me who, as Head of Social Development, had a budget to support a range of Gaelic projects. This work was aided by Myles Campbell, the Board's Gaelic Development Officer who was seeking to foster a number of Gaelic economic initiatives.

With the developing youth emphasis and the Gaelic Arts Project, CNAG opened an office in Stornoway, which meant that John moved his base from Inverness to Stornoway. It is telling to note that in his first year with CNAG, he drove 30,000 miles with journeys covering Edinburgh, Glasgow, Skye and many other places in addition to the shuttling between Lewis and Inverness and flights to and from London. At the same time, whilst much time was spent in urban locations, establishing an office in Lewis allowed John to maintain close links with his roots and an affinity with rural Gaelic-speaking communities. This gave rise to some surprising coincidences.

John's uncle Angus, from whom he took his middle name and who died at sea in the Mediterranean in 1944, had been on one of the ships that shelled Naples as part of the Italian campaign. How John found this out was that CNAG had developed a strategy of using

---

2 The Hielanman's Umbrella is the railway bridge which carries the platforms of Glasgow's Central Station across Argyll Street, where in former times Gaels met during inclement weather.

agricultural shows, nationally and locally, to promote Gaelic medium education. On the occasion of the Carloway Show, CNAG had set up a big tent with television monitors promoting Gaelic medium education and Gaelic television. The weather got bad with wind and rain so that John went to the local shop, run by Donald MacAulay (Dòmhnall a' Bhraisich) to get more rope to lash the tent down. In the shop were two young mothers with children in pushchairs, speaking to Dòmhnall a' Bhraisich in English. As they talked, the children got restless and started crying. John suggested to the women that they buy the children ice cream.

'What do you mean?' was the response of one.

John replied, 'Well as you two are talking to Dòmhnall a' Bhraisich, the kids, at their height can only see posters for ice cream.'

So the women bought ice creams for the children, which had the desired effect of pacifying them.

John then ventured the question, 'Do any of you speak Gaelic?'

Dòmhnall a' Bhraisich said, 'Oh I do.'

And the women added, 'We do a bit.'

The women said a few words in Gaelic to Dòmhnall a' Bhraisich and then left.

Dòmhnall a' Bhraisich then said to John, 'Co thu?' (Who are you?)

John explained that he was John Angus Mackay, that Domhnall's son had worked with him in HIDB and that he had come into the shop to buy rope to lash down the tent.

'That's interesting,' said Dòmhnall a' Bhraisich, 'I've got something for you'.

With that he disappeared into the back of the shop. He rummaged around for a while and came back with a mirror and he said, 'This mirror was made by your uncle Angus, probably the Angus you're named after and I'll tell you what happened. We were both on the same ship, shelling Naples. When the shelling stopped, we went ashore and there were big villas. We went into one of the villas. In one of the rooms, there had been a big mirror above the fireplace, which had been shattered. Your uncle took away a piece of that mirror and using wood from a tea chest fashioned it in the shape of a shield and varnished it. Sometime later, he was transferred to another ship. Before he left, he said, "Take this in remembrance of me, because you'll never see me again." And sure enough, he died of a fever and was buried in the Mediterranean.'

Dòmhall a' Bhraisich continued, 'So I kept the mirror. Many a time I thought, "och, I'll throw it out", but I never did. And now I'd like to give it to you, John Angus, as a reminder of your uncle and namesake.'

John Angus has held on to the mirror to this day and explained to me that it was one of the reasons that he later developed an affinity with Italy which was to influence greatly events in his later life.

With the move back to Lewis, John gave up his house in Invergordon. With his frequent visits to Inverness and the break-up of my own marriage, a room in my own house, which was then in Glenburn Drive, Inverness, had been set aside for John, which was to give me a privileged blow-by-blow insight into John's amazing capacity to achieve extraordinary results in the most challenging of circumstances.

The greatest of these was the achievement of one of CNAG's key aims, namely the securing of a Gaelic television service.

Gaelic Broadcasting Evolution

IT WAS WITH a newfound personal stability with Maria and from his then council house in Arnol that John started to campaign seriously with the Government for a Gaelic broadcasting service, taking on both the broadcasting industry and the Palace of Westminster in the process.

Looking back, John likens the development of Gaelic broadcasting to a marathon relay race run over a course littered with many-faceted obstacles, diversions and dead ends, negotiated by a long line of individuals in which he eventually had the honour of taking the baton from no man's land to beyond the final hurdle, thence to hand to his successor to take it to the finish line. The process started more than half a century earlier.

The first Gaelic broadcast on radio was a 15-minute religious address by the Reverend John Bain FSA (Scot), broadcast on Sunday 2 September 1923. Gaelic radio developed somewhat in the inter-war years in a style that was stilted and aimed primarily at an urban audience rather than Gaelic's rural heartlands. Such limited programming was further constrained during the war to little more than twice weekly news bulletins. With the cessation of hostilities, a more varied schedule recommenced from its Glasgow base, but as often as not in a heavy format made palatable to non-Gaels by the use of English announcements.

The appointment, within the BBC's Gaelic Department, of Finlay J Macdonald was a breath of fresh air. He introduced a more natural, lively and popular approach to Gaelic radio, that was to set a style for others to follow.

Finlay J was succeeded by Fred MacAulay who continued the process of popularisation. Fred had come from the Linguistic Survey of Scotland, an experience that made him all too aware of the fragile state to which Gaelic had declined. This motivated him to provide a lively and more intimate radio service that actually served Gaels and which enhanced the language's standing and validity. The more wide-spread use of tape recordings permitted the recording of stories and songs from Gaels in their own communities, as compared to the stiffly scripted studio-based approach that had been the norm hitherto.

Gaelic radio broadcasting was then limited to about one and a half hours per week but, under Fred's direction, the BBC's Gaelic Department was refocused on increasing output with talented producers tasked with developing programmes in the new more intimate style. This talent included Martin Macdonald, John Alex MacPherson and Neil Fraser who were each to have significant influence on the future development of Gaelic broadcasting.

In 1965, for the first time, a five-minute daily Gaelic news bulletin was broadcast at midday and by 1970 the output had increased to some four hours per week. This was progress, but Gaelic had long been regarded by the BBC's top brass very much as a poor relation, if not as an irritating irrelevance. That was to change with the appointment of Alasdair Milne as controller of BBC Scotland in 1968. Milne was a piping enthusiast, had learnt Gaelic and was unquestionably responsible for developing a more positive approach to Gaelic broadcasting within the BBC's establishment.

By the 1970s, occasional Gaelic television programmes were being broadcast under the auspices of the BBC Gaelic Department. The big development in Gaelic broadcasting at that time, however, was the switch of most Gaelic radio broadcasting to VHF (very high frequency). This move was controversial because at first VHF coverage was patchy, but as coverage improved VHF gave Gaelic radio the room to develop and grow.

A wider range of radio programmes was now available, but as the Gaelic Department was still based in Glasgow with some output from Aberdeen, there was a discontent among Gaels in the rural north and west that Gaelic broadcasting was not as responsive to their needs as it ought to be.

There was also a growing awareness that militant and well-organised activism in Wales had demanded and secured a much-improved awareness of and support for the Welsh language to a scale far in excess of anything that was then presented by the Scottish authorities as achievable for Gaelic. Nevertheless, the ambition for a better deal for Gaelic had been growing among a number of more radical Gaels and their supporters. Demonstrations by Gaelic activists in 1974 and 1975 and submissions from various bodies and individuals to the Committee on Broadcasting Coverage called for expansion and the creation of a proper Gaelic radio service. In November 1974, the committee's report (the Crawford Report) made a number of recommendations including a target that between 13 and 18 hours per week of Gaelic should be broadcast on radio in Scotland. This ambition was quickly downgraded by BBC Scotland's Head of Programmes to an 'ultimate aim' of ten to 12 hours only.

This was way short of the Crawford Report's recommendations for broadcasting in Welsh, for a wholly Welsh language television channel (S4C) and a dedicated Welsh language VHF Welsh language radio frequency.

The issue of the distance of BBC Gaelic programming from its main audience remained and, in 1976, the Gaelic Advisory Committee was created and asked to assess the opinions of the Gaelic community. This brought about the BBC's first official policy on Gaelic. Gaels pressed for something like parity with Wales but, in 1977, a further report on the Future of Broadcasting (the Annan Report) dashed these hopes on the grounds that whereas 20.84 per cent of the Welsh population spoke Welsh, only 1.8 per cent of the Scottish population spoke Gaelic and that increased Gaelic provision would alienate non-Gaelic speakers.

There had been some progress, however. In 1976, the BBC established a radio station with a Gaelic wing in Inverness. Some eight or nine hours per week of Gaelic radio were available as an opt-out in the north-west, but the rest of Scotland, including Argyll, received only three hours per week.

In those years, a number of quite exceptional people did a lot of work in trying to support Gaelic, although it was a relatively lonely business for the individuals involved. John Angus came into that scene in 1979 when things were beginning to hot up and the idea was emerging of developing Gaelic radio as a service – a concept that meant moving from a few minutes a day to a full-blown service, which many at that time found difficult to come to terms with as a realistic proposition. The promoters of the concept argued for it long and hard and, in the end, they won the argument, partly because the BBC eventually conceded that a Gaelic radio service was something that could be achieved.

A clear vision for the future of Gaelic broadcasting was set out in 1979 in an influential report by An Comunn Gàidhealach, written by Martin Macdonald (Survey of Gaelic Broadcasting). Among its recommendations were a new transmission channel for Gaelic, at least within the traditional Gaelic area; programmes increased, initially to around five or six hours daily, with a firm commitment to expand to over 40 hours weekly, and a new station in Stornoway with studios and transmitters in various other locations.

Later that year, the BBC created the Stornoway station in collaboration with the HIDB and Comhairle nan Eilean, the then new unitary local authority for the Western Isles. The new station provided a mix of Gaelic and English programmes which enabled some increase in Gaelic radio, both within the Highlands and Islands and nationally. The irony was that, whereas in the past Gaelic radio had previously been dominated by Glasgow, it now had a northern bias, which was to the detriment of southern Gaels. Nevertheless, there was now an infrastructure in place to enable Gaelic broadcasting to develop if the funding were provided.

There was, however, still no formal BBC policy or plan in place to take Gaelic broadcasting forward to the level demanded by activists. Until 1982 that is, when a report prepared by a Gaelic Study Group, set up by the Broadcasting Council for Scotland, recommended ring-fencing funds specifically for Gaelic. At that time, too, Alasdair Milne, who was by this time Director General of the BBC, made available £100,000 from the DG's war chest for the development of Gaelic broadcasting – a real shot in the arm. After further deliberations, Radio nan Gàidheal was launched in October 1985. For the first time, the basis for a single unified radio service was put in place aimed at the Gaelic community as a whole. For a time, limitations on the capacity of network transmitters meant that some areas continued to receive more programmes than others.

The Gaelic Study Group report of 1982 had also encouraged the BBC to set up a group to look at young people and Gaelic broadcasting. This was taken up by Neil Fraser, now Head of Gaelic at the BBC. It led to the creation in 1986 of Urras Guth na h-Òige (The Voice of Youth Trust), a joint initiative between the BBC and CNAG in which

Neil Fraser and John Angus Mackay were the founding members. Its aim was to strengthen the links between radio and the youth of the Gaelic community. This initiative was highly successful in both creating a range of programming that appealed to young people and in involving young people in producing and presenting programmes such as *Caithris na h-Oidhche*. The reach of Gaelic radio was further broadened in 1985 with the opening of a new studio at Portree followed by Oban and Lionacleit in Benbecula in 1988. At that time, the technical equipment at Inverness and Stornoway was upgraded. Progress with Gaelic radio was to continue through the '90s with the phased introduction of a dedicated VHF/FM frequency and, by 1996, 90 per cent of Scotland was receiving some 45 hours of Gaelic programmes weekly. However, we are moving ahead of ourselves.

As has already been noted, the early to mid-'80s was when the report Còr na Gàidhlig, edited by Martin Macdonald, made a comprehensive set of recommendations for the development of Gaelic, of which the creation of Comunn na Gàidhlig (CNAG) was central. As CNAG's first Director, John Angus was clear that broadcasting was, in his words, 'a key plank in its strategy to helping the language recover some of its strength'. The battle for a Gaelic radio service had largely been won. Attention now focused on television on which Gaelic provision was minimal. Winning a Gaelic television service was to take campaigning to a whole new level.

The Magic Box

THE CONCEPT OF more Gaelic on television had been advocated by several of the same activists as had championed Gaelic radio. By the early '80s, after receipt of a Study Group report, which was presented to the BBC's Broadcasting Council for Scotland by John Angus Mackay as Chair of the Gaelic Advisory Committee, its aspiration was accepted by the Broadcasting Council. This early thinking had been worked up prior to the establishment of CNAG. For a time, however, little progress had been made. The broadcasters were certainly not falling over themselves to increase the then tiny output of Gaelic television programmes.

In 1979, there was, however, one fleeting, almost freakish, glimmer of positivity on the part of BBC One Scotland. That was the screening of *Can Seo*, a televised Gaelic language learning series. The programme lasted for 20 weeks and a textbook, cassette and vinyl LP were produced to accompany the series. The programme was witty and an outstanding success, and seemed to outshine the BBC's other language learning programming of that period. Such was their embarrassment that the BBC perversely refused to screen a follow-up series, despite pressure from viewers keen to learn more Gaelic.

Once CNAG was established and functioning, its broadcasting objective proved much more difficult to deal with than its other objectives. The BBC, Grampian Television and STV (Scottish Television) were effectively closed to any effective outside influence. The problem was much more complex. Whereas Education and the arts were dealt with within Scotland, under the auspices of the Scottish Office, the broadcasting system was controlled from London where all the main decisions were taken. There was some devolved regional decision making at the BBC in Glasgow. The commercial providers, Grampian TV and STV, were of course based in Aberdeen and Glasgow respectively, but the market was a competitive one and there were tensions among the broadcasters. There were also tensions between the existing networks and outsiders trying to get a slice of the action.

Increasing the provision of Gaelic broadcasting became the main priority of CNAG. To advance this, an advisory group was created to consider the best approach. The group included Dr Finlay Macleod, Jack MacArthur, John Murray, Martin Macdonald and Duncan Mac-Quarrie. Papers were prepared, of which *Towards a Gaelic Broadcasting Service*, was influential. It informed discussion at two conferences held to explore a way forward. Meetings were also held with the key broadcasters – BBC, Grampian Television and STV. To be fair, there was innovation and an increase in programming by the broadcasters in the '80s – in the BBC led by Ken MacQuarrie, in Grampian Television led by Bob Christie and in STV led by Alistair Moffat and Rhoda MacDonald, but the aggregate output fell far short of the aspirations of the Gaelic community.

With the aid of his advisors, John started working on a paper to advance the case. One of the advisors who was particularly helpful in developing tactics at that time was Martin Macdonald. As already described, he was the editor of *Còr na Gàidhlig* and several other papers on that theme. John and Martin worked well together over the years. Martin was an experienced broadcaster and journalist who had served the BBC in Scotland and at Westminster – factors which made him an ideal adviser.

Martin had gained insights that he shared with John. One particular experience served to emphasise the point made to him earlier by Dr Finlay Macleod about working on the system from within as well as campaigning from the outside. Martin had been in BBC Scotland headquarters in Queen Margaret Drive in December 1974 when student activists were demonstrating outside in favour of developing Gaelic broadcasting. He overheard a conversation between a television producer and a manager, in which the producer asked if he should do anything. The answer was: 'Ignore them. But if they storm the building and start burning it down, roll the cameras.' The lesson learnt was that much more than a student demonstration outside the BBC was needed to generate positive action.

Knowing how politics and broadcasting worked, Martin came up with a ruse that was eventually to prove a crucial factor in John Angus' quest to gain the support of the Government for developing

Gaelic television. After considering past pleas to the Government for support and discussing why little progress was being made, Martin advised writing to the broadcasters setting out CNAG's aspirations for increased air-time and how they thought they could be met. When asked what he thought would happen, Martin's opinion was that the broadcasters would stonewall, but he concluded, 'We have to pin the broadcasters down, before we can do anything else.'

This was indeed what happened. Letters were written setting out CNAG ambitions for broadcasting, namely a Gaelic television service, and each of the three broadcasters came back saying that in no way could they accommodate such ambitious proposals.

In the same year, John was present at a meeting at the Gaelic radio station between John Murray, Head of Gaelic Radio, Ken McQuarrie, Head of Gaelic Television and Malcolm Rifkind MP, the then Secretary of State for Scotland, when on an official visit to Stornoway. In the ensuing conversation at which the topic of developing Gaelic broadcasting was raised, Malcolm Rifkind's secretary, on seeing a display of Gaelic children's books on the table, confessed that his own children were fans of the cult Gaelic children's television programmes, *Donnie Dotaman* and *Padraig Post*, and was delighted to take books home with him. The consensus of that meeting was that CNAG should liaise more closely with the Government to discuss how Gaelic television broadcasting might be developed.

This contact with Malcolm Rifkind was to prove to be of immense value, as his support, influence and determination were subsequently to prove critical to securing substantial funding, backed up by enshrinement in legislation, for a significant expansion in Gaelic television broadcasting. While the ultimate provision was by no means perfect, this has to be acknowledged as the single greatest boost to Gaelic ever.

The fact of the matter was that politicians are as much a part of the system as are the broadcasters themselves, whereas CNAG was not. Martin and John recognised that the first question a politician would ask is, 'What's the system doing about it?' So when the negative responses were received from the broadcasters, John was able to arrange a meeting with Rifkind's advisors, to be met with the predicted response, 'Why are you coming to us? Why aren't you going to the broadcasters?'

John was of course now able to say, 'We've been there and this is the response we got. They're saying they won't do anything.'

So, while going to the broadcasters may have seemed like a blind alley, Martin Macdonald had in fact been very astute in devising this tactic, which was another step on the long journey to get a step change in Gaelic television broadcasting provision. Indeed, Martin had, over the years, been a great force in articulating through his writings and broadcasts what key individuals were saying about what was needed to progress Gaelic development.

In the beginning, Martin and the other advisors had fields of expertise far superior to John's. As time went by, however, John had absorbed all the relevant information and skills they had and it came to the point that none had actually done what needed to be done. It was becoming clear that while John's work with his advisors had taken the quest so far, the key objective of much greater Gaelic broadcasting provision was very far from being achieved. John now believed that the campaign had got to the stage where, what CNAG could do in Scotland was not enough to change minds in London. He became convinced, therefore, that he had to move on from Martin and his Scottish advisors to find other advisors who had real influence where influence mattered, and that was in Westminster.

Change of Tactics

JOHN HAD READ about, and heard discussed, the hunger strike campaign led by Gwynfor Evans in Wales to secure a Welsh language television channel. This had come about years after Welsh medium education had been established, and against a background of civil unrest in campaigning for language rights. Scotland was different with far fewer Gaelic speakers, little history of militancy since 1746, as well as the fact that the campaign for Gaelic television was to run tandem with the expansion of Gaelic medium education. Both required resources, human and financial, and CNAG's resources were deployed on both fronts. These were to prove to be complementary, politically and practically. After some discussion within CNAG, it was apparent that there was little appetite at the time for running a campaign on the lines of threatening to hunger strike, as this may have proven counter-productive, and in any case it would be an option only if other approaches had failed.

Nevertheless, to keep the idea in people's minds, John thought up a ploy which raised the possibility of hunger strike if all else failed. Organising a seminar on Gaelic broadcasting in Glasgow, hosted by Councillor Bernie Scott of Strathclyde Regional Council, John asked Malkie Maclean to contact the internationally renowned poet Sorley Maclean to request his attendance. Sorley was the closest the Gaels had as an icon to match Gwynfor Evans. The idea was not to put Sorley on the spot should he be asked if he was willing to fast to secure a Gaelic channel, rather that he by his very presence could help to reinforce the possibility, and to this end Sorley was asked not to speak but to look angry at appropriate moments. In the meantime, John had alerted a colleague who had contact with Conservative Headquarters in Edinburgh to the fact that the prospect of a hunger strike by a key individual may be on the cards.

Never before had Sorley, a consummate raconteur and actor, been invited to a public occasion and asked not to speak! He was delighted to help, however, when all this was explained. He turned up, looked angry and went home chuckling. He himself had wrestled with the Scottish Education Department in the past and well knew that lateral thinking was needed if the Gaelic community was to secure concessions from the Government. The seed sown on this occasion was to germinate slowly and bear some fruit more than a decade hence in the new millennium.

John had also reviewed previous arguments and realised that the case for Gaelic had mainly been made on linguistic and cultural grounds aligned with the rights of a distinctive community to have its own service. Realising that this simply was not in tune with the times in Thatcherite Britain, he begun to realise that the argument had to be widened to demonstrate the economic benefits that could accrue to the Highlands and Islands in particular, though not exclusively, through investment in Gaelic broadcasting.

As a starting point, John approached individually Bob Cowan, Chair of HIDB; Sir Kenneth Alexander, former Chair of HIDB and Chancellor of Stirling University; and Sir Alan Peacock, Chair of the Scottish Arts Council and Professor in the David Hume Institute at Edinburgh University. He told them that CNAG was about to launch a campaign of a kind that had not been tried previously for developing Gaelic television broadcasting on a model of delivery not dissimilar to Wales's S4C (a Welsh language opt out from Channel 4).

John explained: 'I know that Malcolm Rifkind and others may ask your opinion of this given your position. All I want you to do if the question comes up "Should we support this Gaelic thing?" is to please say "Yes".'

Each of them asked, 'Why should we?'

In response, John won their support by describing a vision of a channel that would provide an alternative service to Scotland. This channel would feature creative cultural programmes, factual, and outward looking material and coverage of economic issues as well as what would be more traditional Gaelic fare. Perhaps as an opt out on BBC Two or Channel 4 it would require new funding and generate economic benefits through a significant level of new employment opportunities.

John then set out on a new direction to try to identify some means of getting closer to the heart of the Government in Westminster. The way that this materialised was by a happy coincidence.

Having recently moved into his new council house in Arnol, John would sit surrounded by papers, trying to work out a way forward. From time to time, he also took *The Guardian* as a source of information. On one particular issue, there was an exposé about the companies that lobbied and were influencing the Thatcher Government at that time. The thrust of the article was that such lobbying and access to Government ministers was morally dubious. John's take on it, however, was that for the first time he could see now how people could get through to the highest levels of Government with the right support and connections.

Remembering that Comhairle nan Eilean had used a lobbying company in Westminster, John consulted Donald Martin, the Comhairle's Deputy Head of Administration who advised him that they had looked at a range of companies to establish which had expertise relevant to their issue, as each company had particular interests.

With renewed focus, John went back to *The Guardian* and identified Salingsbury Casey as the most likely candidate, as the Chair Michael Casey had been influential in advising Margaret Thatcher to win the 1987 General Election and the company had expertise in the field of the media. So John phoned Salisbury Casey and asked to speak with Michael Casey. He was put through. John introduced himself explaining that he was miles and miles away from London in the furthest Hebrides.

'What can I do for you?' Casey responded.

John said, 'I don't know, but we need to be able to speak to Government ministers and their advisers.'

Casey confirmed, 'Yes. That is what we do.'

John continued, 'I understand, too, that you also have the Prime Minister's ear.'

'Yes, sometimes,' Casey confessed. 'You know, of course, that ministers are very busy and don't have time to speak to everybody, but they will listen to people that they trust.'

Casey then asked what John's particular issue was. John came to the point: 'Broadcasting, but broadcasting to serve the minority Gaelic community. There's an Act coming up soon and we need to get the ear of the Government to make an impression on it.'

John could almost feel Michael Casey smile. 'We have the very man here, working for us who will understand your particular considerations. He's a Welshman and he understands the situation in Wales. His name is Leighton Andrews. I'll put him in touch with you.'

As a consequence of this telephone conversation, Leighton Andrews was engaged as CNAG's parliamentary lobbyist.

The Lion's Den

THE SALINGSBURY CASEY contract, with Leighton Andrews as advisor and lobbyist, was to take the Gaelic television campaign to a completely new level. He was particularly helpful in, for example, introducing John to Graeme Carter, Malcolm Rifkind's advisor, and showing John the ropes about how to handle Westminster contacts placing early day motions and other tricks of the trade.

Leighton Andrews had organised lunches with senior civil servants who had been remarkably open, much more so than Edinburgh civil servants. Through this process Leighton was gleaning information that was helpful to his other clients, so for him it was a win-win situation. John was also advised to try to work on a one-to-one basis and not appear to come mob-handed to meetings with Board members in tow.

In this way, John made good contacts through lobbyists Graeme Carter and Malcolm Rifkind who continued to be supportive.

At one particular meeting, however, he asked, 'What are my back benchers saying?'

John confessed that he didn't know what they're saying.

Rifkind continued, 'Because, much as I'd like to support you, unless the back benchers are behind me, I have a problem. So you're going to have to meet them and talk to them and persuade them that what you are talking about is worth supporting.'

So with Leighton Andrew's help, a meeting was organised with the Scottish Tory Back Bench Committee.

John went along on his own – Daniel in the lion's den as usual. The meeting of these Tory MPs took place in one of the committee rooms in Westminster. The Palace of Westminster in not a place to which most ordinary people go, or in which they feel comfortable. It may be imagined, therefore, how difficult a transition it must have been for John from a croft in Lewis to the hallowed but overbearing halls of Westminster. He had to call on all of his emotional and intellectual resources, while the MPs he was dealing with were in their own comfort zone and familiar surroundings.

John was ushered into the committee room where the MPs were sitting and where they had presumably been having some prior discussion. Fortunately, the Chairman was Sir Hector Munro, whom John had met before, who had been very supportive, kind and courteous. Among those sitting round the room were Alick Buchanan-Smith, Bill Walker from Tayside who had filibustered Donald Stewart's Gaelic Bill, an effusive Nicky Fairbairn and others. The meeting was drawn to order and John was asked to speak.

John outlined the ambitions of CNAG for greatly increased provision for Gaelic broadcasting and for television in particular, after which discussion started with questions led mainly by Nicky Fairbairn. To John, Fairbairn's attitude seemed aggressive and confrontational. At first, John responded defensively, then quickly sensed that this was not the right thing to do. Out of the corner of his eye, he noticed Alick Buchanan-Smith on his left taking it all in. John cooled down and at one stage Fairbairn said, 'Don't worry, old chap, I'm on your side. I'm only asking questions to stimulate discussion.'

At this point, Sir Hector said, 'I'm sorry but I have to go to another meeting now. I must hand the meeting over to the Vice Chair.'

The Vice Chair turned out to be none other than Nicky Fairbairn. Events took a turn for the worse in some ways and for the better in other ways. John was asked various questions, which he tried to answer in a cool and studied kind of way. All the while, he was still conscious of Alick Buchanan-Smith on his left who was very unruffled and didn't say anything but was clearly considering all that was discussed. In due course, John was thanked for his attendance and escorted from the meeting.

It was by no means clear how the presentation had been received, until, a few weeks later when, once more down in London, John met up with Malcolm Rifkind's special adviser who, with a broad smile on his face, said, 'Your meeting was a success. You passed the test. The back benchers will support us and it is now time to move on.'

In the long haul of seeking progress with the Gaelic television campaign, it is not possible to identify what was the defining moment at which it all started to gel. However, this meeting was clearly one of the crucial turning points at which key individuals within the Government of the day were brought on side for, without this back bench support, progress would have been impossible.

The back benchers were one thing, but in the end the real challenge was to win the support of a majority of the cabinet committee on broadcasting. Margaret Thatcher had set this up to deal with the impending Broadcasting Bill. At the early stage of the game, the Gaelic lobby didn't even know that such a committee existed. In fact, its existence was not well known generally. It was, however, a very powerful committee, because broadcasting was a very big issue for that Tory Government. Alongside the Prime Minister, other members of the cabinet committee on broadcasting were: Home Secretary Douglas Hurd with Foreign Secretary Douglas Howe and Economic Secretary Lord Young, and others. Their task was to carry forward one of the Government's main new approaches to public broadcasting through the Broadcasting Bill which would build on the Peacock Committee's report.

The Peacock Committee had been set up in March 1985 under the Chairmanship of Professor Alan Peacock to review the financing of the BBC and public service broadcasting and to try to look at new ways of dealing with it. At first, there was a widespread thought that the BBC would have been done away with. In fact, the Government had expected the committee to report that the television license fee, that was used to fund the BBC, should be scrapped. However, when the Committee took evidence and advice, they realised that the support for the BBC and for the licence fee was very solid.

In the end, Peacock recognised public broadcasting as a public good, but that the commercial market should be freed up. The committee did a *volte face* and favoured retaining the licence fee as they believed it was the 'least bad' option. They then turned the whole emphasis onto the independent sector and recommended that the ITV (Independent Television) franchises, coming up for renewal at that time, should go out to tender. What Peacock sought to do was to balance these two aspects.

In Westminster, John kept in regular contact with the Gaelic Cross-Party Group, chaired initially by Sir Russell Johnston, followed by Calum MacDonald after the 1987 election when he succeeded Donald Stewart as MP for the Western Isles. This provided a forum for briefing MPs on developments, seeking their advice and support for Early Day Motions designed to keep Gaelic broadcasting issues on the radar at Westminster. These motions secured a fair range of cross-party support from MPs across the UK prompted by their colleague members of the group. All the while a wide range of individuals as well as Gaelic and student organisations and local authority members of CNAG wrote a plethora of letters echoing the stream emanating from CNAG's office – to politicians, MPs and Lords and the Press, reinforcing the point that this was an issue that was not going to go away.

Strategies employed also included placing parliamentary questions. All PQs were answered, but only a few were chosen by the luck of the draw from a hat, to be given a verbal response by the appropriate Minister in the House. With one of those, Gaelic struck gold, as a question on Government support for Gaelic placed by Charles Kennedy was drawn for a verbal response from Michael Forsyth as the responsible Minister in the Scottish Office on the last day of Scottish Questions before the summer recess in July 1988. When this came to light, John suggested to civil servants that some of the response should be given in Gaelic to raise the profile of the response. The Minister agreed, but the department had difficulty with the translation as this would normally be undertaken in a confidential manner by Murdo MacLeod, HMI, who could not be contacted as he was on a tour of school inspections. John offered to translate the civil servants' response, did so and to his consternation was then asked to coach the Minister in pronunciation.

This was a risky business, as the Minister was responsible for CNAG funding, and if the affair ended up badly – for example, if the Minister was attacked – the whole thing could backfire. From his home in Arnol, John went over the response with Michael Forsyth. Michael was gracious and after initially struggling with Gaelic double consonants got the hang of it. When asked if it was worth going on with it, John assured him it was, but suggested they go over it again prior to Scottish Question Time.

In the meantime, John contacted Calum MacDonald and asked him for support in ensuring this event proved successful by responding in Gaelic – and positively, in recognition of the Minister's leap of faith. John later had another session with the Minister using the telephone in John Murray's house in Barvas, where CNAG were pro-moting Gaelic education and television at the annual show. In the event, the question was asked in English by Charles Kennedy, Michael Forsyth responded in Gaelic and Calum Macdonald praised him in Gaelic for his response – the first time that a dialogue, however lim-ited, had taken place in Gaelic between opposing factions on the floor of the House. This occasion helped to cement relationships with the Scottish Office Ministers and civil servants.

In contrast, however, John participated in another occasion on which the reality of the mountain to be climbed to secure support for a Gaelic channel was brought home. He was invited to a reception in Edinburgh Castle to celebrate Margaret Thatcher's Government's re-election in 1987. On arriving in the car park, John met up by chance with Professor Donald Neil McCormack who had stood that year as SNP candidate against Malcolm Rifkind and lost. John and Neil had worked together in 1985/86, supported by a Welsh colleague, to do the groundwork for a Gaelic Language Act. The intention had been to dust this off, if and when CNAG had fulfilled the terms of its 1985 agreement with George Younger. Neither of the two were sure why they were invited and they naturally gravitated to a quiet corner from which they could view proceedings through the door. There they chat-ted with two others representing the business community. When the Prime Minister and her husband arrived, they parted company and each worked opposite sides of the room.

Eventually Dennis Thatcher bounced into the corner group, intro-duced himself and spoke to each individually asking what they did. When it came to Neil McCormack, he described his position, com-menting that he did not know what he was doing there as he had contested the election for the SNP.

Dennis Thatcher responded, 'Oh, we are very inclusive in our party, you know.'

When John told him he was involved in Gaelic development, Den-nis Thatcher responded, 'I suppose someone has to', then went on to ask, 'What do you want? You don't want a channel like the Welsh have, do you? It's rubbish and nobody watches it.'

This animosity towards S4C was a warning that John could not ignore, remembering that Gwynfor Evans had forced the Tory Gov-ernment's hand through his hunger strike. John responded to the effect that they did not want what the Welsh had but something similar. Dennis Thatcher then asked if the Gaels had the Bible in Gaelic, and when assured that they had had for hundreds of years, Dennis Thatcher asked, 'What more do you want, then?'

At this point John was rattled, he looked pointedly at the glass of gin held by Dennis Thatcher and was about to ask why he needed gin if he had the Bible in English. Sensing where this was going, Neil McCormack steered the discussion on to a question of human rights in a civilised society. This was not quite Mr Thatcher's territory and the discussion fizzled out.

John thanked Neil for his intervention and they left, not to meet again until Neil was asked many years later to chair discussions between the Gaelic Media Service (described later) with John as Director and the BBC, with a view to establishing a partnership to set up a Gaelic Television channel.

Meanwhile, the magnitude of the challenge that John faced may perhaps be understood from a letter he received from a civil servant in the Home Office early in 1988 telling him that the Government was not persuaded that there was any case for legislation to obtain greater broadcast coverage of the Gaelic language. The official went on to state smugly:

> If you envisage persuading the broadcasting authorities to do more to address the need identified, ie to maximise the provision of Gaelic programmes within the context of the overall remit to provide a proper balance and wide range of subject matter, then it could clearly be accommodated in existing broadcasting arrangements – the only question is the success of your persuasive efforts.

Well, this bureaucratic brick wall was certainly a set-back. It suggested that either John was thrown back on the dubious mercy of the broadcasters to provide more hours and more money for Gaelic, or he had to persevere in trying to find some way of breaking through the Government's intransigence. He persevered – and persevered and persevered.

Most weeks during this period, John would spend between one and three nights in Inverness where he stayed with me in Glenburn Drive. On many occasions, I recall John arriving off the evening London plane fatigued after the kind of negotiations alluded to above. A bottle of red wine would be uncorked and as he relaxed, he would unburden himself of the day's events and then would plot and scheme the next moves. If the plotting and scheming was particularly creative, brandy would be poured and discussion would continue until the small hours. It was a privilege to participate in these inspired episodes.

Notwithstanding these Herculean struggles, the amount of time John was spending in London raised eyebrows and growing criticism to the extent that CNAG's then Chairman Father Calum MacLellan accompanied John on one of his trips to get a feel for what was going on. John introduced Father Calum to several key contacts in the Commons and the Lords, after which he said, 'Now I understand what you are trying to do, how difficult it is, and it must be exhausting. Carry on if you can, but you have already gone further than anyone would expect and if you stop now no one will blame you.'

Stopping was not an option and at least he gained his Chairman and Board's full backing to proceed with his lobbying efforts.

By November 1988, although John had established powerful contacts in Westminster, he had a growing sense that progress in actually delivering a proper Gaelic television service was stalling. In these circumstances, John phoned Leighton to say that as progress had got stuck, CNAG might have to dispense with the services of Salingsbury Casey and shift the fulcrum of the campaign. John asked Leighton, however, if he could recommend someone who could take the matter forward – some kind of amalgam of Saatchi and Saatchi's PR nous and some kind of economic development expertise.

Leighton acknowledged John's position asked for a couple of weeks to think about it. He came back a couple of days later to say, 'I think I've got the very person for you. He's very well regarded by the Government on the broadcasting issue. His name is Cento Veljanovski, he worked with the Peacock Committee and, as it happens, his girlfriend works in our office.'

Lady Luck had combined with Cupid to present a new opening.

Cabadaich 3: *Mun Cuairt a' Chagailte*
Blethers 3: Around the Hearth

ROY: I often think fondly of the time when you were with Commun na Gàidhlig and later with Bòrd na Gàidhlig when you had a sort of home from home at my house in Inverness. I well remember you coming back to Inverness on the late plane from London, knackered after lobbying in Westminster. We would open a bottle of red wine and after a few glasses, you would relax and the ideas began to flow.

JOHN: Yes, I remember it well too. Those chats helped us to stream thoughts, dream dreams and lots of ideas came from that. And after that came actions that made the ideas and dreams become a reality. Gaelic was in dire straits and we asked why are things as they are and then what can we do about changing things? There is no doubt that these discussions gave me inspiration and stimulated me into having a go. I thought of the old quote from *King Lear* that 'nothing will come of nothing', so let's do something. All that was boiling around when I stayed in your house. So you were a source of inspiration and a sounding board for ideas.

That came to a head in a number of ways, but one of the ways was when I told you, having come back from London that I'd spoken to our adviser Leighton Andrews saying 'I'm sorry, Leighton, but we have reached some kind of a stalemate and we need something other than your company. We now need some sort of public relations company like a cross between Saatchi and Saatchi and Deloitte and Touch. Leighton had come back and said, 'Hold on, we don't actually need that. I know the very person you need and that is Cento Veljanovski (the broadcasting guru whose input is described in this book). He's the Director of the Institute of Economic Affairs.' Well as you know, I spoke with Cento and he seemed like the very man to take things forward, but he was expensive and I needed to find the money to pay for his services and we needed to move very quickly. So as the book describes, I came to you.

ROY: Oh, I remember that well. I had delegated powers of up to £10,000, but there were time consuming procedures to go through to process the approval. So the following day, I went to Bob Cowan, Chairman of HIDB, and got his authority for immediate approval of the money.

JOHN: That was the lifesaver. The £10,000 enabled us to hire Cento to come to Lewis and to write the report that was seminal in influencing a reluctant Whitehall to agree funding for a Gaelic television service.

Curiously, following on from that, after the battle had been won and the legislation had been passed which gave us the £8 million a year, later increased to £9 million, to set up and fund the Gaelic television service, I met up with Cento in London to celebrate over lunch in the Chelsea Arts Club. During that meeting, I asked him how the Institute of Economic Affairs worked. Cento explained that it operated as a think tank developing ideas and passing them on to politicians. When I came back to your house in Inverness and we started to ponder, why not create a think tank for the Highlands and Islands? So, as I was Chairman of Sabhal Mòr Ostaig (the Gaelic college in Skye), Norman Gillies (SMO's Director) and I worked up the concept of a Highland think tank which we called Barail. Under the direction of Jim Hunter, Barail led to the creation of the University of the Highlands and Islands.

Also in the course of these discussions, you floated the idea of creating a new Gaelic village in Skye associated with the expansion of the Gaelic college.

ROY: That's right, I felt we needed to create a more sustainable critical mass of energy where Gaelic was the medium of living and of work in a modern setting. I think it was you who suggested pulling together a meeting of the key players to see how the idea could be advanced.

JOHN: Yes. We all met in a Chinese restaurant in Inverness and out of that came the new campus at the Sabhal Mòr and now the village Kilbeg is taking shape.

Aye, one way or another in those evenings in your house we were able to dream dreams and turn them into reality.

Then later when I was having trouble in Bòrd na Gàidhlig with people hiding behind pseudonyms in a campaign to attack and denigrate the work of Bòrd na Gàidhlig, I got so frustrated that I decided to meet with the ringleader for a showdown. I think you got rather alarmed that this might degenerate into fisticuffs, so you insisted in coming along to keep an eye on the proceedings.

ROY: But in the end, I didn't do anything.

JOHN: No but you sat in the corner looking fierce! So in your house what we had was a kind of partnership which led to a number of really positive outcomes.

ROY: I suppose one of the important aspects of this was that my house gave you a kind of base in which you could relax with home comforts, which would not have been the case if you had been staying in a hotel.

JOHN: Absolutely. It created a second home for me and also a colleague support system that I would not have had otherwise. Even although I was tired and stressed, it spurred me on to try to achieve what we were talking about. That was a very important dynamic.

ROY: That was the whole idea and I have to say that I found the whole process not only stimulating, but one through which I learned a lot about how to achieve progress in other aspects of my own professional life.

Alex Mackay from John's father's passport for America in 1929 (Photo: Mackay collection).

Kapitänleutnant Robert Gysae, Commander of U-98 which torpedoed and sank Armed Merchant Cruiser F94 HMS *Salopian* on which John's father served (Photo: www.uboat.net).

John's father and mother binding the sheaves of scythed corn at 43 Lower Shader. Note the size of the peat stack and haystacks all done by hand (Photo: Mackay collection).

Dipping sheep. Back row (left to right): John, aged about 14, holding sheep leg restrainer; his brother Kenny, holding down the sheep; their father. Front row: Ronald Brown, adopted son of John's Auntie Peggy; John Brown; his sister, Annette. Note the height of the hay stack towering over the barn and the bulk of the peat stack, all indicative of hard graft (Photo: Mackay collection).

Bridge House, the Inverness HQ of the Highlands and
Islands Development Board (Photo: HIDB).

Homeward bound from Barra's famous beach
airstrip, the Irish party (including Denis Gallag..
2nd from right) push their Aer Arann Islander
into position for take-off.

The Irish party push the Aer Arann Islander aircraft onto the
beach into position for take off (Photo: HIDB).

Co-op Field Officer for Lewis and
Harris, John Angus Mackay, then
aged 29 (Photo: HIDB).

Back to Lewis. Left to right: John's father;
mother; John's son, Derek; John; his sister,
Annette. (Photo: Mackay collection).

The community co-op team. Left to right: Bob Storey; the author; John; Agnes Gillies; Coinneach Maclean; Chas Ball (Photo: Author collection).

The committee of Co-chomunn na Hearadh with John (centre) in Fairisle cardigan (Photo: Mackay collection).

John and Maria in the early days (1980s) (Photo: Mackay collection).

John and Maria tie the knot (Photo: Mackay collection).

Coming in from the cold. George Younger MP, Secretary of State for Scotland with Donald John Mackay, the first chairman of Comunn na Gàidhlig at Sabhal Mòr Ostaig in 1985. It will be noted, gentleman that he was, that it is the Secretary of State who is holding the umbrella to shelter the CNAG chairman (Photo: CNAG).

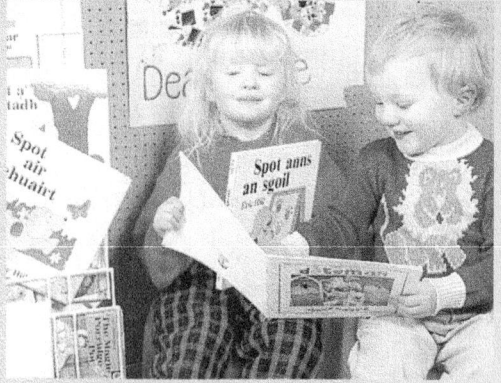

Gaelic playgroups, or *Croileagan*, sparked off the demand for Gaelic medium education (Photo: CNAG).

Gaelic medium education has been the key to creating a new confident generation of Gaelic speakers (Photo: CNAG).

The CNAG board and other attendees with CNAG's second chairman, Father Calum MacLellan (centre) and John Angus (immediately to the right) (Photo: CNAG).

The European Bureau for Lesser Used Languages with chairman the Reverend Jack Macarthur (centre) and John Angus (to his right) (Photo: CNAG).

The Mackays' new house at Arnol (Photo: Author collection).

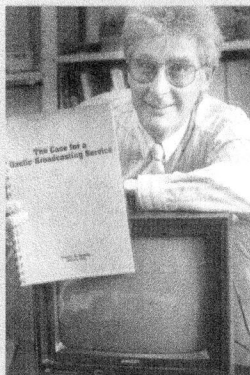

The report that kicked off the long struggle by CNAG for a Gaelic broadcasting service (Photo: CNAG).

Sir Robert Cowan, Chairman of HIDB and Malcolm Rifkind MP, Secretary of State for Scotland, both of whom were very supportive in the struggle for Gaelic broadcasting (Photo: HIDB).

Welsh Wizard Euyrn Ogwen Williams who helped John with planning for the establishment of CTG, its administration and programme funding activities (Photo: Euyrn Ogwen Williams).

Arann Calum Chille, the new campus at the Sabhal Mòr Ostaig that formed a founding part of the University of the Highlands and Islands (Photo: SMO).

The magnificently appointed training and television programme production studio at the Sabhal Mòr Ostaig. Shot taken during the filming of 'Gun Sgot', a Gaelic pub quiz (Photo: SMO).

John Angus and the author share a joke in the 1990s (Photo: Author collection).

The beautiful little medieval town of Pacentro in which the Mackays found their new Italian home (Photo: Author collection).

One of Bòrd na Gàidhlig's successes was in building a close relationship with parliamentarians (Photo: Mackay collection).

John and Maria at the 2015 *Daily Record*/Bòrd na Gàidhlig Scottish Gaelic Awards at which John received the Lifetime Achievement Award (Photo: Mackay collection).

The Mackay family and friends on the occasion John received the Saltire Society Fletcher of Saltoun Award in 2016 for his contribution to public life. Back row left to right: Steven MacIver; Derek; Michael; Peter; Ciaran. Front row left to right: Marie Kilbride; Maria; John; the author; George Adam LLD (Photo: Author collection).

John Angus and Dolina Maclennan at the Saltire Society ceremony (Photo: Author collection).

La Dolce Vita (Photo: Author collection).

Cento Veljanovski

DR CENTO GAVRIL VELJANOVSKI, a neoliberal economist, was secretary to the Peacock Committee. In his wider career, he was an academic and business consultant closely affiliated with the seminal free market think tank the Institute of Economic Affairs and the European Policy Forum. He had written a number of reports arguing for the privatisation and deregulation of the British media, as well as public utilities like gas and telecommunications.

John phoned Cento Veljanovski, introduced himself and said that he had been recommended to speak with him.

'Yes?' came a refined and somewhat detached response. He pronounced it like 'Yeahs'.

'I'm told that you're an economist.'

'Yes.'

'I believe that you're a good economist.'

'Yes.'

John then asked, 'Do you know what our definition of a good economist is?'

'No.'

John continued, 'My view is that any economist can make the big bigger, but it takes a really good one to make the small bigger. Do you think you're up to that challenge?'

'Mm, when you put it that way, I cannot say no. What is this about?'

John then explained that it was about broadcasting, to which Veljanovski acknowledged that he knew about broadcasting.

Having found out a little about Cento Veljanovski, John said teasingly, 'I know that you are of Macedonian decent, that you were brought up in Australia and that you are an Oxford don. I am speaking to you from the Hebrides, from the Isle of Lewis. I come from a family of sailors who have been round the world and know Macedonia and Australia. Do you know where Lewis is?'

'Well,' responded Cento, 'I think it's somewhere near Mull.'

'Well, yes, in that general direction but a bit further north, so if you're going to do a job for us, I think you should come here, because I know more about you than you know about me.'

This was agreed, at which point John asked him what his fee was. Cento replied that he cost a lot. He charged £120.

John signalled that this seemed not unreasonable as CNAG had on occasion paid £120 per day for specialist consultancy advice.

Cento was quick to correct John's misapprehension with, 'No, my fee is £120 per hour.'

John gulped and thought quickly. He knew that at that time, as Head of Social Development in the HIDB, I could authorise funding of up to £10,000 without prior Board approval. On this assumption, John responded, 'If you're that good an economist, you should be able to do this job for us within an envelope of £10,000, inclusive of VAT.'

Cento confessed that this was a challenge and would require thought. After a few days' consideration Cento Veljanovski agreed to these terms, subject to the funds being forthcoming.

John was in Inverness the following day and presented to me the proposition that HIDB hire the Government's own trusted advisor to make the case for the Gaelic television service that was so badly needed in sustaining and developing the language.

Authorizing such a sum for such an unusual purpose, at such an astronomical fee rate, was not a decision to be taken lightly. I wrote a short paper the following day and went to Sir Robert (Bob) Cowan, the Chairman of the Board to explain how this gamble could just swing the Government in favour of supporting a Gaelic television service with the potential for significant consequential employment gains in the Western Isles and elsewhere.

Bob Cowan looked at me in an old fashioned way. After a pause, God bless his memory, he said, 'I hope you're right. Go for it.'

I was on the phone immediately with this news to John, who in turn informed Cento that he had authorisation to proceed.

* * *

It was a cold, wet, windy January morning in 1989 when John Angus Mackay, Malkie Maclean (Head of the Gaelic Arts Project) and myself watched the south plane make its approach to the runway at Storno-way Airport. As the wings see-sawed to the gale, the pilot was clearly struggling to keep his aircraft on line but, with consummate skill, a bump and a bounce, the plane was safely landed.

The white-faced passengers emerged into the terminal build-ing. Among them was a tall donnish looking figure in a long fitted dark overcoat, whom John approached, shook hands, welcomed him to Lewis and introduced Cento Veljanovski to Malkie and me. We repaired to a Stornoway café to allow Cento to recover from the flight over lunch.

Led by John, we then explained the whole background to the social and economic conditions of the Highlands and Islands with particular emphasis on the Western Isles and Gaelic. We described recent initia-tives such as the community co-operative programme and the efforts being made by public bodies, voluntary organisations and individuals to stem the erosion of Gaelic. Of the three main strands of Gaelic development being pursued – education, the arts and broadcasting, it was stressed that broadcasting, and adequate provision of Gaelic television in particular was vital in raising confidence and addressing the powerful erosive effect of English language mass media.

The discourse continued in John's Volvo as he drove our little group through worsening rain squalls on a tour of the sights and to meet interesting people. As we approached Callanish a lightning flash lit up the famous Neolithic standing stones, which John described as 'one of our older developments'. A more dramatic effect could not have been concocted by Shakespeare himself.

The next call was at the end of a winding track over a bleak moor to the isolated but modern house of Alasdair Fraser, fish farmer and Chair of the local independent fish farmers' marketing group. As we were welcomed inside, Alasdair's wife brought us coffee and cake, his two children were kneeling together watching a children's television programme. Cento was very interested to hear about the salmon farming business and he asked where the fish were marketed. Alasdair explained that it depended on the dollar/pound exchange rate on whether the focus was on Boston or Paris and he showed Cento spreadsheets to illustrate these financial characteristics. There was something just a little surreal about our little group observing this international business, being controlled by a very bright man in a boiler suit from a house in the back of beyond in a gale.

Our next call was to the house of Dr Finlay MacLeod, former Deputy Director of Education with Comhairle nan Eilean. By this time, it was dark but the welcome by Finlay and Norma was warm. Finlay explained his progressive take on Gaelic education and cultural development while the ample shelving of books and Finlay's collection of antique maps of the isles conveyed a deep sense of a highly civilised household at ease with its Gaelic roots.

The tour concluded with a dinner meeting with other Gaelic activists and a visit to the radio station, by which time it was late. Cento held up his hand in surrender. 'Do you guys never stop? You fairly want your pound of flesh!'

This we took as a sign that it was time to get some shut-eye.

Next morning, the gale had abated somewhat and, after breakfast, as we strolled seaward, Stornoway's harbour was full of stormbound fishing boats and other vessels of countless foreign flags. In the streets, the Russian, French, Norwegian and Spanish voices of sailors mingled with the Gaelic and English of the locals. It seemed that morning as though Stornoway was some great international hub.

Before we saw Cento Veljanovski off on the southbound plane, John asked if the academic could provide a report that would influence the Government to deliver the kind of Gaelic television service that we sought.

'I'll do my best,' he responded.

Over the next few weeks, Cento remained in contact with John asking for some supplementary information and keeping him briefed on his progress and thinking as he worked. Initially the approach was to examine the possibility of placing a Gaelic television service as an opt-out on Channel 4 or BBC Two. When it became apparent that radical change of the BBC was not to feature in the forthcoming Bill, Cento looked at Channel 4. At one stage, it looked as if that might be possible but there was a big question over Channel 4 – would it be privatised? If so, the prospects of securing a place for Gaelic as an opt-out would not be strong.

The dialogue between Cento and John ran along the lines of Cento phoning to say, 'Good news for you; and bad news for me.'

When John asked what this meant and how he knew, Cento responded, 'It is not going to be privatised; and because I recommended it be privatised.'

Shortly thereafter, Cento rang again: 'Bad news for you, good news for me – it will be privatised.'

Essentially this meant that Channel 4 would be required to raise its own funding from advertising revenue rather than receiving funding from an IBA levy on ITV revenues.

Cento then took another tack and, knowing that the focus of the radical change in the Broadcasting Act would be on ITV rather than the BBC, came up with the proposition of the creation of a Gaelic Television Fund for which ITV broadcasters in Scotland, and independent producers, could bid to make programming to be broadcast on their channels. The fund, he recommended, should be run by a Gaelic Broadcasting Council which followed, to quote 'the spirit of the Peacock Report proposal for a Public Service Broadcasting Council, thus eroding the cultural monopoly of the broadcasters.' This concept was a masterpiece of realpolitik, although not what had originally been envisaged.

The decision to sanction this approach was reinforced for John, when he received a telephone call from the radical playwright John McGrath of 7:84 fame who was by now a Board Member of Channel 4.[3] They met in a café on Great Western Road, Glasgow. John McGrath explained how the new funding model for Channel 4 would be unsustainable if the Scottish advertising revenue was lost through opt-out for Gaelic programming. He made it clear that the Board of Channel 4, whose CEO was Michael Grade, would fight tooth and nail to oppose this – and that they would win. On the other hand, Grade would try to support an alternative argument. It was difficult not to listen to John McGrath, an iconic figure in the Highlands and Islands, with parliamentary connections through his marriage to the sister of the Lib-Dem MP Robert MacLennan, who was later to throw his party's full support behind bids to increase and improve Gaelic broadcasting provision in successive Acts.

---

3 7:84 was a radical theatre group active at that time noted, among other productions, for the acclaimed *The Cheviot, the Stag and the Black, Black Oil.*

Cento's report, which ran to a concise 61 pages, was couched in the Thatcherite mantra of 'privatising the public service broadcast obligation'. To us, and many in the Gaelic world, these concepts were alien and arcane, but the proposal had not come without considerable effort behind the scenes. In the wider arena, many in the establishment were impressed at the audacity of Gaels in making their case by using the Government's own advisor.

In the meantime, aided by Leighton Andrew, John continued to brief ministers, and sought to influence Parliament by working with MPs such as Calum Macdonald to place early day motions supporting the concept of a Gaelic broadcasting service.

Nobbling Ministers

THERE WERE SEVEN key players in the cabinet committee looking at broadcasting. These included Geoffrey Howe (Foreign Secretary), Douglas Hurd (Home Secretary), Malcolm Rifkind, Lord Young and Timothy Renton (Minister for Broadcasting). If the campaign for Gaelic broadcasting was to be successful, it was essential that a majority of these be won round to support meaningful Gaelic television provision. How was this to be achieved? That it was John Angus attributes partly to luck – luck that came about by being in the right place at the right time – and partly to a momentum that was building due to the sustained efforts of John himself.

These key individuals had to be brought round one by one.

Geoffrey Howe

During the lead up to the European Parliament elections, Geoffrey Howe was in Edinburgh to support Catherine Blight, an economist, originally from Lewis, who was standing as a Conservative candidate for that parliament. As it happened, she had been a researcher for a documentary about Gaelic on Scottish Television. As the programme was being developed, she had met John and they had got on well. While STV had originally assumed that Catherine would have been a detractor, she actually became supportive of the concept of Gaelic broadcasting because of the economic arguments that were being employed. While Catherine was campaigning in the streets, with Geoffrey Howe in support, and with TV cameras recording proceedings, a woman started heckling and haranguing them. Geoffrey Howe was somewhat wrong footed.

Catherine came to the rescue by asking the woman, 'Bheil Gàidhlig agad? (Do you have Gaelic?)'

The woman replied, 'Tha. Dè man a tha fios 'ad? (Yes. How do you know?)'

The heckler was deflated and quiet thereafter.

Geoffrey Howe, surprised at this outcome, asked, 'What was that all about?'

Catherine Blight responded, 'I'll tell you later.'

That evening over dinner, she explained and Geoffrey asked, 'But how did you know she had Gaelic?'

And Catherine explained that she knew by the woman's accent that she was a Gaelic speaker, but that she would never have suspected that she, Catherine, with her rather refined accent, also had Gaelic and that this revelation had taken the wind out of her sails.

Geoffrey Howe then asked what the significance of Gaelic was and Catherine had to explain that Gaelic was widely spoken in Lewis where she came from and elsewhere and that there was a campaign running to get support for setting up a Gaelic television service through the forthcoming Broadcasting Act 1990. She revealed that she had been involved on the fringes of the campaign, but that it was being carried forward by a fellow called Mackay.

Howe then said, 'How interesting. You know, my grandmother was Welsh and I have similar leanings, so I'll back you'.

This is how how Geoffrey Howe came on board.

Timothy Renton

Timothy Renton was a more difficult nut to crack. He was broadcasting minister and had made it clear that he was firmly against the whole idea of increased Gaelic broadcasting. In the first meeting John Angus, Roddy John MacLeod and Jack MacArthur (CNAG Board Members) had with Renton, he had said, 'The problem with you lot is you're not as fiery as the Welsh.'

To which John retorted, 'Are you inciting us to arson Minister?'

For some time before that, Welsh language activists had been burning down holiday homes of English owners. Picking up on this insinuation, the Minister responded, 'Oh no, no, certainly not, but you know the Welsh shout for what they want and they get it. You've got a problem. You're not like them.'

Roddy John MacLeod and Jack MacArthur were both appalled at the arrogant way in which that minister had treated them. It was clear that Renton was sceptical and John meantime kept closely in touch with Rifkind and his special advisor.

On a further occasion, meeting with the Minister and a senior civil servant, John had a ruse up his sleeve to try to bring home to them how miniscule Gaelic broadcasting provision was relative to English and Welsh language output. He had looked the previous week at the Gaelic programme listings in the *Stornoway Gazette* and cut them out. At one stage in the meeting, he asked the Minister if he read the *Radio Times*, and the Minister said he did. John then asked if he wanted to see the Gaelic *Radio Times*. When the Minister concurred, John pulled out his wallet and extracted a postage stamp-sized piece of paper which he placed in the middle of the table and said, 'That's it.'

A little later, while looking at Gaelic medium education provision with Strathclyde Regional Council, the question arose of such provision in Tiree. Councillor Bernie Scott, who, as already noted, was on CNAG's board, asked if John would go to Tiree with him and Malcolm Green, who was the council's Director of Education, to address a problem. The issue was that the non-Gaelic-speaking headmaster and his wife had a child going into primary in the coming year and were against the establishment of Gaelic medium in the school.

On arrival on the island, the group met one of the supporters of Gaelic medium, Catriona Maclean, wife of the local garage proprietor, who met them with the hired car. Catriona invited the delegation to her house, although other visits had been organised by the headmaster. They went to the house where Catriona took John to one side and explained, 'There's a lot going on here. There are a lot of people in favour of Gaelic education, but they have teachers and others lined up against us, so it's very difficult for us.'

John recognised Catriona's accent and asked where she came from. It transpired she was from Lenzie and John responded, 'So is my wife.'

Catriona asked, 'Who is your wife?' to which John answered, 'Maria Ferguson.'

'Oh my God,' exclaimed Catriona, 'I know Maria. I used to go out with her brother.'

It also emerged that her sister had spent a summer with Maria in Sicily. As a consequence of these family connections, John and Catriona got on famously.

When Catriona asked what John was doing, he explained that one of his tasks was trying to establish a Gaelic broadcasting service because it was so important for the sustenance and development of the language. Catriona readily understood and agreed explaining, 'My husband speaks Gaelic but I don't and, once the telly goes on, the voice in the house is always an English voice, so I hope that you win with your work.'

John then explained that in his dealings with the Government, some ministers were supportive, but others were not and that Timothy Renton the Broadcasting Minister in particular was an obstacle to progress.

'Timothy Renton!' exclaimed Catriona. 'I know him. He has a holiday house down the road here and I look after it. He hires his cars from us when he comes here.' She went on, 'If you want me to speak to him, I'll speak to him.'

John Angus of course encouraged Catriona to speak with the minister explaining that this persuasive, glamorous and well-packaged voice on the television was competing with the efforts of families in maintaining their native language.

At the public meeting that evening, the community hall was packed and the atmosphere highly charged. Malcolm Green chaired the meeting and, after introductory remarks, a retired teacher acted as spokesperson against Gaelic education with the argument that if Gaelic medium was introduced, it would split the community between those who were in Gaelic medium and those who were not and furthermore that it could be educationally damaging for the children. This performance generated a feeling of gloom among those present.

John asked to speak and was given permission so to do. He countered the negative as follows: 'Well for a start, I'm a teacher, I have taught for years and worked with children from early years to late teens and I have worked with children with special needs, so I think I can speak with a status equal to that of the previous speaker. She does not appear to know anything about bilingualism or the benefits of bilingualism which are known throughout the world, but possibly not to retired teachers in Tiree. There are in fact huge benefits. I have also seen concerns as outlined about the kind of anticipated split in communities. In such cases, the question has been readily resolved once the decision has been taken to commence Gaelic medium education, whereby those who want the Gaelic medium take it, while those who do not don't have to. These communities quickly healed again and stopped being at odds. So I would urge you to go for Gaelic medium education and set aside any thoughts of splitting the community.'

After further discussion, the proposition went to the vote and overwhelmingly the community supported Gaelic medium education for Tiree. Catriona, and the others who were in support of Gaelic, were over the moon.

The delegation left for Glasgow the following day and while John was at the airport waiting for his flight to Stornoway, he spoke to Catriona, who declared, 'You won't believe what's happened here today, John. Timothy Renton has just been on the phone and he's coming here this weekend. I told him on the phone that the community had voted for Gaelic medium education. He had then asked, "But what about those who don't want it?" So I told him, "Oh, that'll be alright. They don't have to take it."'

Evidently the headmaster had been briefing Renton, but John Angus and the Strathclyde delegation got there two days before him to thwart any undermining that the Minister might have undertaken.

Catriona went down to see Renton's wife on the following Sunday while her husband had been out fishing. She started talking about the virtues of Gaelic medium education and explained that there remained a problem in the household.

'Oh dear,' said Mrs Renton. 'What's the problem?'

'Well,' said Catriona, 'our child will get Gaelic from my husband and at the school, but the television keeps spouting English, so no matter what we do to encourage Gaelic, it's negated by the television. So long as there is no Gaelic on the TV, we have a big problem.

By this time the Minister had returned and Mrs Renton turned to her husband and said, 'Really, Timothy we have got to do something about this!'

As Catriona left, she was accompanied to the door by Timothy who said to her, 'Catriona, you are a very persuasive young woman.'

Meantime John phoned Graham Carter to arrange a meeting and in due course met him in London. He reminded Carter about the earlier retort by Renton that the Gaels were not fiery enough. He then said he had just been to Tiree and that he had found Renton's holiday home there.

Carter said anxiously, 'You're not going to, are you?'

John assured him that they were not going to do anything to Renton's holiday home. He said that he had told the people to put a ring of steel round it.

Carter said, 'What do you mean?'

John explained that he had told the people of Tiree that no matter how nasty Renton might be and obstructive to Gaelic television, no one was to dare burn his cottage down.

Carter laughed. 'That's very clever. Just wait till I tell Malcolm. He'll love that.'

Thereafter Renton was told that people up north had found his holiday home, but that they were decent people who fight different kinds of campaigns from the Welsh and have decided to leave his holiday home alone.

Henceforth it appeared that Renton was neutral on the issue of Gaelic television.

Douglas Hurd

Douglas Hurd was contacted through his own constituency. The campaign had reached the point at which, no matter how much the Tory MPs in Scotland had been won round to supporting Gaelic broadcasting, it was an uphill struggle in the south.

However, through CNAG's work with Gaelic learners' groups, John knew that John Angus Macleod had a network of Gaelic learners' classes throughout England. John phoned him and asked if he could help with the campaign to convince people in England as well as Scotland to support Gaelic broadcasting.

John Angus Macleod readily agreed and asked, 'What do you want me to do?'

John replied, 'I'll send you a letter and I'd like you to send copies to all the people in all the classes throughout England that you know of and ask all of them to write to their MPs urging them to support the amendments CNAG sought in the Broadcasting Bill.'

'Yes, sure I'll do that,' responded John Angus Macleod.

So John sat up until 3.00am with a warming glass of sherry in CNAG's Church Street office in Inverness, drafting the letter. It was a cold night and the office heating was off. He felt a shiver of cold going through him as he heard spooky creaking noises and saw shadows flit across the walls of the moonlit room. Alarmed, John looked out of the window to see the trees in the Old High Kirk graveyard creaking and waving in the darkness. It was in the same Old High Kirkyard in 1746 that Jacobite survivors of the Battle of Culloden were murdered by Government soldiers. If the ghosts of Highlanders past were egging him on to right past wrongs, they had a disconcerting way of showing it. The next day John was informed by his PA, Ceiteag MacGregor, that legend had it that Bonnie Prince Charlie had taken shelter in the very building that was now CNAG's office immediately after the fateful battle.

The letter was forwarded to John Angus Macleod, who in turn sent it out to the Gaelic learners in his network. In due course, John Angus Macleod produced a map indicating 263 places in England where there were Gaelic classes or people otherwise interested in Gaelic who had written letters to their MPs urging the establishment of a Gaelic television service. Most of the letter writers, as it happened, were in Tory Party constituencies.

John immediately set off to Dover House in London and showed the map to Graham Carter and said to him, 'Look. We're on the move in England! This is a map showing 263 cells in constituencies where people are writing to their MPs asking them to support Gaelic.'

Graham Carter asked who these people were, to which John replied that he had no idea, but was led to believe that they included doctors, lawyers and other professional people who would be harassing their MPs to support Gaelic broadcasting.

John then excused himself to go to the toilet, and as he walked out, he passed Malcolm Rifkind, who exclaimed, 'Good God; what are you doing here?'

John replied, 'I'm talking to Graham, but actually, I've come to finish the job.'

'What job?'

'The boys stopped at Derby during the '45 uprising and they made a big mistake. I've come back to finish the job.'

Rifkind looked at John with a twinkle in his eye and confessed, 'I often feel the same way myself.'

With that exchange, John's feelings were confirmed that Malcolm Rifkind was on side not least because he realised that what John had been saying to Graham was true, that CNAG was not going away and they were going to get a result – not by burning cottages, but by getting to the heart of Westminster.

A few weeks later, Graeme Carter phoned John to say that Douglas Hurd's advisor had been on the phone to him to ask what on earth was going on with this Gaelic broadcasting business. Graham Carter was able to say:

'It's all right, we know all about it. It's these people we're working with in Scotland.'

'But,' said Hurd, 'do you realise that there's somebody in the Home Secretary's constituency asking to meet him about Gaelic broadcasting?'

Carter responded with, 'Oh yes, we support Gaelic broadcasting and so should the Home Secretary'.

As it happened, Hurd's people also had Welsh connections and, having been presented with CNAG's well-expressed case, Douglas Hurd too became a supporter of Gaelic broadcasting.

Clinching the Deal

WHEN CENTO VELJANOVSKI'S paper was presented, it gave a seal of approval and validity to the concept of creating a Gaelic television service on the back of the forthcoming Broadcasting Bill. Nevertheless, it took considerable pressure from Douglas Hurd and Malcolm Rifkind to convince the Treasury and the Prime Minister that the case for a Gaelic broadcasting service should be supported legislatively and financially. At this stage, John contacted Michael Forsyth MP, then Chair of the Conservative Party in Scotland, reminding him of their previous communication and asking him to intervene with the Prime Minister. Forsyth responded that he would see what he could do.

In the end, Lord Young opposed the inclusion of Gaelic broadcasting in the bill, Timothy Renton probably abstained, but a majority of the committee supported inclusion. As Cento Veljanovski had also been advisor to the Prime Minister Margaret Thatcher, the proposition surely carried some weight with the PM which must have eased its progress through the Government. Furthermore, the tenacity of Malcolm Rifkind in negotiations with Treasury, and the support of Douglas Hurd, were vital in securing a deal, despite strong resistance from the Chancellor of the Exchequer.

Malclom Rifkind was then able to announce at Christmas 1989 that within the Broadcasting Act of 1990, the Government would make provision for a Gaelic television service and that he had secured £8 million to be written into the Broadcasting Act to fund this purpose – a very welcome Christmas present to the Gaelic community. Quite a change in the Government's stance since that civil servant's smug 'brush-off' letter less than two years earlier.

As the act was being drafted, it was decided not to hand the cash to any one broadcaster, but to establish a Gaelic Broadcasting Committee to administer the fund. To cover the cost of administration, training and research activities, a further £1.5 million was to be added to bring the total funding to £9.5 million.

In the negotiations, prior to the passing of the Act, John Angus and his board had sought the support of the broadcasters. At first there was scepticism, but gradually as John and colleagues presented the case, Grampian Television, STV and some people in the BBC became supportive, as were influential individuals such as Sir Robert Cowan, Sir Kenneth Alexander and Sir Alan Peacock.

John recognised that these people could be allies but could also be detrimental if they said the wrong thing out of ignorance. That is why John had been courting them even before the Government itself had been won round. These contacts continued during the gestation of the act and he met face to face with each of them to bring them up to date with progress and in particular to stress the potential economic benefits of the establishment of a Gaelic television service. They were all, of course, economists who were cognisant of economic opportunities when offered.

At the same time, John maintained close contact with civil servants in the Scottish Office in the Arts and Cultural Heritage Department, especially Douglas Miller, from whom CNAG received funding. Maintaining good relations and communications was essential to keeping the atmosphere around the campaign positive. Seminars were held also to bring and keep other Gaelic organisations and interested parties on board.

In his years with HIDB John had been struck by the quietly successful negotiating style of the Reverend Donald MacAulay, Convener of Comhairle nan Eilean, whose mantra was 'Rud nach fhaigh thu le modh, cha ghlèidh thu le mi-mhodh (What you can't win through politeness, you cannot win by rudeness)'.

This had been reinforced by his meetings in Westminster in his early days as CNAG CEO with Donald Stewart, MP, who had given him similar sound advice and tips on how to approach people in a non-confrontational manner. This had been a crucial early initiation in Westminster when John was campaigning in 1985 as the new CNAG CEO for Gaelic to secure recognition in the National Heritage Act.

Another ally was Roy MacIver, former Chief Executive of Comhairle nan Eilean Siar (as the Western Isles Council was by then named) and by that time Chief Executive of the Convention of Scottish Local Authorities (COSLA). When in Edinburgh, John used to call at COSLA to keep Roy in the loop. Roy offered him the use of a hot desk, when in town, sometimes Charlie Gray's, the COSLA leader's desk.

On one occasion, when in Edinburgh, Roy said, 'Och, just use Charlie's desk. He's not coming in today.'

John duly occupied this hallowed space. Half an hour later, Charlie Gray walked in.

John rose and apologised saying, 'Sorry, but I was told you would not be in today.'

Charlie said, 'Oh, you're probably making better use of the desk than I would. Just carry on.'

The Broadcasting Act 1990 passed through Parliament despite opposition from much of the Labour Party and from some Tory MPs, who saw it as representative of a 'dumbing down'. It came into being in 1991 and under its provisions, the television or radio companies, rather than the regulator, became the broadcasters. It allowed for the creation of a fifth analogue terrestrial television channel in the UK (Channel 5), and the growth of multichannel satellite television. It also stipulated that the BBC, which had previously produced most of its television programming in-house, would henceforth have to source at least 25 per cent of its output from independent producers. The Act also reformed the system of awarding ITV franchises, essentially on an auction basis, and allowed companies holding ITV franchises to merge.

Crucially for the ambitions of CNAG, provision for a Gaelic Television service administered through a Gaelic Television Committee with funding of £9.5 million was provided for by the Act. It had been a long and difficult haul, but against the odds, the goal of a new Gaelic television service was now in prospect.

The constant travelling and most weeknights spent away from home were very demanding of John's physical, mental and emotional resources. In particular, the lifestyle placed a heavy burden on his wife Maria, particularly after the birth of sons Ciaran in May 1987 and Michael in September 1990. After the requisite periods of leave, Maria returned to her employment as a social worker, which carried its own pressures. They had also started building a house, hiring local tradespeople, a protracted business which saw mortgage interest rates rise from the initial quotation of 9 per cent in 1987 to 15 per cent by the completion of the project in 1990. As a family, they had been fortunate to secure the friendship and support of a local couple, Ruairidh and Kathleen Macleod, who became effectively surrogate grandparents to the children and, amongst other things, ensured that they grew up fluent in Gaelic from an early age. Without such support, the demands of professional life could not have been sustained by either John or Maria.

The After Eights

NO SOONER HAD the initial £8 million of Government funding been announced, there emerged the phenomenon of individuals and organisations claiming or insinuating that *they* had been responsible for winning this largesse or claiming a right to it. While some of these had been involved, others had been either silent on the issue hitherto or had been censorious or suspicious of John Angus' untiring forensic efforts to win over the London political establishment, even although it was apparent that the campaign had been widely supported. These late-comers to the show came to be known as 'the after eights' – that is to say after the eight million, in two senses of the word 'after'.

Amongst those who shared this newfound enthusiasm for association with the cause of Gaelic television broadcasting was An Comunn Gàidhealach. There is no doubt that many within that organisation had resented the creation of CNAG, all the more so when CNAG was achieving success in Gaelic development when the worthy and well-meaning efforts of An Comunn had been ineffective in stemming the long-standing decline of Gaelic.

In an effort to retrieve a measure of the glory and perhaps even to wrest some control over events, An Comunn decided to host a seminar in Inverness to determine the future of Gaelic television broadcasting in Scotland. Letters of invitation were sent to the conveners of all Scotland's local authorities, broadcasters and other interested parties.

When the invitation arrived on the desk of Strathclyde Regional Council's Convener, James Jennings, he summoned Bernie Scott, Strathclyde's representative on CNAG's board, saying, 'This looks important, you'd better go.'

'But I have to chair the Social Work Committee that day.'

The convener's response was, 'Och, keep it short and go up to Inverness afterwards.'

And so they did. Now Bernie Scott's driving style can best be described as fast and furious. Had his life choices been otherwise, it is likely that he would have made a name for himself in Formula 1. Bernie set off in his Audi Quatro. All went well with his swift sortie northwards up the A9 until he was clocked by the police at Daviot doing 119 miles per hour. This had been the very first day the police had used unmarked cars on that notorious road. As a consequence of this unfortunate incident, Bernie arrived at the seminar half an hour late and not in the best of humour.

By this stage in the proceedings, the Comunn official chairing the meeting was in full flow, extolling the credentials of An Comunn Gàidhealach. He pointed out that, whereas CNAG had been in existence for only a few years, An Comunn had then been around for almost a century. At this remark, John opined that if age was to be the determinant of effective future policy, he should have sent his mother to the meeting as she was almost as old as An Comunn.

At another stage in the presentation, the point was made that, whereas CNAG had only a small board of Directors, An Comunn represented no less than 3,000 members (although it was suspected that a proportion of them were deceased).

In support of CNAG, Bernie Scott interjected. 'If its numbers that matter here, I represent two and a half million people!'

These exchanges were entertaining though perhaps not very enlightening in the circumstances.

One positive aspect of this event was the attendance of Euryn Ogwen Williams, the Deputy Chief Executive of Welsh broadcaster S4C. Euryn was later to have an important role in helping John with the practicalities of establishing the expanded Gaelic television service.

When the seminar was over and it was not immediately clear what, if any, conclusions it had come to, John's first priority was to see what could be done to soften the repercussions of Bernie's speeding charge. Had he been caught in Strathclyde, he may have got off with a warning as he was Chair of the Strathclyde Police Committee, but this cut no ice with the Highland Constabulary. In the end, letters of support were sent by John and Norman Gillies, explaining the extenuating circumstances, highlighting Bernie's charitable work and stressing his exceptional driving skills. In the end, Bernie lost his licence for nine months – a more lenient penalty than might otherwise have been the case.

* * *

An unfortunate fact illustrated by the emergence of 'the after eights' was that the positive results brought about through John's achievement and success could also breed negativity and defamation as a result of jealousy.

Such negativity was further highlighted for John some time later when the expanded Gaelic television service was launched under the auspices of the Gaelic Television Committee, whose creation will be described later, and the new soap *Machair* was in production in Lewis. An evening of entertainment was organised in the British Legion building in Stornoway by the Gaelic Television Committee's PR officer so that the production crew, actors and locals who participated could meet in a social setting.

One local present, who had appeared in a number of episodes of *Machair* and was well known for his wit and anecdotes, was the brawny, bearded Dan Murray. As the event buffet was self-catering, John made his way to the kitchen with dirty dishes and found Dan doing the washing up. To help out, John started drying the dishes and noticed Dan eyeing him from the corner of his eye.

Some exchange of pleasantries took place, and then Dan, ever forthright, looked John in the eye and, translating from Gaelic, said, 'I have to say this, but you surprise me; I always thought you were a bastard.'

When John asked what made him think that he might not be one after all, Dan responded that no one of that kind would do the washing up with him! He then went on to say that he was surprised that John was still alive and standing.

When asked why, he said, 'Have you no idea of the number of knives that have been aimed at your back?'

Nonplussed and shocked John could only respond that perhaps Dan had been keeping the wrong company, thanked him for his openness and left the matter at that – albeit sadder and wiser as a result.

At this time, it also transpired that, disappointingly, there was cynical speculation afoot as to what had been 'sold to the Tories' in exchange for the £8 million Gaelic Television Fund. Those speculating had completely missed the point of the campaign. If anything, what had been 'sold' was the prospect of the economic, employment, social, cultural and linguistic benefits that would accrue to the Highlands and Islands.

One irksome comment made directly to John was that he and CNAG should not have accepted the Conservative Government's legislation and the £8m Gaelic Television Fund but should have waited for a Labour Government to deliver the real goods – a Gaelic television channel. This pitch was especially ironic and incomprehensible as much of John's support had come from the Labour Party, and the Cross-party Group for Gaelic.

Hindsight now demonstrates that without the creation of the Gaelic Television Fund as the cornerstone and stimulus for further developments, the highly successful Gaelic television channel, BBC Alba, would not now exist. Realpolitik can override crude party-political ideology.

As Malcolm Rifkind put it when announcing the Fund, 'This is the biggest boost to Gaelic ever.'

A University for The Highlands and Islands

IN 1991, WHILE the Gaelic Television Fund had been announced, but was not yet in being, there occurred an unexpected congruence of events. At that time, among his many other responsibilities at CNAG, John had succeeded the Reverend Jack MacArthur as Chair of the Trustees of Sabhal Mòr Ostaig, the Gaelic College in Skye, and was close to despair because the finances of SMO were precarious. After much deliberation he and the College Director, Norman Gillies, approached Sir Ken Alexander for advice. Sir Ken agreed to help and prepare a report with the assistance of David Graham, an ex-Chief Inspector of Schools, on the options for developing SMO.

Prior to this, it had been recommended by the previous Principal that SMO be shifted to Inverness or to Glasgow. John and the SMO board could not see the sense in that. At the same time, they couldn't see how to reduce the debt that had accrued when it became apparent that an original plan to attract overseas funding had not worked. Sir Ken Alexander and David Graham came to the view that the only way forward was for SMO to remain in Skye, grow student numbers, provide new living and lecture accommodation, expand the library and trade out of its debt.

After the Government had agreed to pay £9.5 million pounds to fund the forthcoming Gaelic television service, John met up with Cento Veljanovski in London in the Chelsea Arts Club where they had lunch. Both were relaxed as they were no longer in a client relationship, but almost as a couple of buddies celebrating a win. When asked by Cento what else John was involved in, other than broadcasting, John described the efforts to secure a future for Sabhal Mòr Ostaig. He recounted how when Adam Smith, the father of economics, went on his tour of Europe in the 1760s, which resulted in his writing *The Wealth of Nations*, one of his companions was Lord Macdonald of Sleat. On his return to Skye, Macdonald, enthused by 'enlightenment' ideas, initiated the process of clearing people off the land and replacing them with sheep. The steading, which was now the Gaelic college, originated from that era. John described how, when he touched the wall of that building, he felt as if history was speaking to him – his family on his mother's side were Macdonalds – and the time had come to reclaim the heritage that had been taken from them.

Cento was enthralled by this story and asked how much money was needed to expand the college. When told that it would be more than £1 million, he responded that media mogul Rupert Murdoch, to whom he was an advisor, might very well pull out his cheque book on hearing this story and hand over a cheque. He suggested that John think about it and that he would try to broker a meeting with Murdoch if so requested.

With the Gaelic Television Fund in prospect, Norman Gillies was quick to seize the opportunity to secure a slice of the action. He proposed setting up a centre of excellence for training in Gaelic television skills. This proved to be a very good idea, and was implemented in due course after a feasibility study by an independent consultant.

The other interesting thing that happened was that, contemporaneously, the case for a causeway to link the island of Vatersay with Barra had been won and was to be opened by Malcolm Rifkind. John Angus had not been invited to the opening, but he was invited to the lunch to celebrate the event and to sit beside Malcolm Rifkind and the parish priest, local activist, Father Calum MacLellan in the Star of the Sea Parochial House in Castlebay.

John had stayed in Barra the night before and discussed how the whole thing should be handled and what was to happen next. Fortunately, John had been briefed by the civil servants. Father Calum said that his next priority was a causeway to Eriskay. John countered by saying that if he asked for funding for that, it would be very predictable, because now that the Vatersay causeway had been built, the causeway to Eriskay would follow more or less automatically. John then said, 'If you really want to surprise the Minister, you can make a plea for something that's entirely different from the island that you were born on. I suggest you should say "I want you to support expansion of the Sabhal Mòr Ostaig."'

Considerable discussion ensued, because Father Calum was fixated with the pitch for an Eriskay causeway. In the end John put it to

Father Calum, 'Look, are you a statesman arguing for something outside your own immediate area of interest, or are you the local priest arguing for a local amenity in the island that you come from?'

John went on to argue that the Eriskay causeway would happen anyway. If, on the other hand, he argued for Sabhal Mòr Ostaig, there was a chance that the case would be won, whereas it was difficult to see how progress could be made otherwise.

Father Calum thought about it for a while and in the end, he agreed to go along with this tactic, although he confessed, 'This morning I'd never have thought that this is what I'd say to the minister.'

But he did say it.

At the point in the discussion when the pitch for the Sabhal Mòr expansion was made, Rifkind had to absent himself to respond to an urgent phone call and, on his return, he explained that a Typhoon military aircraft had gone down in the Irish Sea. Fortunately, he explained, the pilot and co-pilot were safe as they had managed to eject.

'The thing cost the best part of a billion pounds you know,' he said, 'so bang goes your Gaelic college.'

John then responded that, if necessary, on the basis of his discussion with Cento Veljanovski, Rupert Murdoch might very well provide funding. This alternative was apparently not to the taste of Rifkind.

In the end Malcolm Rifkind agreed to consider the situation and ultimately approved a major contribution to the £1.2 million required for the upgrade of facilities at the college on the understanding that the rest be found from elsewhere and preferably the broadcasters who were to benefit from the £9.5 million Gaelic Television Fund. This negotiation was undertaken by the civil servant Douglas Millar, with whom John had liaised closely over the years, and he persuaded both STV and Grampian to contribute hundreds of thousands of pounds to the Sabhal Mòr Ostaig development.

At the same time, John and Norman Gillies lobbied Highland Council, Comhairle nan Eilean Siar, Strathclyde Regional Council and HIDB for their support, greatly assisted by a striking artist's impression of how the development would look. This was provided free of charge by Donald MacKillop Associates. In due course, funding was agreed to turn the Sabhal Mòr around and, significantly, to create a centre of excellence to train the Gaelic-speaking personnel who would work in the anticipated Gaelic television service. This would in turn generate a new revenue stream for the College.

Thus in his position as Chair of Sabhal Mòr Ostaig, John was able to set in train an initiative which was to have far reaching benefits for Gaeldom and the Highlands and Islands, although the credit for its realisation was to lay with others.

At his meeting at the Chelsea Arts Club referred to earlier, John had asked Cento about the Institute of Economic Affairs of which he, Cento, was a member. What did it do? How did it go about its business? Cento explained than it was a think tank that had blue sky meetings that came up with ideas which they fed into the Prime Minister, which of course was the reason Cento had been employed by CNAG in the first place. In absorbing what Cento outlined as the method by which the Institute of Economic Affairs functioned, John pondered, 'Why don't we have our own think tank to consider ideas for developing Gaelic and the wider Highland economy?'

And that is what happened. John as Chair of Sabhal Mòr Ostaig subsequently floated the idea with Norman Gillies in his role as Director of the College. He and Norman then invited a number of influential individuals, representative of local authorities, HIE and others, to come together over dinner, under Chatham House rules, to look at the idea of a think tank. In the course of discussion and John's description of the way in which the Institute of Economic Affairs worked, those present thought that it was a concept worth following up. They drew up a hit list of things that were important and top of the list came the idea of a university in the Highlands and Islands.

John had already had the positive experience of working with Jim Hunter in setting up the Crofters Union a few years before, and Jim was enlisted to become part-time Director of the new think tank named Barail (Gaelic for opinion or idea). Jim agreed to serve in this capacity and was tasked with setting up a seminar to investigate whether there was any prospect of setting up a university in the Highlands and Islands. A seminar was duly mounted in Portree to which Professor Sir Graham Hills, principal and vice-chancellor of Strathclyde University, was invited as keynote speaker.

Sir Graham was a strong enthusiast for the whole idea of a Highlands and Islands university and this gave the concept a degree of credibility that it had perhaps lacked hitherto. Others increasingly supported the university campaign, and after further seminars and a major conference at Sabhal Mòr Ostaig, a momentum built up. By 1992, Sir Graham proposed that a federation of 13 existing further education colleges that were scattered throughout the region form the structure of the proposed university for the Highlands and Islands. He recommended a small central core, a concept which became known as the 'Polo-mint' model. Among other recommendations, he suggested IT-based distance learning to ease access to learning throughout the large but sparsely populated area to be covered by the university.

The model won the backing of local authorities, enterprise bodies and the Scottish Office, and even persuaded the Millennium Commission to deviate from its policy of not supporting educational projects by securing a grant of more than £33 million. Within a decade, the UHI Millennium Institute had been established and, after a further decade, the college federation gained full university status.

The seeds sown in the Chelsea Arts Club had eventually borne fruit. The new university now has some 7,000 students on 13 campuses and is regarded as one of the most important projects to be created in the Highlands and Islands for a generation.

A Troubled Transition

1991 WAS A year that saw big changes in the Highlands and Islands. On 1 April, the assets of the Highlands and Islands Development Board were taken over by a new Highlands and Islands Enterprise network (HIE) which featured a core organisation based in Inverness and ten private sector-led local enterprise companies whose remit was to deliver development advice and assistance. Bearing in mind the pivotal role of the HIDB in supporting Gaelic development, there was some anxiety at the time as to whether HIE would be as supportive as its predecessor had been.

John Angus and many others knew that the local authorities had long stated ambitions to take over the development role of the HIDB and were especially keen to do so under the forthcoming new regime. John also knew, from his dealings with the Government over broadcasting, that this would be anathema to the Conservative administration then in power. John recognised that if action was not taken then Gaelic would probably lose out. If action *was* taken then Gaelic might gain. So in the gestation period prior to the formal establishment of the HIE Network, John as Chairman of SMO and Norman Gillies as its Director, took the initiative as architects of new local enterprise companies respectively for the Western Isles and for Skye and Lochalsh and that these should have Gaelic at their heart. They also agreed that, contrary to Government proposals, Skye and Lochalsh should be separate from Lochaber in the new enterprise network framework.

Of course, from his former HIDB experience, John knew all of the businessmen, movers and shakers in the Western Isles, so he phoned their numbers, one by one, explaining that the new enterprise network was to be formed and that they should collectively embrace it and set it up for their area. In pulling this together, Agnes Rennie worked closely with John to ensure a successful outcome.

Meanwhile, Comhairle nan Eilean Siar with Angus Graham as Chair of the Development Committee still angled for pole position and called a meeting in the council chamber. Angus MacLeod, Chair of the Crofters Union rose and said, 'We know there's something going on and people are working behind the scenes, but no one is putting their head above the parapet.'

John responded, 'I will. I'm responsible for this, because I know that if we don't do it for ourselves, it'll be done to us. I'm not against local government, but I want the Gaelic voice to be heard and that's why I've been talking to the Government about setting up the new local enterprise company.'

'Oh well,' said Angus MacLeod, 'if you're involved in it, I'll support you.'

It was around this time that John and his cohorts in the Gaelic world became labelled as 'agenda setters' – accurately so.

In due course, the local enterprise company for the Western Isles – Iomairt nan Eilean Siar – was created, as was Skye and Lochalsh Enterprise with Norman Gillies as a prominent promoter. In recognition of his work in setting up Iomairt nan Eilean Siar, John was asked to join the Board of HIE itself. This he agreed to do.

While shouldering his considerable responsibilities in directing CNAG and, most challengingly, the campaign to win a Gaelic television service, John had been striving to keep fit and to alleviate the stress by running. Early in 1991 while on Barra, he took time out to run up the hill road on the east side of the island capital of Castlebay. As he progressed, he felt unwell with pressure on his eyeballs and shortness of breath. Normally he would have pushed himself to get over the pain barrier but on this occasion he realised there was something seriously wrong with his eyes and he gave up the run.

The following day, John was in Inverness and he went to Raigmore Hospital to seek help, explaining that he thought he had serious eye problems. The receptionist asked if John had a referral from his doctor, which he did not, in which case the hospital could not deal with him. John had recently been to his optician in Stornoway, who had identified black spots in his vision, which was causing concern. John phoned the optician and asked if he would fax over to the CNAG office optical diagrams he had developed which showed the blind spots in his eyes. This the optician did and John returned to Raigmore with these diagrams. Within a few minutes of presenting the diagrams, John was told that this was serious and that the consultant would see him immediately.

On examining John's eyes, the consultant explained that it seemed that John had detached retinas in both eyes, but that he needed to seek a second opinion. This was secured and John was told that he needed an immediate operation. There was no theatre space available that day and John was informed that he would have to stay in hospital overnight. On asking why, he was informed that if he was out and about and as much as stumbled, he would probably lose his sight. John explained that he had to get back to the office to give instructions to staff. He did this but returned to hospital where he was kept in overnight. The operation for detached retinas in each eye was carried out the following day.

Around this time, the board of the Gaelic Television Committee or Comataidh Telebhisean Gàidhlig (CTG) was established, with Roy MacIver as Chair. In the spring of that year, the Celtic Film and Television Festival was staged in Inverness and the new Gaelic Television Fund was a hot topic of conversation. Whilst at home recovering, and poorly sighted, John started to get phone calls reporting that a number of people were ridiculing the award of £9.5 million for Gaelic television and the system for deploying it set out in legislation. Prominent among them were sources within the BBC who were rubbishing the whole concept.

It is difficult to understand the motivation of those who sought to undermine this hard-fought achievement before it could prove its worth. Perhaps this was partly due to the internal politics of the broadcasting industry, and jealousy that they were themselves incapable of achieving anything like the successful outcome that John had pulled off. In the face of this small minded but vociferous barrage of disparagement, Roy MacIver was having a rough time even before the appointment of the first Director of the new organisation. It seemed that the job was being labelled as a poison chalice.

Around this time, the West Highland Free Press, which was generally well disposed to Gaelic, carried the headline 'Viewing figures boost case for 'mini-s4c' Gaelic channel'. This was in fact a pessimistic piece about confidential viewing figures obtained by the Free Press casting doubt on the ability of Gaelic programmes on ITV to retain general audiences. The figures, it claimed, were far poorer than the optimistic comments made by Grampian and STV in their franchise bids about the acceptability of Gaelic programmes in their schedules at reasonable viewing hours. Advertisers, it was stated, described the figures as 'appalling'. Another apprehension was that the apparent 'high switch-off rate' would create 'a real danger of a viewer backlash as the sheer quantity of Gaelic programmes, financed by the £9.5 million, grew'.

This was all presented as a dilemma for the fund even before it came into operation. Critics, the article stated, had argued that the idea of transmitting Gaelic programmes at peak hours on mainstream commercial channels was a delusion and that instead a 'mini-S4C' (Welsh language channel) approach, with Gaelic programmes concentrated onto one of the minority channels, such as BBC Two or Channel 4, at fixed times should be adopted. As we have seen, this idea was investigated and was ruled out, much to CNAG's regret. However, securing significant funding was seen as a major step forward towards the eventual creation of a Gaelic Channel. John and others continued to pursue this aim through subsequent Acts of Parliament, until the goal was ultimately reached.

Amid this doom-laden atmosphere, John decided to apply for the job of Director of the Gaelic Television Fund, having previously hoped that a strong candidate would emerge from the ranks of those working in the broadcasting or production sector.

John applied, while recognising that he was unlikely to get the post. In due course, he went for interview at the Thistle Hotel in Glasgow. During the interview, he was asked how he would tackle the job and John said that he would work with broadcasters and producers, but he was under no illusions about where the main interests of the broadcasters lay. While they had been supportive in the later part of the campaign to secure the £9.5 million, they were likely to give priority to majority interests if the funding proved not to be as attractive as it initially looked, and commercial and scheduling priorities changed. The other key point that John made was that, while he was not a broadcaster, he had a track record in setting organisations up – not least CNAG – and had the know-how to set up the new Gaelic Television organisation. He had worked with and within broadcasting organisations, observed management and production processes, and had been planning development of Gaelic television for years. At the end of the interview, Roy MacIver asked John where he would be later that afternoon, to which John replied that he would be in his hotel room.

Roy said, 'I'll come and see you there whatever the outcome.'

At about 5.00pm, Roy appeared at John's hotel room to say, 'Well John, I've got news for you.'

John, resigned to rejection, retorted, 'Ach well, I've got a job anyway, so it doesn't matter.'

'Oh no,' said Roy, 'we want to offer you the job. Do you want it?'

And so John accepted the post of Director of the Gaelic Television Fund.

Comataidh Telebhisean Gàidhlig (CTG)

ON 1 OCTOBER 1991, the 43-year-old John Angus Mackay took up the £40,000-a-year post of Director of the Gaelic Television Fund, or Comataidh Telebhisean Gàidhlig (CTG) to give it its Gaelic appellation. Press reports at the time announced that he would retain his positions on the board of HIE and the Scottish Arts Council, both of which were felt to be relevant to his new post.

It was further announced that the fund, whose initial annual budget was £9.5 million for two years was designed to create up to 200 hours of new Gaelic programming annually. This was over and above the total of 100 or so hours (two hours per week) then produced by the BBC and independent television stations between them. The main challenge was the leap in gearing up to 300 hours of Gaelic programming by 1993, which John described as 'quite a tall order'.

A number of commentators criticised the appointment on the grounds that he did not have first-hand experience of television production.

John's answer was simple: 'There are so few Gaelic programme-makers at the moment that they are as well to stay in programme-making. The fund is about identifying relevant programme strands and funding programmes not producing them.' He cited the example of Channel 4, which commissioned programmes from programme-makers.

As had been demonstrated time and again, one of John's consummate skills was to draw on the expertise of others who knew more about the issue at hand than he did himself. This tactic was to reap enormous rewards in the development of CTG in the form of a certain Welsh wizard. While still with CNAG, and being closely involved as Secretary to the United Kingdom Committee of the European Bureau for Lesser Used Languages, John had got to know and respect Euryn Ogwen Williams, whom he had first seen at the An Comunn Gàidhealach conference in Inverness. Euryn had helped found the Welsh language television broadcaster s4c (Sianel Pedwar Cymru, which translates as 'Channel Four Wales) and had guided it through its first ten years as Deputy Chief Executive. He had subsequently been involved in C3W, a newly formed company bidding for the ITV franchise for Wales and had lost it by a whisker, so was at that stage setting himself up as a freelance producer and looking for a new challenge.

John trusted Euryn and, whilst still employed by CNAG and CEO designate of CTG, he contracted Euryn to help with planning for the establishment of CTG's administration and programme funding activities.

From the start, the aim of CTG was to provide a general service to all Gaelic speakers in fields not previously available, including news, a drama serial and factual programme series, much of which would be broadcast at prime viewing slots on Grampian and STV. As already indicated by John to his critics, CTG would not make the programmes. Instead, it would finance programmes made by the three existing channels (STV, Grampian and ultimately the BBC) or by a beefed-up independent sector. The process of selecting which ideas would be made into programmes would be a joint one between the Committee and the broadcasters.

Euryn proved to be a tower of strength. He knew the industry, the game and the tricks of the trade. The pair of them worked well together and, by the spring of 1992, when the money came on stream, they had already worked out with the broadcasters what the key strands of programming would be. Euryn spent two days each week in Scotland advising John and the committee and helping in the relationship with broadcasters. He also helped with the massive task of building up the cadre of technicians, writers and actors needed to make the new programmes. The magnitude of the task may be understood by the sobering fact that, when CTG started, Equity, the actors union, had just seven Gaelic-speaking actors with television experience on its books and there were virtually no Gaelic language writers with experience in television or drama.

In this period also, in response to the training remit set out in the legislation, CTG Grampian and Scottish Television, in association with Sabhal Mòr Ostaig, set up the Gaelic Television Training Trust with John as Chair to train Gaelic speakers in production skills. By this stage, John had resigned as Chair of the Trustees of Sabhal Mòr Ostaig, to be replaced by Dr Farquhar MacIntosh. By another happy twist of fate, Neil Fraser who had been Head of Radio Scotland and Deputy Controller of BBC Scotland had retired from these positions and was recruited to direct the establishment of the Trust's training programme, supported by Alex MacLean, a former Head of Resources with the BBC. These were of course both Gaelic speakers.

Meanwhile, the board of CTG debated where the company's office should be located. Euryn advised the board to consider a range of factors, such as whether the office should be open-plan. What would be the best location for broadcasters to be able to reach the organisation and so forth? A grid was drawn up setting out a range of potential locations with their attributes. Of the various options, Stornoway and Benbecula emerged as front runners. After a vote, it was agreed that Stornoway would be the location for CTG's offices. In due course, CTG's administration was located in rented new premises at Harbour View.

Prior to the creation of CTG, Grampian Television had no base in the Western Isles and John pointed out that in the competitive licencing market it would be wise for this to be rectified. In response, Grampian Television, led by Bob Christie who had been supportive of John's efforts to develop Gaelic broadcasting, took on the lease of a former engineering workshop on Stornoway's Seaforth Road, which had been bought and renovated by the council. In that building they produced the CTG-funded Gaelic news programme, *Telefios*, the first ever daily Gaelic television news programme. In the course of time, this building was to evolve as part of a multi-purpose Gaelic creative media hub.

Within a year of its establishment, John and Euryn's efforts, with the co-operation of the industry, were starting to bear fruit. Enough new actors and writers had been found to make a major new drama series, *Machair*, inspired by Alistair Moffat and Rhoda Macdonald. This employed 25 actors. Also funded were a drama documentary series on the history of the Scottish clans and a feature film, *From the Island*, partly financed by Channel 4, based on fiction by Iain Crichton Smith about his childhood in Lewis. This remarkable transformation was achieved by holding auditions and camera tests for any Gaelic speakers who fancied their chances on the television, regardless of experience. Housewives and fishermen with backgrounds in amateur acting turned up for these auditions. To complement the assembly of a pool of actors, the team who had produced the successful English language series, *Take the High Road*, was engaged to hold a series of workshops and training courses to create a pool of writers. Teachers, journalists and even former deputy Director of education, Finlay Macleod, attended these scriptwriting courses.

One issue that was to prove controversial initially was whether to provide English subtitles to the new Gaelic programming. Some argued that subtitling would diminish the Gaelic ethos of the service, but in the end the decision was taken to subtitle most programmes, with the exception of children's programmes. This decision was to prove beneficial in both massively expanding the audience figures, but also to expose large numbers of non-Gaelic speakers to the language and the culture it carried.

Another question was whether the expanded Gaelic programming on the existing channels during peak viewing would provoke a backlash among the English monoglot-speaking majority, as had happened in Wales prior to the introduction of the all-Welsh s4c. This did not happen and the new programmes were generally well received.

Some Scottish newspapers at the time like *The Herald* had been opposed to the spread of Gaelic – the editor bemoaning the Government's folly in providing £9.5 million funding and compounding it by giving control to some 'crofter'. Others like *The Scotsman* were more sympathetic. The critics were confounded by the quality of the programmes funded by the committee.

Highlands and Islands Enterprise (HIE)

THERE HAD BEEN a good deal of anxiety among many in the Highlands and Islands about the replacement of HIDB by the Highlands and Islands Enterprise (HIE) Network which, as already noted, would consist of a central organisation and ten private sector-driven local enterprise companies. It was widely recognised that HIDB had developed a strong and successful social role, latterly as a key driving force in the regeneration of Gaelic. As we have seen, the success of this role had been due to the well-focused efforts of a number of highly motivated individuals.

Of these, fortunately John Angus was appointed as a Board member of the new organisation and Iain MacAskill continued as Gaelic-speaking Secretary, but what of the social development role?

Crucial to the future style and focus of the new organisation was to be its new Chief Executive, Iain Robertson, a hardnosed former oil executive originally from Perth, but active most recently in the United States. He had arrived in Inverness in September 1990, to prepare for the formal establishment of HIE half a year later. What would his attitude be to the 'softer' social role and to Gaelic? He certainly came across as a ruthless, 'kick ass' kind of guy, with whom you didn't mess lightly.

On the afternoon of New Year's Day 1991, a first footing visit saw three of us HIDB colleagues foregathered over drams with families: Ken MacTaggart and myself in the house of John Watt, pondering the future and the new, rather scary boss. Then I suggested first footing him. Giggles of incredulity were followed by consideration of the prospect and a defiant 'Why not?'

And so the three of us, plus wives and children trooped to the large and somewhat forbidding mansion on Southside Road where dwelt the designate Chief Executive. While the womenfolk and children concealed themselves on the pavement behind the hedge, the three of us, with bottles in hand, scrunched up the curved drive in the glare of a security light. The doorbell was pressed. Muffled noises were heard within and at length a figure opened the door. It was Iain Robertson bearing a slightly anxious, quizzical look.

'We've come to first foot you Iain.'

A look of relief. 'Ah, we're just finishing our meal, but come into the lounge and we'll join you shortly.'

The distaff side were also ushered inside and refreshments offered.

The Robertsons had house guests – ex oil industry colleagues from America – and soon a convivial party was underway. John's wife Hilary was Canadian and she hit it off with the Canadian wife of one of the Robertsons' guests. Topics of conversation ranged from world affairs to US Treasury stripped interest bonds in which I had been dabbling at the time. In this way, Iain was able to demonstrate to his guests spontaneous Scottish first footing in action. The upshot of the whole affair was that he saw us in us a more worldly and hard-edged side to social development than he had imagined and we saw a more open-minded side to him than we had assumed.

As it happened, Iain was a son of the manse. His father was a Gaelic-speaking Church of Scotland minister from Skye, who had made one of the early Gaelic radio broadcasts in the 1920s. Not only was he well-disposed to Gaelic, although he didn't speak it himself, but he was keen to see the HIE Network play a strategic role in the regeneration process.

The HIE Network commenced operations on 1 April 1991 under the Chairmanship of Fraser Morrison CBE. A new strategy for development was announced with the aim of 'enabling the people of the area to realise their full potential'. This aim was to be achieved by pursuing three overlapping strategic objectives – growing businesses, developing people and strengthening communities. In achieving these objectives, HIE would sustain and enhance the area's unique natural environment and culture which of course included Gaelic.

This promising and well-crafted strategy had been orchestrated by Ken MacTaggart, who had been appointed Head of Strategy. Ken's family origins were of Islay and Loch Fyneside and he too was well disposed towards Gaelic.

And so contrary to worst fears, the HIE Network retained a social development role and a pro-Gaelic focus. This would henceforth fall largely under the new strengthening communities objective and would be devolved to the ten local enterprise companies. One effect of this was that, as the local enterprise companies became established, the Social Development Unit that I headed was gradually to be dismantled.

Until this point, as has been described, HIDB's Gaelic development strategy had been worked as a partnership between the Social Development Unit and CNAG. With the departure of John Angus from CNAG at the end of September 1991 to take up his post with CTG, the future direction of CNAG and HIE's Gaelic development efforts became a main concern.

Allan Campbell was appointed as the new Director of CNAG and much of the organisation's development work continued as before, minus the important broadcasting remit, which had now passed to CTG. One innovation, partly at my suggestion, was the purchase, by CNAG on a mortgage of a large ranch style bungalow at Mitchell's Lane in Inverness, wherein all of CNAG's Inverness-based staff could be relocated from former inadequate accommodation. This Inverness hub of Gaelic activity has been known affectionately thereafter as the Gaelic bungalow.

It was fortunate that, as a Board member of HIE, John Angus was a regular visitor to my home and office. Although less so than formerly, this still facilitated the two-way exchange on intelligence that had always been so vital in maintaining the Gaelic development impetus. By the winter of 1992–3, we had a sense that, while a foundation had been laid for the revitalisation of Gaelic, a more focused effort was now required.

Iain Robertson agreed and in May 1993, a conference called Air adhart le Gàidhlig: Forward with Gaelic was held at Coylumbridge. I drafted the keynote address delivered by HIE Chairman, Fraser Morrison, in which he extolled the importance of Gaelic development as an economic tool. This rather took the breath away from the majority present who had never before heard Fraser speak well of Gaelic.

In a whispered aside, Martin Macdonald said, 'Nice speech, Roy.'

I had been rumbled.

In the course of the conference, my paper, 'The Dynamics of Gaelic Development', written in consultation with John Angus, set out four strategic priorities for rebuilding Gaelic, namely:

Demographic reproduction (through Gaelic medium education)
Cultural motivation (through youth, family, arts, etc)
Wealth creation (through Gaelic media, tourism and other
commercial activity)
Strategic co-ordination (through CNAG partners, funding and
'energy centres')

Iain Roberson regarded this paper, which set out a range of targets, as the basis of a credible business plan for Gaelic development and offered me the prospect of secondment for three years to CNAG. After due consideration and consultation with John Angus, I agreed to this proposal, on condition that HIE enhance the budget.

The HIDB's old Social Development Unit ceased to exist at the end of November, but the secondment did not start until January 1994. During the month of limbo, I drew up the contract between HIE and CNAG, embedding the above priorities and targets in slightly modified form.

Thus, on commencing the new year as CNAG's Development Director I was able to work with Allan Campbell in accepting the contract I had drafted and reorienting CNAG's development focus. Crucially, this move also enabled the partnership between John Angus and I to continue, particularly in trying to align Gaelic broadcasting and the arts within the overall thrust of Gaelic development.

On Air

THE CTG'S FIRST year of operation (1992–3) was described in the committee's first annual report. Launched in Glasgow, it set out how strategic decisions were made as to the types of programmes produced, including the aforementioned *Telefios* Gaelic news service. The report commented on the outstanding success of *Machair*, the soap made by STV, which had utilised £2 million of CTG's budget to finance 30 episodes. Amazingly, it attracted audiences exceeding 500,000 – almost eight times the number of Gaelic speakers in Scotland. In this and other ways, the new Gaelic programmes which came on air in January 1993 had confounded the critics and delighted the audiences.

John Angus commented, 'If you're looking for the type of programme that will attract a family audience with a wide range of ages and be a regular strand on the screen and introduce new people to broadcasting, not just in the sense of audience, but also in the sense of new talent, then a soap fits all those bills.'

The fund Chairman, Roy MacIver, was moved to say, 'There were so many prognostications of gloom by people who said that *Machair* couldn't be done, it wouldn't work and there wasn't the talent there to make it. Indeed, all of our programmes have been more successful than we anticipated.'

One of the most radical and acclaimed programme strands generated early on by the new regime was BBC Scotland's CTG-funded *Eòrpa*, a hard-hitting current affairs series looking at social, economic and political issues across Europe, which put Gaelic into an international context. The budget for the first 32 episodes was £1 million, and very good value for money. Nothing like the coverage of *Eòrpa* had been attempted by the BBC before through the medium of English, let alone Gaelic and such was the professionalism and success of the formula that more than two decades on, *Eòrpa* is still being produced and watched by a large and influential audience, many of whom are non-Gaelic speakers.

Amazingly, one early cookery programme produced by STV attracted 450,000 viewers aided of course by the decision to provide English subtitles, a precedent followed by CTG for most programmes, with the exception of children's and news output.

While celebrating the success of CTG's achievements, a press report at the time by Lorne Macintyre noted that there had been resentment that the CTG money had created a 'gilt-edged' jobs market for young Gaelic speakers. Why this should have been a matter of concern after centuries in which Gaelic speakers had to find their way in a predominantly and alien English-speaking world is difficult now to comprehend. Anyhow, John was quick to respond by explaining that CTG had a remit to finance the training of people who can contribute to the making of the programmes it funded.

He pointed out, 'The Gaelic Television Fund can hardly be regarded as being successful in a general sense if it didn't improve the skills of and increase the numbers of Gaelic speakers who are involved directly in making programmes.'

In fact, of the 450 people, equivalent to 280 full-time jobs, in the media who had gained employment through the activities of the fund over the previous year, only one third were Gaelic speakers. Furthermore, it had been calculated that some £20 million of economic benefit had accrued to the Scottish economy because of the Government's £9.5 million. The economic benefits envisaged in Cento Veljanovski's report had been realised, most notably in the contribution to Skye and the Western Isles where one professional job was equivalent in the local economy to dozens in the Central Belt.

A breakdown of expenditure for the year 1992–3 revealed that the vast majority of the CTG's budget went to programme production – 86 per cent in fact. Of the remainder, 5.1 per cent represented payments to independent companies to enable them to develop programme ideas, 0.6 per cent was for programme promotion, 2 per cent was devoted to audience research, 1.4 per cent on training and 4.9 per cent on administration.

Alistair Moffat and Rhoda Macdonald at STV also struck up a partnership with the Welsh company which had the rights to the popular Welsh language learning series which became known as *Speaking Our Language*, funded by CTG and made by STV, for whom Elen Rhys acted as creative consultant. An interesting effect of the new series for

Gaelic learners was that, in the first three months, three times as many people bought Gaelic learning materials than had bought them in the best year of the BBC's *Can Seo* series in 1979–80. The accompanying books, tapes and videos were produced by Cànan, a company based at the Gaelic college, Sabhal Mòr Ostaig in Skye, who it was stated had been 'deluged by 18,000 enquiries from would-be learners from all over the world'. This had translated into 12,000 sales to more than 6,000 new learners, which included prisoners in Inverness and Shotts jails. Encouraged by this success, a commitment was made to develop a second series of *Speaking our Language* to be shown the following year.

It seemed as though Gaelic had at last come out of the closet, but not without a gargantuan struggle. In Lorne Macintyre's coverage of the first annual report, and referring to the state of Gaelic before the advent of a decent television coverage, he quoted John thus: 'The Gaelic issue was safely tucked away like a mouse behind the wainscot and stuck its head out perhaps once a year and entertained people at the National Mòd, when it was all right because it didn't disturb anyone in terms of their Scottishness.'

Although it was early days for the new television service, CTG's initial output had been a resounding success. And yet carping criticism from some sections of the press continued. Critics again raised the question as to whether or not there should be a Scottish Gaelic channel in the same way as the Welsh have S4C. In response, John had to explain, 'There isn't enough money available to make enough programmes to have a Gaelic channel. We're almost 40 years behind the Welsh.'

After all his efforts to achieve some sort of fairness in the treatment of Gaelic, the ongoing nit-picking by critics angered John greatly. He fumed, 'You have a community that has just managed, by the skin of its teeth to survive an ethnic cleansing exercise in the eighteenth century. There is about £2 billion in broadcasting in Britain. Surely an extra £10 million coming into Scottish broadcasting should be welcomed rather than attacked!'

This may be one of the reasons why, after a year on a budget of £9.5m and despite earlier assurances by Sir Hector Munro when officially opening CTG offices, the fund was cut by £800,000. This was a body blow, but not a fatal one.

Fortunately, the Gaelic Television Fund had the protection of the Broadcasting Act 1990 and was to look forward to a promising future. And it was to provide the spring board from which John Angus Mackay launched a new campaign to secure a place for Gaelic television in successive Acts of Parliament designed to help the British broadcasting and telecommunication industries to meet the challenges, and grasp the opportunities of the new digital era.

Lessons had been learnt and, as John himself said, 'when faced, as a small minority, with a large wave coming in your direction, you either stand and shout "stop" and get swamped, or you get on board and ride the wave'. The latter approach was pursued, which was to keep Gaelic in the frame and to give Gaelic broadcasting access to the airwaves in the unfolding digital environment.

Widening Connections

FOR ALL THE nit-picking, the level and quality of Gaelic programming enabled by CTG represented a step change in the public perception of Gaelic and its credibility as a living component of Scottish life. To John Angus Mackay and his Board, this was a good start, but by no means the end of the road. Something bigger, better and more secure was required and to do that, it was necessary to cultivate influential connections in ways not hitherto tapped.

As a Board member of Highlands and Islands Enterprise (HIE), John seized one opportunity to do so during a ministerial review. Lord Strathclyde was the minister responsible for HIE and after the Chair and Chief Executive had made their presentations and answered questions, it was customary for the minister to have lunch with Board members and senior staff. As it happened, John was placed next to Lord Strathclyde at the lunch table and, naturally, he struck up a conversation with the noble lord, asking how he was enjoying his ministerial duties with responsibility for the Highlands and Islands. To this, the minister replied that he was indeed enjoying the experience especially in getting to parts of Scotland and meeting interesting people that he would not otherwise have the opportunity to encounter. He asked, however, 'Why are people in the Highlands and Islands so depressed and lacking in get-up-and-go, as compared with other areas?'

To this John replied that he had often wondered that himself, until he uncovered the answer from Gaelic poetry.

'Gaelic poetry? How do you mean?' Lord Strathclyde enquired, somewhat nonplussed.

'Well,' explained John, 'after the trauma of the clearances and then the satisfactory outcome of the 1886 Crofting Act when crofters at last got security of tenure, there was a flowering of uplifting poetry and song with a sense of celebrating the environment and better times. Then, more or less a generation later, the First World War broke out and the Highlands and Islands lost a disproportionate number of men, mostly young men, on land and at sea. Depression and a wave of emigration to the USA, Canada and elsewhere followed, which depleted the communities of their life blood – the young, the strong and the enterprising. Although some, like my father, returned, the community was thrown again into...'

'Ah yes,' the minister acknowledged, 'the Second Word War.'

'Exactly – despair really, because of the further heavy losses within another generation. So it is hardly surprising that after such sustained experience of loss, people were not optimistic about the future until my generation who are now trying to do something for ourselves, because we are the first generation that has not known war.'

The conversation went on in this vain with Lord Strathclyde expressing interest, genuine understanding and admitting that he had not realised that these dynamics had been in play. John and he got on well which paid dividends in the future when John and his Board were seeking a place for Gaelic in the new digital environment in the lead up to the Broadcasting Act 1996. This influential contact led to others.

By this stage, too, there seemed to be a genuine feeling among several of the Tories that they should do something for Gaelic, which I believe was in no small measure due to John's persistent and persuasive efforts over the previous decade and a half. That process involved continuously cultivating new connections and allies, since earlier players such as Malcolm Rifkind had moved on to other duties. Lord Strathclyde's support also endorsed the commitment of Lord Jamie Lindsay, who in that period had responsibility for Gaelic.

John's horizons were also broadening and his sense of what was happening in other countries grew as, for example, he was asked to speak at conferences. One such speaking opportunity was a conference in Northern Ireland, where John Hume MP was the main speaker. The purpose of that conference had been to get across the point that Gaeilge (Irish Gaelic) was not just a Catholic preserve. John, therefore, as a Gaelic-speaking Protestant from Scotland was able to demonstrate that Gaelic had a wider relevance than that perceived by most people in Northern Ireland. In this way, Gaelic was presented as a bridge between the two communities, rather than a division. In support of this, John Hume pointed out that the Loyalist march 'Lillibullero', the regimental march of the REME (Royal Electrical and Mechanical

Engineers) that had come out of the Williamite war in Ireland 1689–91, was actually a Gaelic song. The words were in fact a distorted version of the Irish sentence *Leir o, Leir o, leir o, leiro, Lilli bu leir o: bu linn an la*, which translates as 'Manifest, manifest, manifest, manifest, Lilly will be manifest, the day will be ours', referring to a prophecy of Irish victory by the 17th century astrologer, William Lilly.

Meanwhile, the Irish speakers in the Republic had been agitating for a Gaeilge television service for themselves. In considering options, they looked at multi-microwave distribution systems where the signal was thrown from one hilltop to another using a multitude of transmitters. Such discussions with the Irish were useful in informing how John dealt with Westminster because Parliament soon began to think of the multi-microwave as a potential solution to providing a Scottish Gaelic service.

John recalls saying to a minister at the time, 'Well, no, because of our environment. You see, we have a lot of hills, so the system is not robust enough. If a flock of geese flew over or there was heavy rain, which is not infrequent, it would break the signal. Indeed, the geese issue could create even more dissention among crofters because crofters are pretty hostile towards the damage done by geese and the Nature Conservancy at the best of times.'

In the course of all that, Padraig O'Ciadhra who was at the time advisor to Michael D Higgins, the Irish Minister for the Gaeltacht, asked John if he would go to Ireland to explain the impact of the Gaelic Television Fund in Scotland, and suggest what lessons there might be for Ireland. In response, John went over and had lunch with Michael D. John's response was that the fund, although probably not big enough, was necessary and a big step forward. He stressed that what the Gaels in Scotland wanted was their own channel and that was what they were working towards in a step-by-step way. John then recommended that, with the spectrum available to the Irish, they go straight for their own Gaeilge channel. That is what the Irish did in setting up their Gaeilge channel, TG4.

Meanwhile the Welsh channel S4C's former deputy Director Euryn Ogwen Williams, who had helped in so many ways with the establishment and operation of the Gaelic Television Fund, now helped set up an equitable contractual framework for programming. This necessitated working with broadcasters on the one hand and producers on the other so that the most appropriate programmes were commissioned. As a funder, CTG could not itself commission programmes and therefore had to tread a very fine line between producers and broadcasters. To get the optimum results in the circumstances, CTG established a broad framework with the broadcasters and the independent producers as to the types of programmes they would welcome onto their screen, after which CTG put out invitations to bid for making the programmes. It was then open to the broadcasters and the independent sector to make the programmes. S4C's commercial and legal experts, including their London-based legal eagle Mike Hendry, were crucial in setting up these arrangements. Mike Hendry, as legal brief also to the Independent Producers' Association, was an expert in matters such as intellectual property rights, which gave the Scottish independent producers confidence that the system was fair and robust. S4C and its advisors were particularly helpful in looking at stands of programming that could be jointly funded between S4C and CTG. They also helped on how complimentary materials (books and DVDs) for programmes like *Speaking our Language* could be produced at Sabhal Mòr Ostaig by the SMO's subsidiary company Cànan, thereby creating additional economic activity and jobs.

In this spirit of inter Celtic co-operation, CTG made contact with Bretons who were attempting to establish a Breton language television service, offering access to some of the programmes that CTG were promoting. This mutual support proved to be useful to all the Celtic minority language parties in raising political profile and in learning from shared ideas and experiences. One of the issues that emerged in Brittany and in Scotland was whether it was feasible to have a Gaelic or Breton television service operating on commercial lines. In both cases, the audience, in truth, proved to be too small for this to be commercially viable. The irony was that CTG was effectively embedded within the commercial sector simply because the door of public service broadcasting through the BBC had so far been all but closed to it.

Contact was also established with the Manx Gaelic-speaking community which had established Manx Gaelic education at primary school level in the Bunscoill Ghaelgagh at St John's. There is a close relationship between the Scottish and Manx Gaelic – the former in written form being almost intelligible to a Scottish Gaelic reader as its spelling resembles a phonetic version of Scottish Gaelic. After a visit to the Isle of Man, John and his staff provided DVD copies of Gaelic programmes to Manx educationalists on behalf of the Gaelic Television Committee.

All in all, not only did these wider contacts help inform how CTG developed, but they anchored Gaelic and CTG in the broadcasting landscape and gave it a profile in these Celtic countries that was helpful in strengthening the case for minority language broadcasting in general. Such contacts had already existed between the BBC and the Irish broadcaster RTÉ and also the Welsh S4C, particularly at the Celtic Film Festival but, hitherto, a Gaelic body did not have a profile in that broadcasting club. Now it did.

This underlined the fact that for centuries up to this point, Gaelic had no official supporting institutions. So, what had happened in Scotland since the creation of Comunn na Gàidhlig and then the first Gaelic institution created by act of Parliament – the Gaelic Television Committee – was that Gaelic was beginning to develop an institutional support structure that was being recognised, not only in Scotland as an important force in national life but one of international significance.

Digital Developments

IN THE PAST, new technologies had entered the broadcasting industry slowly which meant that there had been fairly extended periods between broadcasting acts. For example, there was a period of ten years between the 1980 Act, which had led to the creation of the Welsh channel s4c, and the 1990 Act, from which CTG emerged. In order to keep pace with the speed of technological developments, however, the need for new legislation grew within shorter periods. This meant that, although in its infancy, it was necessary for John Angus Mackay on behalf of CTG to consider what steps needed to be taken to secure and enhance Gaelic's position in the lead up to the forthcoming Broadcasting Act 1996.

Each Act was normally proceeded by a green and/or white paper, which gave clues as to the Government's intentions. The important and revolutionary new development was the proposed creation of five new Digital Multiplex Services. This represented a technical step-change compared with traditional analogue television channels that were transmitted 'uncompressed' as a single programme service, which filled the entire 'bandwidth' available.

Bandwidth can be defined as the amount of data that can be transmitted in a fixed amount of time. For digital devices, the bandwidth is usually expressed in bits per second (BPS) or bytes per second.

Digital television channels can be 'interleaved' in a highly compressed format. The bandwidth they require varies due to the bitrate provided to each channel, such that it is possible to transmit several channels together by sharing the same bandwidth. A group of programme services transmitted within a particular bandwidth allocation is known as a multiplex which is much more cost efficient, as the bandwidth of one analogue broadcast is sufficient for several compressed digital channels.

This presented an opportunity for an increased output of Gaelic television broadcasting, but only if a fresh lobbying campaign were initiated. Inevitably this task fell to John and once again, he drew on past contacts.

One particularly useful contact was Murdo MacLean whose office was at 12 Downing Street. Murdo, amongst other things, was the parliamentary 'fixer' for debates in the House of Commons with strong contacts in both the Commons and the Lords. John got to know him and his value was not so much in advising as in posing challenging questions that others would ask, such as 'How do you respond to the claim that Gaelic television is not commercially viable?'

The Conservatives were still in the Government at that time, and while broadly supportive of Gaelic broadcasting, they needed guidance on how to proceed. As it happened, Lord Strathclyde was Chief Conservative whip in the Lords. In view of past contact, John was able to get meetings with him for some 15 minutes at a time to explain issues. Lord Strathclyde showed a generosity of spirit and would then say, 'I see, then you need to speak to...'

The organisation John used, however, to advise and make amendments to clauses in the Bill was a firm called Westminster Communications whose main advisor was Murray Elder. He had formerly been General Secretary of the Scottish Labour Party and was Chief of Staff to the then Labour leader John Smith MP. With this experience, Murray Elder had a close inside track on the inner workings of Westminster politics.

With the aid of these high-level contacts, John commenced the lobbying campaign as before using early day motions and making direct contact with politicians. In the course of all this, to help organise meetings with key politicians and officials, John worked with Iain MacLeod, who was then an officer in the House of Lords. As had been demonstrated in previous campaigning, cross-party support was vital if the cause of Gaelic was to make progress against competition from a myriad other issues, many of which would have been regarded as more important by the body politic.

On one occasion, to reinforce the case, John phoned Lord MacAulay of Bragar to ask him to go to the House of Lords to speak in support of Gaelic. He was not at home, but John spoke to his wife who said to him, 'Well he doesn't do broadcasting, but if it's essential, I'll speak to him.'

In the event, Lord MacAulay agreed. John Angus met him in the bar of the House of Lords. The first thing Lord MacAulay said was that his general rule was 'If you don't know what you're talking about, don't open your mouth, so I'm wary, but will try to do what I can to help.'

An enjoyable couple of hours of conversation ensued during which time a number of Lords came and went. There was an air of excitement in the corridors because there was a chance that, because of the numbers present, the Labour Lords might just win an important vote.

When the debate started, there was no sign of Lord MacAulay, and John thought, 'Oh ho; something has gone wrong here.' It was, however, another Lord who spoke. His topic was support for Grampian Television, but he attached to his speech support for Gaelic broadcasting, which actually came across better than if someone had spoken about Gaelic only. Lord MacAulay had found a suitable substitute advocate.

The Labour spokesman responsible for broadcasting was Lewis Moonie. Interestingly, he had been named Lewis because he had been born in Lewis. His father had been a banker there. John made an appointment with him, explained what the campaign was about and found support in that quarter. As the issue was a very complex one, John wanted to make sure that Moonie kept this in mind as the Bill progressed. To ensure that things kept on track, John attended nearly every committee debate – an onerous and at times soul-destroying process. Aware that Lewis Moonie was a heavy smoker, John went out to the corridor in anticipation of the time when Moonie would need to go out for a cigarette. The point of that was just to be seen, to reinforce the point that he (John) was present and watching. From the outset of the campaign in the '80s leading up to the Broadcasting Act 1990, Alasdair Darling had been a Labour member of the Parliamentary Committee dealing with broadcasting and his supportive stance had been carried through by himself and others over the years.

The cross-party group was chaired by Calum Macdonald MP. With John's input, a consensus of support emerged, reinforced particularly by Liberal Democrats' Ray Michie MP and Robert Maclennan MP, because the case for increased Gaelic television broadcasting had now been taken on board by the Liberal Democrat side. In the course of debates, Robert Maclennan spoke very strongly in support of the Gaelic cause. This commitment earlier manifested itself through intervention by Charles Kennedy who asked John to write him a short paper outlining the case for supporting and developing Gaelic Television. To John's amazement, the piece he had written appeared in *The House*, the magazine of the House of Commons. What John had not realised was that Charles was the deputy editor of *The House*, and that he had intended to use his role to raise the profile of Gaelic. Years later, at an event at Sabhal Mòr Ostaig and shortly before Charles' untimely death, the two of them had a long chat and a good chuckle about this escapade.

The net effect of all this, was that there was broad cross-party support for Gaelic broadcasting, but nobody knew quite what that meant in terms of practical proposals in the new digital environment. This was partly because it was difficult for members to get their heads round the new and complex technicalities thrown up by the potential change from five channels to 200.

The minister for Gaelic was Lord Jamie Lindsay who was also supportive. John had of course also been speaking with the civil servants including those of the Scottish Office, but he became more and more aware of the lack of practical progress and he sought the advice of Murdo Maclean. It was through his good offices that the issue came to a climax.

John arranged to meet Murdo at the House at around 5.00pm. He duly arrived, but there was no sign of Murdo. There was still no sign of Murdo at 6.00pm. After that, a secretary came out to say that Murdo had been tied up at a meeting, but that he shouldn't be too long. At 7.00pm, the secretary came out again to say that Murdo was still tied up. 'Do you want to leave it for today to see if we can fix up another meeting?' to which John said, 'No. I'll hang on for as long as it takes.'

At 8.15pm, Murdo came out and said, 'Oh you're still here, I'm very sorry but the meeting went on much longer than I had anticipated.'

Murdo then took John through a maze of corridors and backstairs from the House of Commons to the House of Lords into the office of the Chief Whip and, who was standing in the room but Lord Jamie Lindsay. He had his jacket off and was wearing his 'trademark' grandfather's trousers with braces to hold them up because they were too big for him and he was pouring himself a dram.

Murdo said, 'You two probably have something to talk about. I have other business in this office.'

Jamie said, 'Good to see you, John. Would you like a dram?'

'Yes. Thanks.'

'The thing is,' said Jamie, 'we have done what we can for Gaelic. I don't think we can take it any further. The broadcasters already think they have too much Gaelic on their screens. We can't get any further concessions from them.'

'I know that,' agreed John. 'That's the old analogue system which is on the way out. What I'm interested in is the digital system.'

'What do you mean?'

'The new Act is to do with digital broadcasting. We know there's no more space on the analogue system, but the digital system is going to have loads of spectrum available. So we want a foothold in that digital spectrum.'

'Oh,' said Lord Jamie. 'I didn't realise that. What can we do for you?'

John replied, 'Well, s4c will have its own channel on one of the multiplexes. Surely we can get space for Gaelic.'

John explained the opportunities that the digital multiplex system offered, to which Lord Jamie responded, 'Oh well, we'll see what we can do.'

So, as a result of John's dogged perseverance and that dram, things took a leap forward.

Digital Foothold

THE BROADCASTING ACT 1996 duly became law. Under its terms, the Gaelic Television Committee was renamed the Gaelic Broadcasting Committee and given responsibility for administering the Gaelic Broadcasting Fund, as it had been renamed. In addition to funding television programming, the committee was given the additional responsibility of funding radio programming.

More importantly, the intensive and persuasive lobbying had produced practical results. As a springboard to future development in this new digital era, Part 1 Section 32 of the Act provided for digital broadcasting of Gaelic programmes on Multiplex A (one of six multiplexes) provided by the broadcasters. This provision was for an admittedly disappointing minimum of 30 minutes per day but it was a start. Space on the Multiplex was to be shared by Channel 5, s4c, Gaelic and commercial ventures. The Gaelic Broadcasting Committee acquired a significant new role in this setup as the Act stipulated that the providers of the digital Gaelic service should consult the Gaelic Broadcasting Committee on the quantity of Gaelic programmes to be broadcast and the schedules for these programmes. An innocuous enough requirement, but the Gaelic Broadcasting Committee took full advantage of this as events unfolded.

John Angus found himself travelling back and forth to Westminster just as much as he had on previous lobbying ventures. It is perhaps difficult for those who work 9–5 in an office to understand just how energy-sapping and at times dispiriting such travelling and hanging around waiting for opportunities to meet and persuade contacts can be. John had been doing this now for over a decade, as well as thinking through strategies, tactics and technicalities, demonstrating an unusual level of stamina as well as political nous.

While this was going on, John had been working closely with s4c colleagues, Emyr Byron Hughes, their corporate affairs manager, and Ann Beynon, their press officer. s4c were, of course, trying to consolidate as much as they could for themselves.

On one particular day, John spotted Emyr Byron and Ann coming out of the House in the company of Prys Edwards, Chair of s4c and other s4c Board members. He went over to congratulate Emyr Byron on the way he had dealt with the intricacies of the Bill and what he had achieved for s4c.

'Really?' said Prys Edwards.

'Oh yes,' said John, 'you should be really proud of how s4c has carved out a space for itself on digital broadcasting.'

Prys Edwards replied, 'I'm really pleased to hear that' and away they went.

This turned out to be a fortuitous move, for, unknown to John, the s4c Board members had been finding it difficult, as were many others, to grasp fully the implications and technicalities of the new digital setup. By his genuine words of praise, John had helped to validate Emyr Byron's efforts to secure a good deal for s4c under the new legislation.

The next day when John was back in Scotland, he phoned Euryn to tell him of the chance meeting. As it happened, Euryn was with Emyr Byron at that time and both were delighted and toasting John's intervention at Westminster. Seemingly, John's words of wisdom had made a difference and caused a change of attitude within the Board of s4c. Now that the s4c Board grasped the potential of the digital system, this gave Emyr Byron more room to manoeuvre, at which he was very adept.

Once again, a chance meeting and an instinctively kindly but incisive intervention by John had turned a negative into a positive.

Another happy coincidence was that Ann Beynon was later to marry Leighton Andrews, John's former lobbyist prior to the 1990 Act. Leighton became a Labour Minister for Education in the Welsh Assembly. John was delighted and privileged to attend the couple's wedding.

Sometime after the passing of the Act, John phoned Euryn Ogwen to ask how s4c was getting on with the bid to run Multiplex A. Euryn's response was that they had felt that the whole thing was too complicated and had decided not to bid. John responded that that was a pity as there did not seem to be any competition for a licence to run Multiplex A. On Euryn questioning this, John pointed out that, in the light of the requirement under the 1996 Act, the licence holder of Multiplex A had to broadcast at least half an hour of Gaelic programming and had to consult the Gaelic Broadcasting Committee on scheduling. No potential bidder had contacted the Gaelic Broadcasting Committee. The point of this was that any likely bidder would have at least to make some contact with Gaelic Broadcasting Committee if they had been serious bidders.

On hearing this, Euryn and Emyr Byron put their heads together, decided to review their strategy, contacted NTL (National Transcommunications Limited) for technical support, enlisted other potential partners and wrote a draft bid which was approved by the S4C Board the following week. This bid by S4C was successfully approved by the ITC (Independent Television Commission) and a new subsidiary company SDN (S4C Digital Networks) was established to run Multiplex A.

By this stage, Neil Fraser and two others had set up a company S4A to bid to run the Gaelic service on Multiplex A, but negotiations with SDN did not bear fruit and, in discussion with John as Director of the Gaelic Broadcasting Committee, SDN began to look elsewhere for support. The problem was that SDN was a commercial operation, and its Board had to be convinced that the service would be run as cost effectively as possible to meet all licence requirements.

Thus, SDN looked at various options for creating programme schedules and transmitting the service. A proposal that Gaelic Broadcasting Committee-funded programmes could form the basis for the schedules was ultimately the chosen option, and a new entity TeleG was established in Stornoway in partnership with SDN. This operation was led by Murdo MacLennan, an ex BBC television engineer. He recruited staff to draw up schedules, source programmes in association with the CTG and then to send finished tapes to SDN's transmission centre. In the ten years that this service ran, the arrangement brought £2.5 million to the local economy in Stornoway.

Significantly, the spectrum that TellyG had filled formed the space and the basis on which BBC Alba was subsequently established as

Channel 7 on digital terrestrial television services – an absolutely prime location on the television listings.

In the meantime, the Gaelic Broadcasting Committee and its staff were to face a series of scheduling and financial difficulties from which the committee was to emerge, in John's words, 'dented but undaunted' and even more determined to pursue the goal of a Gaelic television channel.

Scheduling and Financial Difficulties

AS THE 1990S progressed, circumstances became more difficult for the Gaelic Broadcasting Committee in relation to programme scheduling and finance. The BBC was taking programmes funded by CTG, notably *Eòrpa* and the Children's series *Dè a-Nis?*, and scheduling these on a fairly consistent basis.

As the decade progressed, however, commercial considerations began to impact more and more heavily. The audiences for Gaelic programmes, funded by CTG and shown at peak times on ITV/STV were considered too small to be attractive to advertisers. Even although the television companies made some of these programmes themselves, there was pressure to shift them to non-peak times in the schedules. Initially, the Grampian Gaelic news service *Telefìos*, for example, had a good slot at around 6.00pm, but then came pressure to move the programme to around 5.00pm, when, of course, very few of the core Gaelic audience would be able to view it. Inevitably, this caused a lot of debate about scheduling and reducing the number of minutes of the programme. The outcome of these arguments was that the CTG, with deep regret, decided to stop funding *Telefìos* – a decision forced on the Committee by the circumstances. In essence, neither the Gaelic audience, the broadcaster nor the public purse was going to get value for money by continuing with *Telefìos*. CTG inherited the lease of the Grampian studio building and moved its offices there.

At the same time, changes in personnel at Scottish Television resulted in the levels of finance for *Machair* being questioned under a new financial regime. There were therefore calls for increased funding from the CTG. The costs of *Machair* were already high, because a fairly high proportion was shot in different locations throughout Lewis. Costs had admittedly started to increase because the owners of buildings, which had originally been made available for shooting at relatively modest fees, now sought more money.

It has to be understood that the regime under which STV made *Machair* (with finance from CTG) was different from STV's relationship with ITV for other types of network programmes. When STV made the crime drama series *Taggart*, for example, with its UK-wide reach, ITV paid STV in proportion to the advertising revenue likely to be generated. This difference began to grate on the STV management. The problem with *Machair* was resolved partially by filming more of the programme in the one studio with fewer location shots. Rather than have those shot in Glasgow, CTG sought funding from Western Isles Enterprise, European funding and a bank loan to create a studio on Lewis. A separate company, in which CTG had a share, was set up and a new Studio Drama Gàidhlig created in Seaforth Road in Stornoway behind the existing Grampian news studio. This then became the main location for filming *Machair*.

Unfortunately, after the new Labour Government was elected in 1997, the then minister for Gaelic, Brian Wilson MP, who had been supportive of Gaelic, proposed to reduce CTG's funding by £1 million. This came to light with a phone call, after 10.00pm on a Sunday, to John by a concerned BBC employee who sought clarity as to what such a cut would mean in practical terms. To this John responded that it would mean the cessation of *Eòrpa* because, technically at that time, CTG was tied to ITV and, although not prevented from doing so, were not required to fund BBC programmes. The proposed million-pound cut was subsequently reduced to a less severe but still damaging £550,000.

In hindsight, it seems that what motivated this cut was resentment that a Tory Government had created the CTG system. There was, furthermore, criticism that the Conservatives had not given the Gaelic community a channel of their own, or a slice of BBC or Channel 4. There had, indeed, been a school of thought, as previously mentioned, within some circles that the Gaelic community should have hung fire and waited for a Labour Government to have delivered the goods. That the Gaels had not waited seems to have caused resentment in some Labour quarters, with the result that money was taken from CTG and given to other Gaelic organisations. What made this worse for Gaelic television was that this latest half-million-cut followed the earlier cut in 1993 of £800,000.

It was unfortunate that the cut in funding came at a time when *Machair* audiences had been dropping to around 200,000 from the initial viewing figure of 600,000. As STV asked the CTG for more money than it could muster, the decision was taken to discontinue *Machair* from April 1999. This was not a decision taken lightly. *Machair* had been a great vehicle for talent development as well as making a major contribution to the Western Isles. There was widespread disappointment amongst the production people and supporters of the project.

These were difficult and frustrating times for John and his committee. They were caught between reduced overall funding from the Government on one hand and the independent sector, who were increasingly unhappy with the level of funding that was coming their way, on the other. In this environment, however, the original aim of securing a Gaelic television channel had been kept alive. This aspiration grew in strength and in 1997 Neil Fraser was commissioned to write a report on the way forward.

The Fraser Report recommended the creation of a Gaelic channel. In response, the Secretary of State for Scotland, Donald Dewar, created a committee, chaired by Alasdair Milne of the BBC, to work up a report on the feasibility of the establishment of a Gaelic channel. In 2000, after due deliberation, the Milne Report recommended the establishment of a Gaelic television channel with a budget of £43 million per annum. Unsurprisingly, in view of the earlier cuts in budget, the Labour administration considered the proposed sum unrealistic.

The new Scottish Parliament was finding its feet at that time and in 2001 its Education, Culture and Sport Committee conducted an enquiry into the Gaelic Broadcasting Committee. The CTG Chair did not appear and John was advised to answer all the Committee's questions himself. This he did. He must have been persuasive, because the Committee found that:

> ...the Gaelic Broadcasting Committee and those it has funded
> have, through their work, made a highly positive impact on
> Gaelic language, culture, education and society. (Paragraph 70)

Thus, George Younger's sage advice a decade and a half before to work up practical initiatives and CNAG's wisdom in following it by concentrating on developing Gaelic Education, Broadcasting and the Arts had proven to be strategically effective.

While all this was going on, John had had cataract operations on both eyes which meant that he had to spend a lot of time at home. The upshot of the eye operations was that, after a life since childhood of severe sight impairment, John suddenly had a quality of vision that he had never previously experienced. I recall him telling me of the amazement and pleasure he felt on seeing sheep on distant hills and picking out other details that had formerly been hidden from him. All in all, a welcome boost of confidence at a time when he would have to rally to new challenges.

The Gaelic community had been fortunate to have able representatives appointed to the Gaelic Television Committee by the ITC. It should be noted that, from the outset, the quality of staff recruited by the committee, played no small part in the success of the organisation as a funder of programmes, training and research in a sometimes fractious industry environment. This inherent strength gave John a sound platform from which to launch initiatives, and also helped to ameliorate the disappointments experienced along the way.

The ever-increasing pressure of events was also lightened by the appointment in 1997 of John Alex MacPherson as Deputy Director of CTG, who took on the responsibility of directing funding strategies. A former and very able BBC radio broadcaster, and also formerly the Public Relations Director of the Canadian Nuclear Energy Agency, John Alex was highly respected and proved to be a steady hand on the tiller in his ten years of tenure.

Assorted Activities

WHILE GAELIC BROADCASTING had been John Angus' overriding professional preoccupation since the mid-'80s, he was also active in a number of other fields connected with Gaelic development. As the '90s progressed, he was Chair of the UHI (University of the Highlands and Islands) Language Policy and Plans Working Groups, a Board member of Lews Castle College and pro tem Chair of the multi-agency National Gaelic Education Strategy Steering Group.

John was also appointed as a member of Scottish Arts Council and succeeded Elizabeth Fairbairn (sister of the Chief of the Clan Mackay) as Chair of the Combined Arts Committee. In this role, he reviewed arts centres all over Scotland, giving him unprecedented insights into the perplexing workings of the world of the arts.

One arts project was particularly close to John's heart, namely the creation of an arts and cultural centre in Stornoway which was to become An Lanntair. A development committee was formed and John was elected as its chair. It was to be a ten-year slog of promotion, lobbying and fundraising but, in October 2005, the magnificent new An Lanntair multi-arts venue opened on the Stornoway seafront with a co-commissioned play, *It Was A Beautiful Day*, in conjunction with Traverse Theatre. The building includes a 220-seat auditorium, contemporary gallery, office space, shop and café bar that functions as a theatre, a cinema, a dance studio, a concert hall, a platform for poetry and literature and is one of the largest arts developments in the Highlands and Islands. The centre's varied programme has featured performances and events from all over the world including The Wiyos (USA), Nablakov Quartet (Bulgaria), The Moscow Ballet, Kakatsitsi (Ghana) and Genticorum (Quebec). Over the years, major awards and endorsements have been received from, among others, Arts & Business, Arts and Tourism (Trophy), Art Partners and, in 2007, Traditional Music Venue of the Year.

In 1997, a new opportunity presented itself when Mary Robinson, the then President of Ireland visited the Sabhal Mòr Ostaig to give the annual lecture. She was a gracious and engaging speaker and her theme was the shared Gaelic culture of Ireland and Scotland. The address was well received and an important outcome was the idea of a project to foster support for the Gaelic language and develop links between Gaelic Scotland and Ireland. The idea was supported by Brian Wilson MP, who was then Scottish Minister of State for Education, Industry and Gaelic and so the inter-governmental Iomairt Cholm Cille or the Columba Initiative was officially launched in December 1997.

The initiative receives state support from Scotland, the Irish Republic and Northern Ireland and since its foundation has fostered links and funded projects between the Gaelic-speaking areas of the participating communities in a variety of areas, including music, sport, heritage, the economy and other areas of people's lives. Projects range from school exchanges and smaller ventures to the large-scale such as the annual student parliament which involves large numbers of Irish and Scottish Gaelic students coming together to debate and discuss topics of relevance and importance to them.

John Angus was nominated as Chair of the initiative, a role, which, bearing in mind a range of political sensitivities, he handled with skill and tact. In 2001, when Brian Wilson MP was minister in the Scottish Office and Alasdair Morrison MSP was the Gaelic minister in the Scottish Executive, Northern Ireland hosted a meeting of the Columba Initiative which was for the first time, held in Stormont. John knew that three ministers representing each of the jurisdictions covered by the initiative were scheduled to speak and he knew that as Chair of Colm Cille, he would have to thank the ministers afterwards.

John's dilemma was how to follow three ministers without upsetting anyone or repeating what had already been said. As he thought about this in the weeks beforehand, John looked for a way of tackling the issue. He looked at anthologies of Irish poetry and came across a poem in Gaeilge that he thought would fit the bill. He then asked Michelle Ni Chróinín, the Colm Cille worker from the Republic, to coach him in the correct Irish pronunciation.

On the day of the meeting, after the ministers had given their respective speeches and John thanked them, he duly recited the short poem:

Anoís

Anoís tá gach ní slán,
Cá bhfios an mbeidh arís go brách?
Blais nóiméad seo an ghrásta –
Taoi arís id naíonán fásta

Which translates as:

Now

Now everything is well
Will it ever be again?
Take this moment, then, and taste –
Man again a child of grace

When he finished, a member of the audience leapt up and with a whoop and clapped his hands. John asked the individual afterwards why he had clapped.

He responded, 'This is a first. Nobody has ever recited a Gaelic poem in Stormont before. It was wonderful.'

Raising the Stakes

TIME AT HOME after his cataract operations gave John Angus an opportunity to think through strategy and tactics on how to address what was coming next – the 2003 Communications Act, which was already under consideration by ministers and officials.

In order to keep up with the fast pace of developments in broadcasting and digital technology, John decided to take on the challenge of studying for a Masters degree in Media Management, an online course through the University of Stirling– gaining an MSc with distinction, the first in the inaugural year of the course. This gave John access to the foremost thinking of the day on digital developments and gave him the terminology and capacity to discuss broadcasting and technical issues in any forum. This proved to be a boon when, a few years later, he started negotiations with the BBC about jointly establishing the long-sought Gaelic channel.

John's dissertation had examined the programming and scheduling recommendations in the Milne report, using extensive surveying through questionnaires and individual interviews of the Gaelic audience panel in Scotland and the potential audience of London-based Gaelic speakers and supporters. One interesting departure from the conventional view of peak-time broadcasting commencing at 6.00pm emerged in the research: both the Scottish audience and the London-based respondents preferred a 'Gaelic news peak time' start of 8.00pm to fit in with existing viewing patterns and availability to view. The Gaelic news programme *An Là* was scheduled for 8.00pm when BBC Alba was launched. This neatly avoided potential conflict with the news on the established channels.

From 2000 onwards, following the Milne Report, a new campaign commenced with a view to influencing the 2003 Communications Act. Once again, Calum Macdonald MP was Chair of the Gaelic cross-party group in Westminster. A Lewisman himself, he was very supportive of John's efforts as were the Crichton brothers, also from Lewis – Donald Crichton who worked for the Labour Party in Milbank and Torquil Crichton who was a London-based journalist.

On a visit to London, talking to Calum Macdonald and working out how they could phrase amendments to the forthcoming Act, it was decided to seek powers that they did not then have for the Gaelic Broadcasting Committee to commission programmes and the capacity to apply for a broadcast license. These were two crucial powers that would greatly strengthen the Gaelic Broadcasting Committee's hand.

On another visit to Westminster, John, sitting in the bar with Donald and Torquil Crichton, said, 'Look I need to get a chance to speak with the Chancellor of the Exchequer, Gordon Brown. I'm not sure how to do that but I know that Alasdair Darling and Murray Elder are close to him.'

As this discussion continued, one of the Crichton brothers said, 'Look, Murray Elder's sitting over there. Do you want to speak to him?'

In the course of the previous campaign, Murray Elder had of course been John's adviser through Westminster Communications. So John and the Crichtons got up, went over to Murray Elder's table and John said hello.

'Oh hello. What are you doing here?'

'Well,' John replied, 'I've come back to finish the job we started in 1996.'

'What do you mean?' retorted Murray.

'Well, as I said, to finish the job we started, but didn't finish – to secure adequate funding for Gaelic broadcasting and to create a dedicated digital channel.'

'That's interesting. Let's meet again to discuss this.'

Sometime afterwards, John did meet with Murray Elder, who went through the issues and he asked what sort of figures John had in mind. John knew that they could not get the £43 million stated in the Milne Report, but the committee had commissioned a report from Deloitte which calculated that £21 million would be a good step forward.

Murray Elder felt that such a sum was not impossible but would need to check with Treasury. This he did and, after discussion with Gordon Brown, he came back in a further meeting saying that Gordon Brown and others were receptive, but there was a technical difficulty between Treasury and Edinburgh. The problem was that, under the Barnett Formula, Edinburgh had been getting increased funding for Gaelic television, but had not been passing it on to the Gaelic Broadcasting Committee. Treasury would not, therefore, give a penny until Edinburgh made up the shortfall.

During this period when John had been lobbying in London, he had also been busy with contacts in the newly created Scottish Executive. The Minister for Gaelic, Alasdair Morrison, and Education Minister Peter Peacock were kept in the loop and were supportive, as was Frank MacAveety, the Scottish minister with a responsibility for the arts who had to put a case to Finance Minister Andy Kerr.

In view of the ultimatum from Treasury, John met with Scottish ministers to set out the proposition that if the Scottish Executive (as it was then termed) was to come up with a certain amount of money, Treasury would also do so. The matter was progressing well when Brian Wilson, with no doubt the best of intentions, was able to get a late-night debate in the House of Commons in which he made a pitch for funding for Gaelic broadcasting. The minister attending the debate knew nothing about Gaelic, could not understand where Brian was coming from and said, 'Why don't you get Sean Connery to fund Gaelic broadcasting?' This was anathema for Brian, Sean Connery being a supporter of the (hated by Labour) SNP and the debate descended into farce.

Unfortunately, a journalist, Catherine MacLeod, who was in the know about what was happening, went to Tessa Jowell to tell her about the farcical debate that had taken place about Gaelic broadcasting, to which Tessa retorted, 'But I'm the minister responsible for Gaelic broadcasting.'

This appeared on the front page of *The Herald* the following morning and when it was drawn to Andy Kerr's attention, he retorted that there was no reason for the Scottish Parliament to come up with funds for Gaelic broadcasting when the Westminster Government was clearly responsible for it. And so, the whole carefully assembled plan fell apart, losing the committee and Gaelic broadcasting the £6 million that had seemed potentially in the offing.

This was a big blow, but John continued nevertheless to argue the case, in the course of which there was the usual round of seminars. One such, organised by Robert Beveridge, head of media studies at Napier University, was attended by John and representatives from BBC, Grampian Television and STV.

The question was asked, 'What do the Gaels really want?'

To this, John replied that what they wanted was a Gaelic channel of their own, notwithstanding the fact that neither the BBC nor the ITV companies had been supportive. John went on to say that the set up was not sustainable the way it had been going, the scheduling had largely collapsed, the funding was inadequate and a new solution needed to be found.

It was then pointed out that when the Welsh had met with an impasse regarding the establishment of their own channel, Gwynfor Evans had gone on hunger strike. John was then asked, 'If it came to the bit, would you go on hunger strike?'

There was a camera on John. His reply was, 'If you put it that way, and it comes to that point, I cannot say no.'

The stakes were getting high. On return home, John told his wife Maria what had transpired. John thought she would say, 'Oh, please don't' (or words to that effect). What she did say was, 'Well you do what you have to do' – a brave and supportive response.

When John informed his Chairman Iain MacAskill of this, he got angry and said, 'Look, you, as an officer, should never have been put in that position. If push comes to shove, I'll do it.'

John said, 'Are you serious?'

'Yes, I am serious.'

A little after that, John was in the Scottish Parliament after a schools debate, walking down a corridor with Alasdair Morrison who said that he was sorry about what had happened at and after Brian Wilson's late night debate. John pointed out that Iain MacAskill was getting so angry that he was threatening hunger strike.

As they proceeded down the corridor, they met Peter Peacock. After exchanging pleasantries, while thanking Peter for his support, John explained that things had taken an ugly turn because there was talk now of hunger striking to get what the Gaels wanted. Peter asked who was going to go on hunger strike. On being told that it was to be Iain MacAskill, a very large man, Peter, perhaps not wholly believing in the threat, jested that the process would take some time.

To this John retorted sharply, 'Well, all the worse for you, because it will be spun out, just as Gwynfor Evans had spun it out in Wales.'

Peter then acknowledged the seriousness of the issue and said that he would see what he could do.

The Scottish Parliament ultimately came up with £2.5 million in 2006/07 to which Westminster added a further £1 million.

The (Westminster) Broadcasting Minister in the lead up to the 2003 Communications Act was Dr Kim Howells and Calum Mac-Donald was able to broker a meeting for John with him. After the committee ceased the funding of *Telefios* in December 2000, Grampian Television no longer had use for the studio facility on Seaforth Road in Stornoway. The Gaelic Broadcasting Committee took over the lease of these premises, which were owned by Western Isles Council, refurbished the premises and relocated its office there. In April 2002, Dr Kim Howells officially opened the new office, and was fully briefed and lobbied for support for expanded powers for the committee. The Minister, from initial scepticism, became sympathetic and this was to prove critical in the course of the drafting of the Act.

All of the lobbying, the amendments and the gaining of support from the Labour Government, through Calum Macdonald, Murray Elder and Kim Howells eventually bore fruit in the 2003 Communications Act.

Cabadaich 4: *Foghlam Fad Beatha*

Blethers 4: Life-Long-Learning

ROY: You're an educated man who had achieved a great deal by your mid-career. Why did you decided to do a Masters degree?

JOHN: This goes back to my school days when I was in my sixth year at the Nicolson Institute in Stornoway and a number of us had won places to go to university. The rector of the Nicolson at the time, Addison, who had goodness knows how many degrees and letters after his name, gave us a sonorous lecture about how important university was, but that how difficult Honours degrees were and unless you were really gifted, you shouldn't attempt an Honours degree – the exact opposite of what you would have thought a rector of such an institution would say. Some of us who came from crofts thought, that's us, there's no point in us going for Honours degrees.

Years after that, I began to think, hey, that wasn't right. At a later stage in my life when I was over 50 years of age, I was a Board member of Lewis Castle College and at that time the concept of encouraging life-long learning was very much in vogue and I was part of a committee that was working on trying to encourage it. So I espoused the idea and decided to lead by example, because I was trying to encourage my own staff to upgrade their skills and academic qualifications.

ROY: If I may say so, that is very much in your character – not expecting others to do what you wouldn't do yourself.

JOHN: So, having spoken with Frank Rennie, who was then a lecturer in the college, I decided to do a PhD and then perhaps a change of career after I was finished doing the media work and maybe get some lecture work with the UHI. The idea I hit on was to do a history of the HIDB in the Western Isles over its first 20 years. I spoke about that to my then Chairman Iain MacAskill, who had been secretary to the HIDB and Iain, typically in his straightforward gruff manner said, 'Why don't you do something useful?'

I said, 'What do you mean?' he said, 'Well you can write a PhD on the HIDB and I sure you'd do it well, but it would end up on a shelf somewhere and very few would read it. Why don't you do something that's useful for the work that you're doing at the moment?'

I was still working for Gaelic Media Services at that time. So I thought about that and decided, yes. I looked at the options and Stirling University had at that stage just launched a new online Masters degree in media management. I applied for that and was one of three people in the first year of that course. It was online which of course suited me as I could work from home and it proved very helpful.

Iain MacAskill was prescient as usual because there was new legislation round the corner to do with digital media.

ROY: So that gave you an understanding of the technicalities of the new phenomenon of digital broadcasting and how the industry needed to change.

JOHN: Yes and it gave me new confidence and access especially to the new terminology associated with this new idea and also the thinking about this fast-changing environment and what the issues were around that. What was most important was that it gave me insight into how we could win the argument for Gaelic Media Services to get access to airtime and capacity to fund programmes in our own right which we won with the 2003 Act. So in the end that worked and it was even more pleasing to me because I got a Masters degree with distinction, having put so much work into it at a time when I had serious problems with a detached retina.

ROY: I would expect no less from you. But seriously, what an achievement that led to the creation of BBC Alba. It astonishes me that hardly anyone realises the pivotal role you played in bringing about this revolution in Gaelic broadcasting that is so vital in sustaining and growing Gaelic. That is why I was determined to write this book.

Goals Achieved

JOHN ANGUS'S EFFORTS had not been in vain. The campaign had been successful in winning major concessions under the 2003 Communications Act which set out measures 'to secure that a wide and diverse range of high quality programmes in Gaelic are available to persons in Scotland'.

In addition to the former mandate to fund programme production and development, training, audience research and related activities, the new service got additional powers to make, schedule and commission programmes and the authority to seek a broadcast licence.

In light of these changes, the CTG was renamed the Gaelic Media Service (GMS) because, with its new powers, it had the potential to maximise the impact of the public funding given to the service. These were radical changes.

Compared with the provisions of the previous legislation, the Act changed the responsibilities placed on the independent broadcasting companies to schedule Gaelic programmes. This meant, however, that whilst the original GMS could continue to fund the broadcasters to make programmes, it was in a much weaker position than formerly to negotiate appropriate schedule slots when the target audience was available to view. Another potential future challenge was that the BBC's license renewal settlement might cause the BBC to be less accommodating to Gaelic programming than had been the case hitherto.

To address these challenges, John Angus Mackay planned a two-pronged approach. With its new status resulting from the concessions won by the 2003 Act, the GMS was keen to pursue the option of establishing a channel and favoured trying to establish a partnership with the BBC. It was by no means certain, however, that the BBC would agree as this would be an entirely new departure for the cautious state broadcaster.

Knowing full well that a proposition of this kind would present the BBC with a considerable challenge and that it would be tactically unwise to go into negotiation without a fallback position, John had earlier opened negotiations with Channel 4 in anticipation of a positive outcome from the 2003 Act. As it happened, Channel 4 had established a small contribution studio with up-to-date technology in Belfast and John's contact in Channel 4 saw no difficulty in doing something similar in Scotland.

Another element in the back-up plan was that, with the CTG now relocated in the former Grampian studio, the opportunity was presented for the GMS, as successor to CTG, to put together a package with the support of Channel 4 that would fund and commission programmes and draw up schedules which, with a technical plan, would form the basis of an application to Ofcom for a broadcast license to establish a Gaelic channel.

A partnership with the BBC was still the preferred option, however, and the then Chair of GMS, Neil Fraser and the controller of BBC Scotland, Ken MacQuarrie, agreed that a working group be set up between the two parties to consider the options for such a partnership. One of the main points of discussion was whether a partnership service, if established, would be run under a GMS license from Ofcom or under the auspices of a BBC licence. To be fair to the BBC, and in recognition of the longstanding relationship between that body and the GMS and its predecessors, John let Ken MacQuarrie know at an early stage that he had prepared the groundwork for an alternative option in partnership with Channel 4, should a partnership with the BBC prove not to be a feasible proposition.

There followed nearly three years of protracted, though amicable, negotiations between the small GMS team, supported by legal advice from McGrigors, a team of Glasgow-based lawyers, and BBC Scotland policy and production staff with strong input from the BBC Deputy Head of Policy based in London. The relationship of mutual respect built up between John and that Deputy Head of Policy, David Fawcett, was to prove crucial towards the end of the proceedings. To facilitate discussion from a neutral stance Professor Donald Neil MacCormack had agreed to act as Chair of the online meetings whilst more informal discussions took place between meetings to clarify points of fact and clear up any misunderstandings. A report on the options and costs for setting up a Gaelic Digital Service was commissioned from Deloitte MCS Ltd to inform discussions.

The outcome of these negotiations was a report drafted by BBC Scotland staff with input from GMS. This described the background to discussions between GMS and the BBC and made positive recommendations regarding establishment of a partnership between the BBC and the Gaelic Media Service.

The GMS board accepted the report's recommendations which were then to be presented to the Board of Management of the BBC in London. At a crucial stage, before the report was circulated, however, having reread it, John realised that, whilst the report lead to positive recommendations, the lengthy description in its earlier pages of the complex issues discussed could seem to include many negatives that might prejudice the view of a reader coming to it for the first time. John phoned David Fawcett to point this out and proposed putting the positive recommendations up front instead of at the end. Fawcett agreed in principle but feared that it was too late to change the report. However, John had already redrafted it and forwarded this revised version to Fawcett, who further improved on the layout by removing much of the contorted arguments to an appendix and submitted the report to BBC management.

Thankfully, in 2006 the powers that be in the BBC approved the report, which recommended a partnership between the BBC and GMS to set up a Gaelic channel. By this stage, John felt that in many ways, after years of hard slogging, the job was done and that it was time for someone else to take things forward. John stood down from GMS in April 2006 and was succeeded by Donald Campbell who had previously been a Board member and one of the group that had negotiated the agreement with the BBC.

On 14 November 2006, John and Maria, Derek and Ciaran travelled to Buckingham Palace where Her Majesty the Queen awarded John the OBE for Services to Gaelic Broadcasting in Scotland.

* * *

Over the years, John, and especially Maria who was, of course, fluent in Italian, had become very attached to Italy and returned often to rent a house in the south in the small village of Morigerati which they had visited with the Western Isles group on the first exchange visit. The house, which had originally been a barn, was very basic and water was drawn from a well and heated for bathing in tin baths out in the sun. This took John back to his Hebridean childhood in the 1950s, and to his delight he discovered in an outhouse sickles, a scythe and a machete with which he spent early mornings clearing weeds from the overgrown vegetable and fruit garden adjacent to the house. When the house came up for sale, they nearly bought it but were put off by the logistics of getting from Lewis to Naples and then driving for three hours with two small children to their destination.

The dream persisted, however, and when John left the Gaelic Media Service, they were in a position to consider looking again for a bolthole in Italy. They spoke with a number of Italian friends that they knew and asked, 'If you were buying a house in Italy, where would you go?'

Naturally the usual answer was the part of Italy from which their advisors originated themselves or based on other prejudices such as advice to avoid Tuscany because there were too many foreigners, or the north because people were too snooty, or the south because – well, they were too southern. This really left the centre of Italy.

John and Maria adopted a more structured approach in which they set out their requirements on a checklist. Among these requirements was reasonable access to one or more airports, at least two bedrooms, a *terrazza*, a view, reasonable access to skiing and to the sea, which narrowed the search down to the Province of Abruzzo and the Peligna Valley in particular. Maria then searched the internet and narrowed the focus down to two selling agencies. It transpired that the parents of a partner in one of the agencies had a B&B in the picturesque village of Introdacqua, so that is where they based themselves for the search.

The first property they looked at in Introdacqua was a furnished four storey traditional Italian house on the market for €35,000. They nearly bought it on the spot but it didn't fit all the required criteria – no *terrazza*, inconvenient layout and not much of a view. Another two or three properties were viewed but were also found to be unsuitable.

On the first morning, John had got up early and had gone to a little square to have a coffee. While drinking the coffee and enjoying the scene, he spotted a poster with a picture of a man holding a child by the hand and heading back to a hillside town. The poster was advertising the Festa del Ritorno in the little town of Pacentro which lay on the other side of the valley. The festival was aimed at emigrants and their families offering an opportunity for them to return to visit their homeland. The picture was the exact opposite of a print of an iconic poster titled 'l'emigrante' from an original painting by the artist Giulio Greco that John had bought about 20 years earlier in Caselle in Pittari in Campania. That painting featured a man in the act of emigration, with suitcase in hand striding out from his hometown – a scene only too reminiscent of emigration from John's own island community – and was designed to draw attention to the flow of emigrants from the south of Italy.

John was struck by the irony of the contrast between the two images. He drew Maria's attention to this place called Pacentro and the fact that there was a festival there. On enquiring further, Clive, one of the property agents, took them to Pacentro and showed them a small flat. On entering and opening the shutters, the view over the Peligna Valley and the mountains beyond was magnificent. The flat, however, was too small. Then they discovered that the owner had another two properties as part of the same development. The lower one was better but the third was just right. It ticked all the boxes, having a *terrazza*, a wonderful view, three bedrooms and everything else that they sought. By the time they were ready to leave Italy for home, they had signed an agreement to purchase.

John and Maria have since spent as much time as they could in their lovely home in Pacentro and have become well integrated within the local Italian community. After a few years, they were invited to participate in the annual outing of returnee Pacentranni who, after a meeting with the Mayor, had a *festa* of their own at Passo San Leonardo in the mountain above Pacentro. John and Maria continued to attend such events in subsequent years. In 2017, as adopted Pacentranni, they were invited to participate in the Class of '52, the celebration of Pacentranni born in 1952 – Maria's birth year – in the renowned Caldora restaurant in the historical heart of Pacentro.

That the Mackays are well integrated in Pacentro's community life was demonstrated this summer of 2019 when John participated in the town's medieval street play costumed as a Knight Templar. I am told he looked most fetching in red tights – a far cry from his part as an oil rig roustabout in *Na Moireasdanaich* all those decades ago in Glasgow.

BBC Alba

ALTHOUGH JOHN ANGUS had left the world of Gaelic broadcasting behind, his spirit was to live on due to the deep and strong foundation he had created and was to bear fruit in the form of MG Alba and later BBC Alba, the long-awaited Gaelic television channel.

MG Alba became the operating name GMS/Gaelic Media Service (Seirbheis nam Meadhanan Gàidhlig). The organisation's remit under the Communications Act 2003 was to ensure that a wide and diverse range of high-quality Gaelic programmes be made available to persons in Scotland. In addition to the former mandate to fund programme production and development, training, audience research and related activities, the new service was given new powers to make, schedule and commission programmes and the authority to seek a broadcasting licence.

In 2007, the BBC Trust opened a consultation for the proposed Gaelic digital service in partnership with the GMS. In November 2007, in the light of this consultation, the Audience Council Scotland recommended their support for the creation of the service on 7 December 2007, stating that the Trust should pursue carriage of the service on digital terrestrial television and that existing 'Gaelic zone' programming on BBC Scotland should remain after the launch. On 28 January 2008, the BBC Trust gave the go-ahead for a Gaelic channel.

The channel began broadcasting on satellite at 9.00pm on 19 September 2008 with a launch video featuring a new rendition of the Runrig song, 'Alba'. The first part of a live ceilidh from Skye, presented by Mary Ann Kennedy, was followed by a specially produced comedy drama entitled *Eilbheas* (Elvis) at 9.30pm, starring Greg Hemphill as Elvis Presley. The channel's first independent commission, *Peter Manuel – Deireadh an Uilc?* (*Peter Manuel – The End of Evil?*), a drama documentary produced by STV Productions, was shown at 10.30pm before the opening night closed with the second half of the live ceilidh from Skye. The launch night was simulcast on BBC Two Scotland between 9.00pm and 10.30pm and there was a launch event held at the National Museum of Scotland, which was recorded by the channel's news service *An Là*.

A study demonstrated that 650,000 people had watched BBC Alba per week in the first two months of broadcasting, in spite of only being available to around a third of Scots at that time. In 2009, after a review by the BBC Trust and a recommendation from the Audience Council Scotland, a plan was announced to broadcast the channel on Freeview in Scotland from the 2010 digital switchover, under the proviso that the reach of the service should extend beyond the core Gaelic audience to 250,000. After BBC Trust approval, the service was launched on Freeview on 8 June 2011. By 6 November 2012, the channel was also made available nationwide on the Virgin Media and Sky platforms.

BBC Alba combines television, radio and online programme content and is financed by the BBC Scotland budget and by MG Alba, which itself is financed by the Scottish Government. There are four studios across Scotland, located in Stornoway, Glasgow, Inverness and Sleat (Skye). In addition to programme-making, continuity and channel management are based in Stornoway in a building adjacent to the former Grampian Television studio, while the news services are based in Inverness. BBC Scotland's headquarters at Pacific Quay in Glasgow are used to transmit the programmes.

Output on the station consists of news, current affairs, sport, drama, documentary, entertainment, education, religion and children's programming, broadcast on most days between 5.00pm and midnight. Around 90 minutes of television content daily is new material.

Children's programmes are shown for two hours every weekday, between 5.00pm and 7.00pm. These are not subtitled and, besides their entertainment value, reinforce the language immersion programmes of Gaelic medium schools and nurseries. Most other programmes are subtitled in English which enables non-Gaelic-speaking viewers to access the channel's unique content. The nightly half-hour news programme, *An Là*, on weeknights at 8:00pm covers local, national and international events. The Gaelic adult learning programme, *Speaking our Language*, is re-broadcast on weeknights at 7.30pm and the distinctive series *Eòrpa* which, using a format not found on any other channel, covers otherwise unreported political, social and cultural issues across Europe, is shown on Thursday nights on BBC Alba and also later on BBC Two Scotland. BBC Alba broadcasts more Scottish sport than any other channel. On Saturday nights, there is coverage of a selected Scottish Premier League football match not otherwise covered on Sky Sports with Gaelic commentary, with coverage also of key rugby and shinty fixtures. There is, of course, much else in terms of documentaries, drama, humour, discussion, religious programmes and regular music slots from traditional Gaelic to country and western and, what is more, almost all of these programmes are made in Scotland.

This is clearly a winning formula because on occasion viewership has reached as high as 900,000, many, many times the total number of Gaelic speakers in Scotland. One advantage that BBC Alba has is that it is, as already mentioned, located at the prestigious Channel 7 slot on the electronic programme guide having inherited the slot that had previously been held by TeleG following the successful campaign mounted by John Angus to secure a place in the then emerging digital TV environment under the Broadcasting Act 1996.

There is no doubt that BBC Alba has had a positive impact at many levels including increasing artistic and technical skills, extending economic opportunities in fields that never existed before for Gaelic speakers, stimulating parents' interest in Gaelic medium education, appealing to and serving adult learners of the language and strengthening Gaelic acquisition, usage, vocabulary and transmission of Gaelic. It should perhaps be noted, however, that there has been criticism by Gaels about a dilution of commitment to Gaelic, citing statistics of 70 per cent English content in BBC Alba programmes.

Nevertheless, for the relatively modest £15 million per year that the channel costs, it has been calculated that, besides the many positive social and cultural benefits, the economic multiplier benefit since the establishment of the Gaelic Television Fund has been in the region of £1 billion.

That surely is some legacy for the years of hard and at times lonely slog against huge odds that John Angus Mackay expended in making it happen.

Health Board

JOHN ANGUS HAD half a year's peace following his retirement from GMS, pursuing his various interests which included tending his small flock of sheep held on the croft he had purchased at Arnol in 2002, and spending time in Italy which was to become a haven to which to escape from the maelstrom of events which were to follow.

In the late autumn of 2006, John was contacted by a man who explained that he was a head-hunter working for a recruitment agency on behalf of the NHS (National Health Services) who were looking to recruit a Chair of the Western Isles Health Board. John was already aware that the previous chair, David Currie had resigned.

In response to the man from the agency, John suggested and named a number of people that he try to ascertain if they might be interested.

The response was, 'I've already spoken to all of these people and they all said to speak to you.' The recruitment agent then tried to persuade John to apply. John was not keen because, from his understanding, the situation in the health board had been toxic. The agent persevered, however, and John was eventually persuaded to apply.

An interview was arranged, at which it was explained that a new Chief Executive had already been appointed and John was asked how he felt about that.

John replied that most people would not be very happy with such a situation in which the Chair did not have a say in the CEO's appointment. He continued, however, that he would have to accept the judgement of the panel and hope that it was sound. On the other hand, John pointed out that if the panel had made the wrong choice, then that would be on their heads, not John's.

The outcome of the interview was that both John and the new Chief Executive, Laurence Irvine, started almost simultaneously in January 2007. John was not impressed with what he found. The organisation was in debt and governance was not functioning effectively. Matters had come to such a pass that the staff had put forward a vote of no confidence in the management of the organisation. At the same time, John could see that the medical staff were doing a good job.

John found early on that, while the post was supposed to be for three days a week, it was in fact a six- or seven-day job. Being a local man, he made the effort to go round all the Western Isles Health Board's facilities and GP practices with Laurence from Vatersay in the south to Ness in the north. They sought to meet with and get to know as many of the staff as possible and to understand their issues, to gain their confidence and to demonstrate that they were a listening and caring board.

One of the issues at that time was cleanliness and guarding against hospital-acquired infection. John, therefore, volunteered to go on an infection control course, which entailed 16 hours of study, after which he passed the exam and proudly wore the badge of Infection Control Champion. Thereafter, John was able to go round wards and other facilities engendering a feeling of solidarity with the frontline personnel. This he regarded as an important role of the Chair.

The difficulties of the 'failing board', however, were well known in Scottish Government circles and had been the subject of much coverage in the national and local press. Audit Scotland had issued a Section 22 report and referred the board to the Audit Committee of the Scottish Parliament for scrutiny and an investigation commenced into the workings of the board. This was inevitably to lead to an investigation by the Scottish Parliament Audit Committee.

In the meantime, another challenge emerged. Two individuals separately signalled to John that they suspected that the information provided by the Chief Executive in his application for the job was incorrect. John started to investigate this firstly using the HR Director of another health board who interviewed both John and Laurence Irvine and drew up a report that was inconclusive. John decided to pursue the matter further because he felt that if the situation was left hanging and if there was a problem subsequently then he would be seen as letting everyone down.

John then referred the matter to the fraud section of the NHS in Scotland and they started an investigation. At the same time, John asked Laurence, 'Please tell me if there is an issue because if there is, these people will pursue you, so it will be best to come clean now.'

'No, no,' said Lawrence, 'I have done nothing wrong.'

By this time, some seven months had elapsed since John's appointment and Nicola Sturgeon MSP, then the Health Minister, was due to visit the health board in September as part of the annual review. The week before the review, the fraud section phoned John to say that they had evidence that Laurence had been manifesting himself to the Western Isles Health Board differently from his persona in England where he had worked previously.

John then questioned if he could stand on the same platform as Laurence in public in front of Nicola Sturgeon, thereby affirming his credentials. He considered the risk to be too great, the stakes were high as both his own and the Health Secretary's credibility were potentially in jeopardy. John suspended Laurence pending the outcome of further investigations. He then informed the NHS in Edinburgh and it was decided to postpone the annual review.

In the event, Kevin Woods, Director General of NHS Scotland, came to Stornoway without the minister but brought with him someone he thought might be a good interim Chief Executive – John Turner.

John interviewed John Turner, introduced him to the Board and recommended that he be appointed as interim CEO. The Board agreed.

There was a further complication, however. The Chief Executive who had been in post before Laurence Irvine had been stood down from his post in the Western Isles and had been seconded to work on projects for the NHS in Edinburgh. Technically, he was still an employee of NHS Western Isles. Thus, John found himself within the first eight months in post with *three* Chief Executives.

John Angus and John Turner formed a good working relationship, rolled up their sleeves, tackled the finances, staff and clinical governance issues and created a stable operational regime. Meanwhile, the non-executive Board members who had been in post during the previous regime stood down when their term of office came to an end. A new Board was appointed which, with the new Chief Executive, was able to face an investigation by the Scottish Parliament's Audit committee – an excruciating process held in public in the Council Chamber in Stornoway. John Angus and John Turner, however, had a good story to tell about the changes they had put in place and the Chairman of the hearing was able to say that he had been pleased to hear the evidence provided and that the Western Isles Health Board was not the 'basket case' he had been led to expect.

Meanwhile, Laurence Irvine appealed against his suspension and an appeal panel was set up within the Board. The appeal was reviewed and the panel upheld his suspension. Laurence appealed against that, after which there was an independent panel established to review the case, which led to an investigation that both John and Laurence were required to attend. Again, the panel found in the Western Isles Health Board's favour. Despite delaying tactics by his lawyers, Laurence Irvine's contract was terminated.

Then there was the case of the original Chief Executive who was on secondment. The issue was that once the two-year secondment had ended, he was presumed to be able to return to the Western Isles Health Board. As this was hardly a practical proposition, John negotiated with him and reached agreement that he would forego any claim to entitlement of employment with NHS Western Isles.

With the organisation now functioning much more smoothly under John Turner's management, when the job as Chief Executive of NHS 24 came up, John Turner applied and got the job.

Before John Angus took over as Chairman, the NHS had set up a support team to provide leadership in lieu of the departed Chair and Chief Executive. One member of this group was Gordon Jamieson, an enthusiast for good clinical governance. He knew his way around the organisation and, when the Chief Executive post was advertised, Gordon applied and was appointed – the fourth Chief Executive under John Angus' watch.

From the outset, John and Gordon set out to provide a quality service to the people of the Western Isles, articulating the aspiration to be 'The Best at What We Do'. Staff relations were critical to success in ensuring good clinical and financial governance, and gradually morale improved, as did performance. With no previous background in the health service – except as a patient – John had a steep learning curve to climb, both in dealing with local issues from the Butt to Barra, and in participating in external events.

The first Monday of every month the chairs of all Scottish Health Boards met with the Minister and officials to discuss current issues and future prospects. John was also for some time the 'small board' representative on the NHS National Performance Management Committee which monitored pay awards for the Executive cohorts in each Health Board. A partnership agreement with Highland Health Board required regular dialogue and knowledge sharing.

Continuous improvement in governance was an NHS wide imperative. The Board of NHS Western Isles embraced the concept and worked assiduously with the Governance Development Unit set up by NHS Scotland. The growing confidence of the board became manifest in its taking the decision to press ahead with ambitious plans to create a new, state of the art, dental treatment and training facility in Stornoway. Over the years, this centre has attracted students from other centres, and allowed local people to undergo training without needing to give up their home life on the island.

All in all after three years of intense activity as Chair of NHS Western Isles, John had helped to turn around the financial affairs of the organisation and had seen improvements in service delivery, staff morale and overall governance.

Ever the multi-tasker, John had also been a Board member of Bòrd na Gàidhlig (BNG) before he left GMS and joined NHS Western Isles. BNG was going through a difficult stage. The CEO had left, and the organisation was managed by an interim support team. When the CEO post came up, John's four-year term as Chair of NHS Western Isles was due for renewal. He was encouraged to do a further term and had to make up his mind whether to stay with NHS Western Isles or apply for the Bòrd na Gàidhlig post. In the event he stood down from the Health Board, applied for the Bòrd na Gàidhlig post and was appointed.

Bòrd na Gàidhlig

BÒRD NA GÀIDHLIG (BNG) had been created by the Scottish Government in 2006 as a non-departmental public body responsible for implementing the Gaelic Language (Scotland) Act 2005 and specifically, as stated in the Act, 'securing the status of the Gaelic language as an official language of Scotland commanding equal respect to the English language'.

One of BNG's early tasks was to create a National Gaelic Language Plan, as stipulated in the Gaelic Language (Scotland) Act 2005. The purpose of the five-year plan, which had to be approved by Ministers, was to set out the rationale for increasing the number of Gaelic speakers and users and to provide a framework of activities in fields such as education, social, economic and community development which all interested parties could develop as appropriate in their own fields of operation. Although developed and promoted by the Bòrd, it was designed to be a plan for all of Scotland, showing what the Bòrd would do at its own hand and indicating what was expected of others, for example Local Authorities and other public bodies.

John Angus took up post as Ceannard (CEO) of Bòrd na Gàidhlig in October 2010 for an initial period of three years, later extended to four and a half years. This was to prove to be another extremely challenging period in John's working life. From the commencement of John's tenure, the Bòrd was faced with building up a new management structure. At the same time developing the second National Gaelic Language Plan had become a priority whilst simultaneously implementing the first. The 2011 Census was imminent, heralded by prognostications of doom in some sections of the media, and the Bòrd became subject to criticism through the development of social media, which gave oxygen to anyone who wished to voice a negative opinion.

John's strategy for dealing with the difficulties that lay ahead had been conceptualised at his interview as formulation of a 'war plan' which took account of goals to be achieved, territories on which to go into action and measures to combat immediate threats.

The recruitment of key management staff was a priority for John and the Bòrd was fortunate to recruit able professionals to the posts identified in a revised staffing structure plan. To create mutual understanding amongst senior managers of administrative and developmental sections of the Bòrd, a senior management team was created which shared with the Ceannard responsibility for major decision making, whilst inevitably the final onus fell on the Ceannard. John's ultimate aim was that all senior managers understood how each piece of the BNG jigsaw fitted together in delivering the aims of the National Plan and the governance requirements of a public body. In other words, it was important that each could speak knowledgeably about all aspects of the organisation's remit.

John made early contact with the Census Office with whom an agreement was struck that BNG would work closely to publicise the importance of the census and encourage as full a return as possible. To assist in this work Allan Campbell, a former Ceannard of BNG, was contracted to coordinate publicity in communities and schools throughout Scotland. Despite fears that the 2011 Census would see a further marked decline in the numbers of Gaelic speakers, there was some hope that the signs of slowing down in decline seen in the 2001 Census would be replicated in 2011 due to the growth in Gaelic medium education. Census analysis by Dr Kenneth MacKinnon, a BNG member, underlined this hypothesis. In the event, it proved to be correct – the under-20 age group showed growth, despite the loss of older Gaelic speakers, and the 2011 Census showed that the overall numbers of Gaelic speakers in Scotland had almost stabilised.

Another early challenge was that the Bòrd, prior to John's appointment, had decided after a number of meetings to discontinue funding for TAIC, previously under the name of Comhairle nan Sgoiltean Araich (The Gaelic Playgroups Association). This organisation created by Finlay MacLeod had, since 1980, pioneered the development of Gaelic medium pre-school groups throughout Scotland, which had then laid the foundation for Gaelic medium primary school education. By 2010, however, Local Authorities had increasingly assumed responsibility for early years education as feeders to Gaelic medium Primary School units. Divisions had arisen between TAIC and the local authority system which appeared to threaten future seamless transfer from the one level to the other. Understandably, in recognition of the pioneering work of Finlay MacLeod, the Bòrd was faced with a continuous barrage of criticism, locally, nationally and internationally – for example, from no less than the world-renowned linguist Joshua Fishman – for the decision to cease TAIC's funding. Fortunately, the Bòrd had the full support of the Scottish Government.

The Bòrd's response was to establish a new framework for Gaelic pre-school provision entailing appointing a small team of early-years workers, working in partnership with local authorities to ensure effective transition from pre-school to Gaelic medium primary school. The ultimate result was that there was a steady year on year increase in uptake of Gaelic medium education from 2012 onwards.

The adult Gaelic learners sector also proved to be something of a minefield. BNG had been asked by the Minister, Michael Russell, to accelerate growth in this field and the Bòrd had invested considerable sums in a joint scheme with HIE and Skills Development Scotland to support the development, introduction and implementation of the language scheme Ulpan, under the aegis of a company named Deiseal Ltd. Ulpan was a method of teaching and learning which originated in Israel and had been successfully adapted in Wales. It entailed providing training for tutors who subsequently set up classes locally with fees supported by Local Authorities. Targets were set for recruitment which were met by and large, but initial estimates of retention of students and numbers which would become fluent proved to be optimistic. Critics were quick to seize on this and waged war on the Bòrd in the press and social media, though the Bòrd was able to demonstrate value for money in comparison to the costs of institutional-based adult education, and in terms of tutor jobs created in communities.

One unfortunate aspect of this saga was that the Bòrd came under constant pressure from certain individuals who had an axe to grind with Deiseal for personal reasons and used a constant stream of Freedom of Information (FOI) requests to gather information for use as ammunition. This was hugely frustrating and counter-productive, to the extent that John resolved to engage more directly at a personal level with the protagonists. He discovered that two people who were submitting FOIs for similar information were, in fact, married although they had managed to obfuscate this fact.

I became aware of the growing tension, and when John told me that he had arranged to meet with the husband in a neutral location – a café in Nairn as it happened – I resolved not to let him go alone and persuaded him to let me accompany him. Thus, I found myself sitting in a corner of this café observing the interaction between John and his thorn in the flesh, fearing the worst and hoping for the best. In the event, whilst some argument ensued, both protagonists dealt with the meeting in a civilised fashion, and better understood each other's positions as a result.

In fact, the meeting ended with John's companion saying, by way of recognition of how difficult things had been, 'I guess when this is all over, I should buy Alasdair MacKinnon a bottle of whisky.'

John acknowledged this gratefully but did not wish to spoil the moment by saying that Alasdair MacKinnon, the Bòrd officer who dealt with FOIs, did not drink whisky!

Not for the first time, John had risked taking an unorthodox route to solve a problem. In similar fashion, on another occasion he contacted another individual in Berwick upon Tweed by telephone who was regularly criticising Gaelic and its promoters in letters to the press. Press rebuttals had served only to fuel more argument. After a long conversation, where both parties eventually agreed to disagree, the other party congratulated John on his determination to have it out with him. The correspondence in the press stopped.

Then a tabloid columnist mounted a sustained series of bitter, prejudiced and misinformed pieces attacking Gaelic and Gaelic broad-casting – a classic example of biased journalism focusing on what had been perceived as a soft and easy target. Not so soft and easy as it transpired, as Bòrd Chairman, Arthur Cormack, fought back, vigor-ously and relentlessly rebutting every line of misinformation penned by the journalist. In due course the vitriol ceased.

As local authority, colleges and individual tutors set up classes throughout Scotland, the future of the Gaelic Learners' Association, CLI (established in 1984), became increasingly precarious, and its funding from sources other than Bòrd na Gàidhlig began to diminish. This led to prolonged discussion between the Bòrd and CLI. Ultimately CLI decided to cease teaching classes and to provide an online service to its members. Again, these processes were subject to considerable negative media coverage.

It will be readily understood that much time and energy was expended by BNG management in dealing with media coverage and FOI requests, whilst still pursuing development goals. A further blow in the winter of 2011/12 was that BNG Chair Art Cormack had to resign for health reasons. Art had been a pillar of strength during his period as Chair, and the Ceannard now had to establish a relationship with the Interim Chair Betty McAteer. This was duly accomplished but the loss of continuity resulted in a further unsettling period for BNG. Indeed, as events unfolded, in his four and a half years as Ceannard, John served under four different Chairs, Betty McAteer being followed by Ian Campbell, to be succeeded by Allan MacDonald as Interim Chair and then as substantive post holder. In these circumstances, John's previous experience of working under numerous Chairs and of chairing other organisations proved invaluable in maintaining leadership and stability and keeping up the morale of the organisation.

The Government push to ensure efficiency savings on a year on year basis was an additional financial challenge for BNG, especially with increasing demands on its grant aid to other organisations. In the lead up to the halfway breakpoint in the Bòrd's office lease, the Head of Finance and Corporate Affairs, Alasdair MacKinnon, initiated a review of costs and examined options for reduction and relocation. After considerable debate, the decision was taken to relocate offices to the spectacular Scottish Natural Heritage (SNH)-owned property, Great Glen House, under a management agreement, which crucially included new IT systems and other support. Whilst releasing significant savings, this process was in itself challenging for staff, although it facilitated open-plan working which was more in keeping with the new ethos of the organisation.

Bòrd na Gàidhlig's Stornoway personnel were also relocated to the former *Machair* studio, by now redeveloped as An Tosgan in which are located a number of other Gaelic organisations, such as Comunn na Gàidhlig, publishers Acair, educational resource producer Stòrlann Nàiseanta na Gàidhlig, in addition to BBC Radio nan Gàidheal located across the road. When taken together with the MG Alba/BBC Alba Studio building next door, this hub of Gaelic activity now employs in the region of 100 skilled and well-paid people – surely a testament to John Angus' foresight years before in persuading Grampian

Television to open their studio in Stornoway, and subsequently relocating CTG there.

One area of governance that normally goes unnoticed by the public, but which is vitally important to the efficient running of any organisation is financial control. When John's tenure at BNG commenced, the accounting system was not providing as clear a picture of performance as was desirable. To address this issue, John brought in outside expertise to re-jig the financial control mechanism. Once operational, Audit Scotland officials declared BNG's accounting system to be a model of best practice to be emulated by other non-departmental public bodies.

The development of the second National Gaelic Language Plan 2012–7 was a legislative responsibility of the Bòrd. It entailed considerable discussion with the Government, engagement and ultimately formal engagement with communities, Gaelic organisations and other interested parties including local authorities and COSLA (the Confederation of Scottish Local Authorities). These activities gave a new focus for the BNG senior management team who travelled the length and breadth of the country holding meetings. The plan which eventually emerged, as approved by ministers, gave priority to growth in Gaelic medium education which in turn refocused BNG's strategy for the coming years.

This required a major system change in national educational circles. Here the groundwork laid by John as Ceannard and the BNG Head of Education and learning, Màiri MacMillan, formed a foundation for significant development. An extensive process of relationship building was undertaken with individual local authorities, COSLA and major national education institutions, such as Education Scotland, the Scottish Funding Council, the Scottish Qualifications Authority, Sabhal Mòr Ostaig and a range of colleges and universities. The National Gaelic Language Plan included a Gaelic Education Strategy. To ensure buy-in from the outset, these institutions were invited to become members of the National Gaelic Education Strategy Steering Group which the Bòrd convened, to share in the formulation of the strategy and ultimately to participate positively in its implementation, with meetings held at intervals to review progress and discuss future action.

One noteworthy initiative to emerge from these discussions was a new scheme called GIFT, which would provide training and support for existing teachers to cross over to Gaelic medium education teaching. This was but one of a range of activities sponsored and spearheaded by the Bòrd to encourage teacher recruitment. Major promotional campaigns were launched under the banner 'Thig gam Theagasg!' ('Come and Teach Me'), which featured pupils in a range of situations. These campaigns used television advertising, billboards in major centres and the underground trains in Glasgow as well as a range of localised venues. Teacher numbers gradually grew, but to this day there is a need to maintain robust efforts to ensure supply of teachers to meet the demand from the ever-increasing numbers in Gaelic medium education.

The profile of Gaelic was further raised by the Bòrd's Corporate and Communications Manager, Steven MacIver, in engaging with the *Daily Record* to create an annual Gaelic Awards scheme which was widely publicised by that newspaper. This scheme, which featured a range of category awards, engaged with communities, schools and individuals who were contributing to Gaelic development and acknowledged their achievements in a major showcase event, in an atmosphere which equalled the BAFTAs and other such events in intensity, celebration and enjoyment. It came as a surprise when the *Daily Record* editor recommended John Angus himself for the prime award – the *Daily Record*/Bòrd na Gàidhlig Duaisean Gàidhlig na h-Alba 2015 Urram nan Gàidheal/Lifetime Achievement Award which John, accompanied by his wife Maria, was honoured to receive. At last, after years of criticism and undermining, there was growing recognition of John's efforts and hard-won achievements.

In the meantime, partnerships were established with MG Alba and Creative Scotland to help maintain momentum in the development of the Gaelic media in the increasingly complex digital media environment. Furthermore, as Creative Scotland reviewed and refocused its funding strategies, John and his team gave a fresh push to make sure that the Gaelic arts would continue to be supported. This area of activity, the Colm Cille project and managing the programme of public bodies' Gaelic language plans fell within the extensive remit of David Boag, Head of Gaelic Usage.

The formal establishment of the Senior Management Team (SMT) of which all senior management personnel were members, chaired by the CEO, was crucial in tackling the challenge of co-ordinating development activity across such a broad range as required by the National Gaelic Language Plan. The SMT also fulfilled the vital function of shared corporate responsibility for financial governance in considering grant awards, and in managing budgets. This mechanism, whereby Bòrd members participated in development and audit committees combined with the skills and commitment of the individuals involved, ensured that the Bòrd's governance arrangements were recognised by auditors as exemplary.

As seen earlier, cross-party-political support for Gaelic in Westminster had been sought and gained in the 1980s. Once BNG had been put on a relatively even keel and confidence in signs of successes in initiatives grew, knowing the importance of briefing Members and fostering support, John resolved to engage with the Cross-party Group in the Scottish Parliament. In this he was fortunate to gain the support of successive Chairs of the group, Dave Thomson MSP and Angus MacDonald MSP. From discussion with Angus MacDonald as to how the group could help to create wider interest in Gaelic in the Parliament, it was agreed that BNG should mount an exhibition in the Parliament and staff it so that Members could engage and be briefed on issues of interest.

In the event, the exhibition in the Parliament proved to be very successful in raising the profile of Gaelic and BNG in the Parliament. Knowing that members would ask why BNG was doing this, John branded it as an exercise in accountability to show the Parliament that much progress was being made with the funding provided – and to thank the Parliament for its support. This was genuinely meant, as he well remembered the days when there was no parliamentary support at all for Gaelic. It would be interesting to know how many other organisations had thanked the parliamentarians for their support.

Over three successive years, professional exhibition materials were created and John and other BNG staff, supported by colleagues from the media and universities, displayed the exhibition at the Scottish Parliament on a daily basis Tuesday to Thursday, in the process meeting with members of all parties. In the first year, the exhibition – a joint effort with MG Alba – demonstrated year-on-year increases in the numbers of children entering Gaelic medium primary education and enhanced audience viewing figures for Gaelic television programmes which greatly exceeded the numbers of Gaelic speakers in Scotland. In the second year, the growth over a period of all Gaelic education was covered. In the third year, the exhibition showed the correlation between the growth of Gaelic medium education and the near stabilisation of the number of Gaelic-speakers in Scotland as shown in the 2011 Census. At times the exhibitors faced some tough questioning, but the general support across parties was demonstrated by the messages of goodwill left by party leaders and members from the First Minister and many others.

The advent of the Independence Referendum posed BNG with an interesting dilemma, as the issue of whether the referendum question should be bilingual English/Gaelic became a hot issue. It was argued that it should be bilingual if Gaelic had, indeed, official status in Scotland and equal respect as enshrined in the Gaelic Language (Scotland) Act 2005. To demonstrate how this would look in practice, John provided the Government with a bilingual version of their original copy. This spawned badges and other manifestations of the positive 'Bu Chòir' – the 'Yes it should' response favoured by the pro-independence lobby.

In the event, this version was not used, the argument being that it may have caused resentment in some circles and that, if the referendum result proved negative, Gaelic would be scapegoated. Who knows if that would have been the case, but certainly political pragmatism won the argument over pure principle in this instance.

By the end of John's tenure as Ceannard of Bòrd na Gàidhlig, despite setbacks, the Bòrd's profile was infinitely more positive than when he started. Much, of course, still remains to be done and it will be for future generations to take forward the foundation that John has laid.

The Legacy

JOHN ANGUS MACKAY had taken the decision to apply to be Chief Executive of Bòrd na Gàidhlig because he believed it could be turned around.

He had turned the health board round with the help of good people for, as John said, 'You can't do these things on your own. You have to leave yourself bare, put your heart on your sleeve, surround yourself with good people and trust them and also know that some people will let you down. When things go wrong, you have to pick yourself up and lift others up too.'

He did turn Bòrd na Gàidhlig round; again, by surrounding himself with good people. His desire was to leave a legacy that others could build on.

Looking back over his 25 years at the helm of dedicated Gaelic organisations, semi-official and public, and Chairmanship of a range of others, it is clear that huge advances have been made in areas where previously such developments would have seemed inconceivable. John is the first to acknowledge that his input was largely spurred on by the guidance and support of others from whom he drew inspiration and which provided the impetus for creative thinking and decisive action and that there would not have been such success in the ventures described in these pages without the tremendous support of Board members, staff, colleagues, friends and family.

That is why it is important that John's story be told – so that others can understand how so much has been achieved and perhaps the best of them may emulate John's technique.

The battle for Gaelic media development and the ultimate outcome as manifested in BBC Alba and related digital media developments has been described above in some detail. In the field of education in which John commenced his professional career, the outcome has been no less remarkable.

By 2017, there were 3,145 children in Gaelic medium primary education in Scotland, 1,272 in secondary GME and a further 3,195 learning Gaelic ab initio in secondary schools. In addition, there were approximately 1,900 children below school age at Gaelic medium playgroups or nursery and another 7,000 in primary getting a taster of Gaelic songs, phrases and traditions. Thus, all in all, there were some 16,500 children in Scotland receiving some form of access to Gaelic. At the time of writing, in addition to 52 Gaelic medium primary units in schools in 14 local authority areas, there are dedicated Gaelic medium primary schools in Inverness, Edinburgh, Fort William and two in Glasgow – which also has a dedicated Gaelic medium secondary school on the same campus in the north of the city – with further Gaelic medium primary schools due to open in Glasgow and Portree.

It is to be hoped that some young person reading this may pick up the threads of John's methodology: tenacity and clarity of purpose, networking skills, cultivating friends in high places and the acumen to read the political winds.

As John himself said, 'What needs to be done to save a language, is not to put your head down, but to jump up above the parapet and get on with the job.'

A Well-Deserved Accolade

IT IS FITTING to end this account of the life and achievements of John Angus Mackay by noting a special event which took place on 7 December 2016 in the historic Town House at Aberdeen. On that day, John was presented by the Saltire Society with the 2016 Fletcher of Saltoun Award for his contribution to public life.

Jim Tough, Executive Director of the Saltire Society, outlined the proceedings. Lord Provost George Adams welcomed those present to Aberdeen and before Saltire Convener Professor Alan Riach made the award, I was honoured to be asked to summarise, in a few words, John's accomplishments. It went as follows:

> Lord Provost, Professor Riach, ladies and gentlemen – John Angus Mackay has been a colleague and friend for almost 40 years – and I have no hesitation in saying that he is the most remarkable person I have been privileged to know. It is especially fitting that the 2016 Fletcher of Saltoun Award for John's contribution to public life should be presented here in Aberdeen, his alma mater where, next door in Marischal College, he received his Degree of Master of Arts.
>
> Our paths first crossed when we were both called by the good old Highland and Islands Development Board to work with remote communities to develop community co-operatives. John's beat as field officer was his home territory Lewis and Harris. This was pioneering work and many were the doom mongers who said it would never work. It did work, in no small measure due to John's magic touch – an ability to work as a double agent, as the community's man who could convince the Inverness bureaucrats and the HIDB's man who had the respect of the crofting communities.
>
> John soon expanded this Social and Economic Development role with HIDB to Senior Administrative Officer Western Isles

and then as Organiser and Founder member of Western Isles Enterprise and Board Member of HIE (which replaced HIDB).

Then in the 1980s, a number of us realised that Gaelic was declining fast and in mortal danger. A new Gaelic development organisation Comunn na Gàidhlig was created with John as CEO. The focus was Gaelic medium education (to create a new Gaelic-speaking generation), arts and broadcasting. It was in the field of broadcasting that John was to engineer the most astonishing triumph. In fact, earlier in the 1970s he had presented a Gaelic Radio Requests programme, acted in a Gaelic radio soap and was Chair of the BBC Gaelic Advisory Committee.

But the big coup was spearheading the political campaign and negotiations that in 1990 secured £9.5 million for establishment of the Gaelic Television Fund and subsequently BBC Alba. Cumulatively, this has brought some £250 million plus into Scottish broadcasting with an economic impact of £1 billion.

John was then recruited to become the first CEO of the Gaelic Television Committee and its successors, founder and Chair of the Gaelic Television Training Trust (training young people in the arts of TV broadcasting), Chair of the Programme Committee of the Fort William Celtic Film Festival which he successfully reformatted and refreshed. While all this was going on, John undertook a Masters degree in media management and passed with distinction. He received an OBE for services to Gaelic Broadcasting.

John's achievements do not stop there. John's early career was as a gifted teacher in Glasgow and at various times a youth club leader, a ski party leader for young people and holding after-school drama clubs for teenagers,

He was to return to education as Chair of Trustees of the National Gaelic College SMO based in Skye and with the SMO Director founded the think tank Barail, which revisited the concept of a Highlands and Islands University. Out of this, the UHI was ultimately created. John was subsequently Chair of UHI's Language Policy and Plans Working Groups, a Board member of Lews Castle College and pro tem Chair of the Multi-Agency National Gaelic Education Strategy Steering Group.

Then there are the Arts: John was a Member of the Scottish Arts Council and Chair of the Combined Arts Committee (succeeding Elizabeth Fairbairn, sister of the Chief of the Clan Mackay!). In this role, he reviewed arts centres from the Borders to Orkney, Edinburgh to Glasgow and points in between. He was also Board member and Chair of the development committee for An Lanntair Arts Gallery in Stornoway and latterly Chair of the Board. He was also founder member and Board member of The National Gaelic Arts Agency (Proiseact nan Ealan) and Board member and Chair of the publishing company, Acair.

On retiring from the field of Gaelic broadcasting, John was persuaded to become Chair of NHS Western Isles, which at that time was in a sorry state. In three years, he turned it round into a model health board. In this time, he was also a member of the NHS Scotland National Performance Management Committee.

The world of Gaelic called again and after serving as a Board member of the new statutory Bòrd na Gàidhlig, John was appointed as CEO, once again turning the organisation round to become a model of good practice. In so doing, John is so far the only person to be CEO of the only two statutory Gaelic organisations GTC and BNG.

In the course of all this, John also strode the international stage as a Member of the European Bureau for Lesser Used Languages, and Secretary of the UK Committee. He Liaised with Ireland, Wales and Brittany on language and broadcasting matters sharing platforms with John Hume MP and Michael D Higgins – now Irish President. This led to the creation of the Irish Gaelic channel TG4. John was also Chair of the Columba Initiative established by Irish President Mary Robinson and UK Minister Brian Wilson.

The real accolade to John Angus Mackay's astonishing range of achievements is the large number of talented young Gaelic speakers who have been inspired to carry forward the Gaelic tradition in new and inspiring ways through teaching, broadcasting, music and the arts, not least through the achievements of his four sons, who are present here today.

As living proof of all this and the efficacy of these inter-related development activities, I would now like to bring it all back home and ask Steven MacIver to say a few words.

Steven MacIver, a most talented young man, proved to be a shining example of the young Gaelic-speaking generation whom John had nurtured throughout his career. As he spoke, his youth, speaking skill and musical ability struck just the right note. He ended by singing 'Thoir dhomh pòg', a moving version of Burns' 'Ae Fond Kiss' that had been translated by John Angus' own great uncle, the Shader Bard Murdo Morrison.

Also present at the event was the redoubtable Dolina MacLennan who had all those years before scripted the Gaelic radio soap, *Na Moireasdanaich*, in which she spookily predicted in fiction John's factual move back to a new career in Lewis. That fact is indeed stranger than fiction is borne out by the subsequent exploits of the remarkable John Angus Mackay.

Cabadaich 5: Prìomh Threòraichean

Blether 5: Main Influences

ROY: You have achieved an awful lot in your professional life. Who were the most influential and helpful people in that journey?

JOHN: This reminds me of the words of the old song, 'It takes people like you to make people like me'. And that goes for a lot of people I met along the way over the years. From the time I got involved with HIDB, I learned a lot from yourself about being positive about making things happen and not knowing what the result was going to be. So you and our boss, Bob Storey, were great influences.

ROY: Wow! That's good to hear. You know, you were a huge influence on *me* over that period. You were able to grasp that nettle and, especially with your understanding of how rural communities worked, I learnt a lot from you. So there was a mutual learning thing in facing the challenges of trying to encourage development where others could not – and in the end being successful.

JOHN: The thing is, moving to HIDB from the kind of environment I had worked in before was a life changing experience. I met people like you and Bob Storey who wanted to make things happen and were really positive. That was totally outside my experience up until that point. And I'll throw this in – somewhere along the line Iain MacAskill, the Secretary of HIDB and another long-standing influence, quoted to me JF Kennedy's words – 'Some people look at things as they are and ask why. Others dream about what could be and ask why not.' And that was the ethos of the HIDB. That is what inspired me from lacking in confidence to being able to make things happen. In that way we fostered the creation of community co-ops when most people said it couldn't be done. Honestly, I could not believe to begin with that someone could work in an organisation like HIDB and push that kind of notion and not get sacked. That is true.

ROY: It was wonderful, wasn't it? I used to think myself how amazing it was to be paid to follow my dreams.

JOHN: While talking about co-ops, our colleague Bill White should get a mention. He gave me the idiot's guide to profit and loss accounts and balance sheets. This stood me in good stead over the years, as well as a course on management accounting I attended. On that course, we were given case studies based on applications to HIDB for funding, and we had to work out whether the investment ideas were sound. One case was especially hilarious as my colleagues worked diligently on returns on investment and such like. I gave up after reading the case application. When it came to assessment time, I was asked why I had not done any calculations. The reason was that the application was for growing lobsters in *fresh* water, which of course was a biological impossibility, which goes to show that common sense needs to be applied to finance applications as well as formulae.

ROY: Well I didn't know much about accounting either until we got into the co-ops. I had to learn bloody quick too.

JOHN: That was wonderful. So that's the first great influence – the HIDB and these people – you, Bob Storey and HIDB's secretary, Iain MacAskill, were the people who changed me from lacking in confidence to willing to have a go.

As you know, my job interview didn't go well and I asked Bob Storey when I had such a bad interview why he employed me. And he replied, 'It was that streak of madness in you.'

ROY: Yes, well I suppose we all needed to be a little bit mad to do what we did. Thank goodness for the madness.

JOHN: So that was the HIDB, that gave me a strong footing and a belief that I could change things. In fact, even after I had left HIDB, Iain MacAskill was an ongoing influence until 2006. But in my HIDB time, there was the day Bob Storey said that Iain MacAskill wanted to see me in his room. This sounded ominous. Anyway, I went to his room and Iain said, 'Would you like a dram?' I didn't know if this was a trap so I said, 'What are you having?' He said, 'I'm having a malt' to which I said 'Well I'll have a malt too.' After pouring the drinks, Ian said, 'The situation in the Western Isles is pretty dire. You're doing reasonably well but watch what you're doing. I know you don't like the rules but the rules are the rules. Don't break the rules but use them to do what needs to be done.' When I got back to Bob Storey's desk, he asked, 'How did it go?' I told him that he had offered me a dram to which Bob said, 'Well, in all the times I have been in Iain MacAskill's room, I've never been offered a dram. Clearly, I don't merit a malt.'

When I moved to Comunn na Gàidhlig, the first Chair of that was Donald John Mackay. He kept saying to me, 'Feumaidh tu bhi seòlta.' I though he meant that I had to be sly as that is one meaning of the word. I said, 'No, I'm not a sly or underhand person.' But there is another sense of the word that means an ability to think and work laterally – out of the box, as we would say today. He was right. Duncan Macquarie was the secretary. He too was a huge influence and advisor – no doubt about it. Once the organisation was up and running, Jack MacArthur was a great advisor on how to handle politics.

ROY: Oh, you're talking about, the Reverend Jack, the former councillor with Comhairle nan Eilean and the education convener with Highland Council and Highland Council's representative on Comunn na Gàidhlig.

JOHN: That's right and he was the one who took me by the hand, so to speak, and into St Andrew's House in Edinburgh. I remember going through the doors there for the first time with Jack. Jack said, 'Are you worried or frightened?' I said, 'Absolutely, both'. He said, 'Don't worry. You'll be coming through these doors in a few years' time as if they were your own.' So as we walked into the place and a door opened, just along the corridor a guy came out and said, in Gaelic, 'Hello Jack, how are you?' Jack replied that he was fine. This was HM Chief Inspector of Constabulary and he asked, 'What are you doing here?' to which Jack replied, 'Och we're coming along to a meeting here.' Of course, the chief inspector was Alec Morrison from Ness, and Jack, as a schoolmaster's son, knew the family. So when we went into the meeting with the civil servants, the senior civil servant said, 'I hope you haven't come here just to meet with me' to which Jack replied, 'Oh no, we have just been speaking with the Chief Inspector of Constabulary.' Which of course was no lie.

ROY: An example of being *seòlta*.

JOHN: I suppose so. Then veteran Strathclyde Councillor Bernie Scott was another astute political operator who was both enormously helpful and a great inspiration.

As is described in the book, we were in Scotland trying to work out how to achieve a Gaelic television service. Martin Macdonald was the prime advisor to Comunn na Gàidhlig and to me about how we would tackle the broadcasters. Martin came up with the ruse of sending a letter to them to ask if they were willing to expand their Gaelic television programming. He hit the nail on the head: they responded that they could do no more for Gaelic but then at the time we couldn't see how to take things beyond that.

Really, lots of people were helpful and influential in their own way – Dr Finlay MacLeod, John Murray, Lisa Storey, Dolina Maclennan, Ceiteag MacGregor, Malcolm Maclean, Ken MacQuarrie, Neil Fraser, Jo Macdonald and Margaret Mary Murray, Kenna Kennedy, Chrissie Dick, Margaret Mactaggart and Norma Macleod to name but a few. Then at a later stage, Sir Ken Alexander, Sir Alan Peacock, Bob Cowan and Bob Christie of Grampian Television all gave insights in their own ways. So the way the whole thing worked was along a trajectory. The people who were helpful earlier on became less so as we moved on because they took things as far as they could, but we had to move on. That's why the relationship with you was so helpful, as we yarned in the nights in your house.

ROY: So the way of dealing with the issues and problems as they emerged required new sets of actions and advisors.

JOHN: Yes, we had to shift the focus from Scotland to Westminster. That's why I linked up with lobbyist Leighton Andrews who introduced me to Graeme Carter, advisor to Secretary of State for Scotland, Malcolm Rifkind MP. Graeme in turn showed me how to influence events in Westminster. Donald Stewart as MP had given me guidance on how to behave in Westminster, and his successor Calum MacDonald MP continued in his footsteps in arranging meetings and helping to draft amendments to legislation and to propose support through Early Day Motions which won support from all parties and, indeed, MPs from Wales, Northern Ireland and England, as well as Scotland. Ray

Michie was also very active and helpful in this regard. When we were looking at legislation in the 1990s Murray Elder also helped greatly. Lewisman Iain Macleod, who worked in the House of Lords, was a great help in keeping me right on how to do business with members of that house and in facilitating contacts. Torcuil and Donald Crichton, also Lewismen, were invaluable sources of advice and guidance with regards to the internal politics of Westminster at a crucial stage in the lead up to the 2003 Act. Another most important influencer at that time was John McCormick, later BBC Controller for Scotland, who coached me in the thinking of that organisation. Indeed, listing all those who advised and supported me would require a book in itself.

ROY: Looking back on your lobbying campaign for a Gaelic television service, the Welsh example must have been an inspiration.

JOHN: Yes, absolutely and, just as Iain MacAskill was like a thread running through my professional journey, so was Euyrn Ogwen Williams. You see, it seemed that Gaelic Scotland did not have the confidence to take a bold step until CNAG was set up. While An Comunn Gàidhleach had been agitating for a radio service, they didn't spot the potential in the Broadcasting Act 1980 for a Gaelic television service, or if they did, nothing came of it. It was that Act that got the Welsh television channel S4C established, after Gynfor Evans went on hunger strike, way ahead of anything that Scotland could dream of at that time. It was into that we walked and tried to make sense of what it was all about and how to emulate the Welsh.

ROY: Well it was a long and difficult haul but you got there in the end. We now have BBC Alba. What an achievement. The Gaelic community should be eternally grateful to you.

JOHN: What we set out to do was like trying to climb Ben Nevis in the dark. But if I managed it to the summit, metaphorically speaking, I owe a huge debt of gratitude to the Gaelic community for its support, to the Board members I worked for and the staff who worked for me, to the many others who were involved, directly and indirectly, supporting and agitating in their own ways, as well as all those mentioned here and in the book. There are too many to name, but those still around know who they are. All I can say is Mìle taing, a' chàirdean.

Bibliography

Basini, Mario, Western Mail, Helping a Second Language Survive, Cardiff, 1992

BBC Annual Report and Accounts (various)

BBC, Broadcasting Council for Scotland, Report on the study group on the future of Gaelic broadcasting, 1992

BBC, Extending Choice: the BBC's role in the new broadcasting age, London, 1992

BBC, The BBC beyond 2000, London, 1998

Carter, H.C., Culture, language and territory, London 1989

Comunn na Gàidhlig, Draft brief for a Gaelic language act, Inverness 1999

Comunn na Gàidhlig, Gaelic 2000: a strategy for Gaelic development, Inverness 1994

Comunn na Gàidhlig, Gaelic broadcasting and the BBC, Inverness 1993

Comunn na Gàidhlig, Gàidhlig plc; Plana leasachaidh cànan, Inverness 1997

Comunn na Gàidhlig, Inbhe thèarante: Secure status for Gaelic, Inverness 1997

Comunn na Gàidhlig, The case for a Gaelic radio service, Inverness 1994

Comunn na Gàidhlig, Towards a Gaelic television services, Inverness 1988

Comunn na Gàidhlig, Towards a national policy for Gaelic, Inverness 1986

Creighton, Sir Kenelm, Convoy Commodore, London, 1976

Fishman, J.A. Reversing language shift, Clevedon, 1997

Herald, The, Glasgow, various

HIDB, Staff Paper 3339, Community co-operatives – review of progress, Inverness, 1979

Highlands & Islands Development Board, Annual Reports (various)

Highlands & Islands Development Board, Cor na Gàidhlig, Inverness, 1982

Highlands & Islands Enterprise, Annual Report's (various)

Highlands & Islands Enterprise, Strategy for Development, Inverness, 1991

HMSO, Highlands and Islands Development, (Scotland) Act 1965

Hutcheson, Roger, A Waxing Moon – The Modern Gaelic Revival, Edinburgh, 2005

Macdonald, D, HMS Salopian, Back, 2008

Mackay, Derek K, The History of Gaelic Radio Broadcasting by the BBC, Glasgow, 1998

Mackay, I and Maclennan, C, Oran a' Chrùsair, 1941

Mackay, J, 9 Upper Barvas, Letter describing the sinking of the Salopian, 1941

Mackay, John A, Dissertation presented in part submission towards the Award of the Degree of Master of Science in Media Management, Stirling, 2002

MacKinnon, K., Gaelic: a past and future prospect, Edinburgh, 1991

Macleod, Charles, Devil in the Wind, Edinburgh, 1979.

Milne, A., Gaelic Broadcasting Task Force; Gaelic television; a dedicated channel, Edinburgh, 2000

Morgan D, and Taylor B, U-Boat Attack Logs, 1939-1945Roll of Honour Ness to Bernera, For King and Country, Stornoway1939 to 1945

Osborne, R, Spong, H, and Grover, T, Armed merchant Cruisers, 1878-1945, World Ship Society, Gravesend, 2007

Pedersen, Roy, The Dynamics of Gaelic Development, Coylumbridge, 1993

Saltire Society, The, Why Scottish Broadcasting Matters, Edinburgh 2007

Scotsman, The, Edinburgh, various

Stornoway Gazette, Roll of Honour, Ness to Bernera, For King and Country 1939 to 1945

Stornoway Gazette, Stornoway, (various)

Thomson, D.S., Gairm Vol 21, Air an Spiris, 1957

Thomson, F., The history of An Comunn Gàidhealach; the first hundred years, Inverness 1992

Veljanovski, Cento, The Case for a Gaelic Broadcasting Service, Inverness, 1989

West Highland Free Press, Broadford, (various)

Luath Press Limited

committed to publishing well written books worth reading

LUATH PRESS takes its name from Robert Burns, whose little collie Luath (*Gael.*, swift or nimble) tripped up Jean Armour at a wedding and gave him the chance to speak to the woman who was to be his wife and the abiding love of his life. Burns called one of the 'Twa Dogs' Luath after Cuchullin's hunting dog in Ossian's *Fingal*.
Luath Press was established in 1981 in the heart of Burns country, and is now based a few steps up the road from Burns' first lodgings on Edinburgh's Royal Mile. Luath offers you distinctive writing with a hint of unexpected pleasures.
Most bookshops in the UK, the US, Canada, Australia, New Zealand and parts of Europe, either carry our books in stock or can order them for you. To order direct from us, please send a £sterling cheque, postal order, international money order or your credit card details (number, address of cardholder and expiry date) to us at the address below. Please add post and packing as follows: UK – £1.00 per delivery address; overseas surface mail – £2.50 per delivery address; overseas airmail – £3.50 for the first book to each delivery address, plus £1.00 for each additional book by airmail to the same address. If your order is a gift, we will happily enclose your card or message at no extra charge.

Luath Press Limited
543/2 Castlehill
The Royal Mile
Edinburgh EH1 2ND
Scotland
Telephone: +44 (0)131 225 4326 (24 hours)
email: sales@luath. co.uk
Website: www. luath.co.uk